Poor and Paying for It

THE PRICE OF LIVING ON A LOW INCOME

Edited by Gillian Fyfe

Scottish Consumer Council

EDINBURGH : HMSO

305.56969411

© Crown copyright 1994
 First published 1994

Applications for reproduction should be made to HMSO

ISBN 0 11 495206 X

CONTENTS

	Page
About the Scottish Consumer Council	vii
About the contributors	viii
Acknowledgements	ix

1 Life on a Low Income
by Gillian Fyfe.

1.1 Introduction	1
1.2 The book's purpose	2
1.3 Living on low incomes	2
1.4 Low incomes, low pay and poverty	3
1.5 Social and economic trends	5
1.6 Scotland in context	7
1.7 Household expenditure	9
1.8 Redressing detriment	11
1.9 Characteristics of consumer detriment	11
1.10 Summary	15

2 Housing
by Robina Goodlad and Nicholas Williams.

2.1 Introduction	17
2.2 Tenure change and its effects	19
2.3 Housing needs	23
2.4 Housing finance	26
2.5 Advice, information and support	28
2.6 Conclusions	31

3 Energy and Fuel Consumption
by Bill Sheldrick.

3.1 Introduction	34
3.2 Fuel expenditure	36
3.3 Insulation, heating, and the cost of fuel	39
3.4 Cold comfort	43
3.5 Other costs	49
3.6 Conclusions	51

Page numbers for chapter openings: 1 — 17 — 34

4 Food and Nutrition — 54
by Damian Killeen.

4.1 Introduction — 54
4.2 Low income, inadequate nutrition and poor health — 55
4.3 What do low income households eat? — 56
4.4 Influences on food choice in low income households — 58
4.5 Welfare benefits and food poverty — 59
4.6 The cost of a healthy diet — 59
4.7 Access and choice — 62
4.8 Planning, regulation and food poverty — 63
4.9 Responses to food poverty — 64
4.10 Conclusions — 67

5 Health and Welfare Services — 70
by Lisa Curtice.

5.1 The challenge of health in Scotland — 70
5.2 Health services — 75
5.3 Community care — 78
5.4 Consumer participation and advocacy — 81
5.5 Conclusions — 82

6 Education — 87
by Sheila Riddell.

6.1 Introduction — 87
6.2 Educational outcomes of children from low income families in Scotland — 88
6.3 The extent to which schools are responsible for educational disadvantage — 95
6.4 Factors within schools which tend to help or hinder pupil progress — 97
6.5 Equalisation of educational opportunities — the present and future policy context — 99
6.6 Conclusions — 102

7 Transport — 106
by John Farrington.

7.1 Introduction — 106
7.2 Transport and the needs of low income consumers — 107
7.3 Transport policy — 109
7.4 Car ownership and public transport use — 113
7.5 Conclusions — 118

CONTENTS

8 High Street Goods and Services — 121
by Keri Davies and Mark Gabbott.

8.1 Introduction	121
8.2 The low income consumer of goods and services	122
8.3 The provision of high street goods and services in Scotland	125
8.4 Problems of access to the market	128
8.5 Price-quality and price-volume relationships	129
8.6 Access to market information	131
8.7 Conclusions	132

9 Social Security — 135
by Angus Erskine.

9.1 Introduction	135
9.2 The extent of dependence	137
9.3 Claimant need	140
9.4 The workings of the benefit system	142
9.5 The Social Fund	143
9.6 The interaction between National Insurance and income support	144
9.7 Occupational and state welfare	146
9.8 Appeals, adjudication and policing	147
9.9 Advice, information and services for claimants	148
9.10 Conclusions	149

10 Credit and Debt — 153
by Michael Adler and David McMillan.

10.1 Introduction	153
10.2 The extent of consumer credit and consumer indebtedness	153
10.3 Credit scoring	156
10.4 Patterns of indebtedness	158
10.5 Debt advice	160
10.6 Debt enforcement through the courts	161
10.7 Convenient credit	163
10.8 Alternative forms of credit	164
10.9 The regulation of consumer credit	166
10.10 Conclusions	169

11 Legal Services   173
by Elizabeth Macdonald.

11.1 Introduction   173
11.2 Legal aid   174
11.3 Alternatives to court procedures   178
11.4 The legal profession — effect on the delivery of
     legal services   180
11.5 Other factors limiting access to legal services   182
11.6 Alternative forms of provision of legal services   183
11.7 Quality of service   185
11.8 Conclusion   186

About the Scottish Consumer Council

The Scottish Consumer Council (SCC) was set up by the Government in 1975 to give a vigorous and independent voice to consumers in Scotland. Our purpose is to promote the interests of Scottish consumers with particular regard for those people who experience disadvantages in society.

The issues affecting those on low incomes have always been of concern to the Council. This book provides an overview which draws together many of the facets of life on a low income. Although the book focuses on Scotland, much of the material is of relevance throughout the UK and beyond.

Chapter 1, which contains the views of the SCC, outlines the main trends that have had an impact on the number of people living on low incomes and summarises the main characteristics of consumer detriment. Chapters 2 to 11 were commissioned from individual experts whose findings and views are personal to them and do not necessarily represent the views of the SCC.

The entire project was overseen by the SCC's Economic Affairs Committee chaired by Gordon Smith. The other members of the Committee were Pat Cooper, Peter Edmondson, Deirdre Hutton, Tom O'Malley, Yvonne Osman and Ralph Palmer. The project was managed by Gillian Fyfe, the SCC's Senior Research Officer. The chapters were originally commissioned by Graham Atherton, then the SCC's Senior Research Officer. The text was edited by Gillian Fyfe, copy edited by Katie Carr and prepared for publication by Jackie McCrea and Audrey Paterson.

The members of the Scottish Consumer Council (Autumn 1993) are Deirdre Hutton (Chairman), Winnie Sherry (Vice-Chairman), Joan Aitken, Pat Cooper, Kim Donald, Peter Edmondson, Cowan Ervine, Bernard Forteath, Tom O'Malley, May Kidd, Yvonne Osman, Ralph Palmer, Gordon Smith and Mark Steiner.

The Scottish Consumer Council publishes a wide range of policy papers and reports on consumer issues. Most of them are on sale from the Council's office. Please send for a publication list to:

Scottish Consumer Council
Royal Exchange House
100 Queen Street
Glasgow G1 3DN.
Tel: 041 - 226 - 5261.

About the contributors

Michael Adler is Reader in Social Policy in the Department of Social Policy and Social Work at the University of Edinburgh.

Lisa Curtice is a Research Fellow in the Research Unit in Health and Behavioural Change at the University of Edinburgh.

Dr Keri Davies is a Lecturer in Marketing in the Institute for Retail Studies at the University of Stirling.

Dr Angus Erskine is a Lecturer in the Department of Social Policy and Social Work at the University of Glasgow.

Dr John Farrington is Senior Lecturer in the Department of Geography at the University of Aberdeen.

Dr Gillian Fyfe is Senior Research Officer with the Scottish Consumer Council.

Dr Mark Gabbott is a Lecturer in Marketing in the Institute for Retail Studies at the University of Stirling.

Robina Goodlad is a Senior Lecturer in the Centre for Housing Research at the University of Glasgow.

Damian Killeen is the Director of Strathclyde Poverty Alliance.

Elizabeth Macdonald is Acting Legal Advisory Officer with the Scottish Consumer Council.

David McMillan is a Research Assistant in the Department of Social Policy and Social Work at the University of Edinburgh.

Dr Sheila Riddell is a Lecturer in the Department of Education at the University of Stirling.

Dr Bill Sheldrick is Research Manager with Heatwise Glasgow Ltd.

Dr Nicholas Williams is a Senior Lecturer in the Department of Geography at the University of Aberdeen.

Acknowledgements

The Scottish Consumer Council would like to thank all the authors for their contributions to the book. The SCC would also like to acknowledge the help of the following people for their comments on earlier drafts of individual chapters: Gillian Bull, Deborah Khudabux, Suzi Leather, Jeremy Mitchell, Peter Sherry, Robin Simpson and Beti Wyn Thomas. The SCC would also like to thank Professor Ian Willock of the University of Dundee for preparing a background paper for the chapter on legal services.

Michael Adler and David McMillan would like to thank a number of representatives of consumer credit institutions and money advice agencies for providing information and Lyn Thomas (University of Edinburgh), Andrew Fleming, Sue Morris and Alison Platts (The Scottish Office Central Research Unit) for their helpful comments on an earlier draft of chapter 10.

Lisa Curtice would like to thank Carolyn Thomson for literature searching, Fiona Clark and Alex Watson for secretarial assistance and Xanthe Fry for editing. Brian Chaplin, David Donnison, Vivienne Nathanson, Alison Petch, Jenny Popay and Penny Richardson generously provided helpful comments but bear no responsibility for the final text of chapter 5. The Research Unit in Health and Behavioural Change is funded by the Chief Scientist Office, the Health Education Board for Scotland and the Economic and Social Research Council. However, the opinions expressed in chapter 5 are those of the author and not the funding bodies.

John Farrington gratefully acknowledges the help received during the course of research for his chapter from many Regional and Islands Council officers, Strathclyde PTE officers, transport operators, the Transport Users Consultative Committee for Scotland and academic researchers.

Robina Goodlad and Nicholas Williams would like to thank Ade Kearns and Moira Munro for their helpful comments on an earlier draft of chapter 2.

Elizabeth Macdonald would like to thank the Scottish Legal Aid Board which made available an unpublished draft of its *Research Report on the Distribution of the Supply of Legal Aid in Scotland*.

Sheila Riddell would like to thank Dr Lindsay Paterson for permission to reproduce Figures 6.1, 6.2, 6.3 and 6.4.

# Life on a Low Income

by Gillian Fyfe

1.1 Introduction

In 1977 the National Consumer Council published a book *Why the Poor Pay More*[1] which examined the extent to which those on low incomes were disadvantaged, not only by having less money to spend, but also by being more likely to receive poor value for money or poor quality services.

This double disadvantage of having less money and getting less for it in terms of both quality and quantity has been called consumer detriment[2]. This detriment applies to goods and services paid for directly, for example food or transport, and also to public services paid for indirectly, such as the education or health services. In relation to public services it may be harder to see how the poor can be at a disadvantage or receive a service of lower quality. Many of our public services are based on the ideal that all those who use them should receive services that are of an equal standard and that they are equally accessible. However, as we will see in some of the following chapters—for example on education, and health and welfare services—this is not always the case.

Since the publication of the National Consumer Council's book, much has changed in the UK. Many more people now own their own homes and possess expensive consumer durables such as cars, video recorders and washing machines (Figure 1.1). Despite this general growth in material prosperity average incomes have grown at a lower rate for those in the lower half of the income distribution[3]. A large number of people still live on low incomes (32.4% had less than £175 per week in 1990/91)[4] and social security benefits made up 10.8% of average gross weekly household incomes in 1990/91[5].

1.2 The Book's Purpose

The Scottish Consumer Council decided in 1992 to commission a series of papers to assess the extent to which the poor still pay more. The SCC has a particular remit to represent the interests of those who are disadvantaged. In commissioning this book we have established how disadvantage is experienced in Scotland today and the findings of the book will help inform the future policy of both the SCC and others at all levels from national government down.

This book is not concerned with the extent of poverty nor with its explanation; instead it documents the way in which those on low incomes experience disadvantage every day and throughout their lives. Living on a low income and living in poverty are not synonymous. The book focuses on low income consumers but references to those who are poor or living in poverty are made where appropriate by individual authors. It concentrates on Scotland but almost all the issues raised and problems identified are common to the whole of the UK. The contributions to the book cover a very wide range of service sectors and touch on most facets of daily life.

Ten service sectors were chosen and specialists in each field invited to contribute a chapter to the book. The subject areas covered are housing, energy and fuel consumption, food and nutrition, health and welfare, education, transport, high street goods and services, social security, credit and debt, and legal services. Much has been

Figure 1.1 Percentage of households with certain durable goods, 1964 to 1992

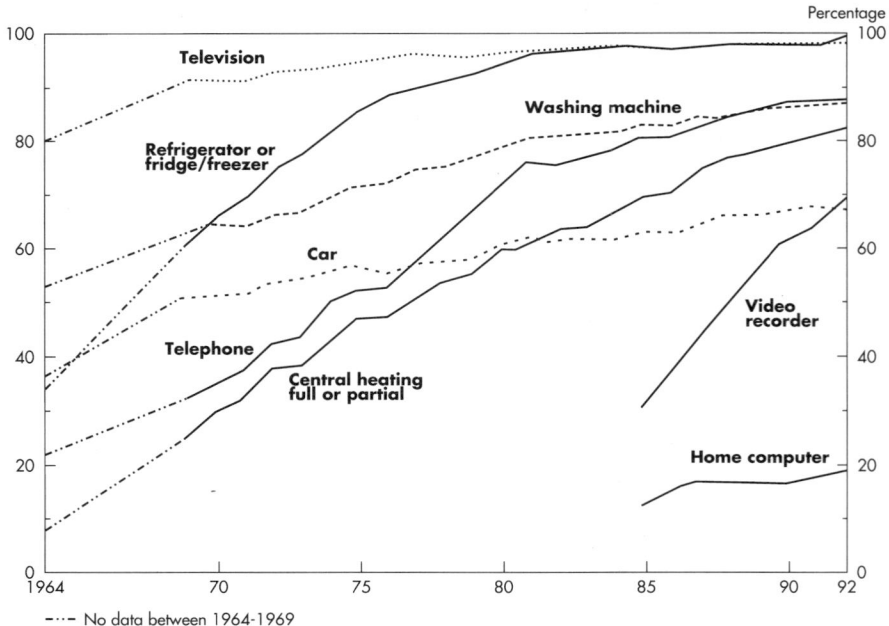

--- No data between 1964-1969

Note: Percentages are a percentage of all households with certain durable goods.
Source: Central Statistical Office, *Family Spending: A Report on the 1992 Family Expenditure Survey*, HMSO, 1993, Chart A.

written about each of these topics individually, but few attempts have been made to address all the issues together so that the connections between them and the complexity of multiple disadvantage are highlighted.

We hope that the book will both stimulate discussion and encourage action to tackle the problems identified. Those on low incomes face a wide, complex and interconnected range of problems. Imaginative and far-sighted solutions are required at *national* level to overcome this web of detriment. Identifying these large scale solutions is beyond the scope of this book but they should be addressed as a matter of urgency by the relevant agencies and organisations.

1.3 Living on Low Incomes

Throughout the book the term 'low income consumers' is used in its widest sense to include not only those who are in employment and paid low wages, but also those who have to live on very little money from whatever source. This includes the elderly, people with disabilities, single parents, students, those who are unemployed and those who are homeless.

Everyone, whatever their income, has basic needs that have to be met throughout their lives. Predominant among these needs are adequate food, warmth, light and shelter. Beyond these basic needs people aspire to a good education, to be looked after by health services and to be able to travel to get to work, go shopping or visit friends. When people can no longer meet their basic needs on their existing incomes they need help to make ends meet in the form of social security benefits. As this book shows, whether our basic needs and aspirations are met, or not, largely depends on how much money we have to spend and what choices are available to us.

For many people, living on a low income is a lifetime experience; for others, a sudden change in circumstances such as losing a job, family break-up, retirement or sickness results in a loss of income. Whatever the reasons involved, and whatever the income available, everyone makes use of a wide range of goods and services every day. All these goods and services need to be accessible and for consumers to get a good deal they need to be able to choose from several options. With public services there is often no element of choice and issues of quality and value for money become more important. For some services it is important that consumers have an official body to represent their interests, for example Local Health Councils or the Transport Users Consultative Committee for Scotland. Representation is particularly vital in relation to services where consumers have no choice at all. Whatever the goods being bought or the service being paid for (directly or indirectly) clear information is essential so that informed choices and decisions can be made. When things go wrong, simple complaints systems and appropriate forms of redress or compensation should be available.

Disadvantage and detriment permeate daily lives and restrict opportunities from birth until old age. At the day to day level those on low incomes spend proportionately more (but usually less in actual money) on household goods and services, fuel, light and power, and food than those who are better off[6]. Despite spending so much on these basics many people still live in damp houses that are difficult to heat and eat food which is nutritionally inadequate.

Children growing up in households with low incomes often leave school with fewer qualifications and as they move into adult life have very constricted levels of mobility, poorer health and lower life expectancy. Dependence on social security benefits is unavoidable for many and shortage of money forces people to borrow at high rates of interest which may ultimately lead to debt. When problems arise redress is often hard to get in situations ranging from exchanging a faulty toaster to getting compensation for an injury. Access to legal services is very difficult and too expensive for many people.

1.4 Low Incomes, Low Pay and Poverty

There are many quantitative and qualitative definitions used to delimit low pay and poverty, although not low incomes. Although there is no official definition of low pay in the UK, definitions have been developed by the Council of Europe and the Low Pay Unit. The Council of Europe's 'decency threshold' set at 66% of adult full-time earnings was equivalent to £207.13 per week in September 1993[7]. A commonly used definition of low pay is that used by the Low Pay Unit of two-thirds of median (mid-point) male earnings. In September 1993 this was £197.27 per week, slightly lower than the Council of Europe's decency threshold[8].

The European Commission (EC) defines the poverty threshold as 50% of the average disposable income per head in the country in question. Using this definition, one in five people in Britain are poor and nearly a quarter of all poor households in the EC are British[9].

As well as definitions that give exact sums of money which delimit low pay or poverty there are those that give an indication of quality of life. One definition identifies people as being in poverty "when they lack the resources to obtain the types of diet, participate in the activities and have the living conditions and amenities which are customary or at least widely encouraged or approved in the societies in which they belong"[10]. A similar qualitative definition has been developed by the EC which identifies the poor as "persons whose resources (material, cultural and social) are so limited as to exclude them from the minimum acceptable way of life in the member states in which they live"[11].

Using the lowest 30% of the income distribution in the UK the population living on low incomes can be looked at by household composition. Table 1.1 shows which types of household are most likely to be in different income categories. Those represented most strongly in the lowest 30% of the household income distribution are single pensioners and pensioners in general. In the lowest decile group (lowest 10% of the income distribution), about three-fifths are retired and a quarter are single people below retiral age. In the second decile group (lowest 10%-20% of the income distribution), half are retired people and a fifth are single adults with dependent children. In the third decile group (lowest 20%-30% of the income distribution), the distribution is more evenly balanced with a lower proportion of pensioners and a higher proportion of couples with children.

Table 1.1 Proportions of households on low incomes (percentages)

Composition of household	Decile Group of the Household Income Distribution		
	Lowest 10 per cent	Second decile group	Third decile group
One adult, retired	58	36	15
Couple, retired	1	14	28
Couple with children	2	8	16
Single adult with children	7	20	11
Couple, non-retired without children	3	7	11
Single adult, non-retired	27	12	11
Other	–	–	2

Note: Figures have been rounded and percentages may not add up to 100%.

Based on: Central Statistical Office, *Family Spending: A Report on the 1992 Family Expenditure Survey*, HMSO, 1993, Table 6.

1.5 Social and Economic Trends

Demographic and economic changes throughout Britain in the last 16 years since *Why the Poor Pay More* was published have had wide-reaching consequences. Some of the changes are the result of ongoing trends that will continue to be important in the future. Of relevance here are the changes that have had an impact on the number of people living on low incomes and their characteristics.

(a) An ageing population

Over the last 16 years, the number of people over 75 years old has steadily increased and in 1991 7% of the British population were over 75[12]. This general ageing trend is expected to continue. More women (8%) than men (5%) are over 75 and represent about three-fifths of this age group[13]. Since 1977 those in the 65-74 age range have stayed roughly constant at about 9% of the population[14].

As we have seen in section 1.4 above, pensioners are the largest group living on low incomes and single pensioners are particularly vulnerable. Of these pensioners more are women who may also have lower incomes than men of the same age because they have not worked at all or for so long. An increasing proportion of the population is now reliant solely on income from a pension. The ageing population is now under debate in relation to the Government's intentions to alter the balance between state welfare provision and what individuals provide for their old age through private insurance[15][16].

(b) Household size

There has been a general decrease in household size so that by 1991 14% of the British population were living alone[17]. Half of those aged 75 or over live alone. There has also been a decrease in the number of households consisting of a married or cohabiting couple with dependent children. By 1991 only a quarter of all households consisted of this 'traditional' family[18].

Much of the increase in people living alone has been among those over pension age who, it has already been noted, are likely to be living on very low incomes. Single people below retiral age are also vulnerable and a quarter of the poorest tenth of the population are single people.

(c) Single parent families

There has been a steady increase in single parent families from 8% of families in 1971 to 13% in 1981 and 19% in 1991[19]. (The term 'single parent family' is used to refer to any family with children headed by one adult.) The increase is accounted for by more families headed by single, divorced and separated mothers. The number of families headed by single fathers has stayed constant at 1% or 2% since 1971. Half of all single mothers are aged between 16 and 24 and single parents in general tend to be younger than the heads of other families.

Single parent families have lower incomes than other families with a much higher proportion (68%) having a weekly household income of less than £150 than other families (10%)[20].

(d) Unemployment

Rates of unemployment in the UK have risen since the late 1970s peaking in 1987 at 10.9% before falling again to around 6% in 1991. Since 1991 unemployment has risen again to around 10.6% in January 1993[21] and stood at 10.4% in August 1993[22]. This rate of unemployment masks higher rates of unemployment among some categories of workers. For example, in 1991 the rate in Britain for semi-skilled manual workers was 13% and for unskilled manual workers 16%[23]. The unemployment figures also do not include many people who are not registered as unemployed but who nevertheless do not have a job.

(e) Employment

Many changes in the nature of employment have also taken place. The deregulation of the labour market, including the removal of protective legislation and the abolition of Wages Councils, has meant that more workers are now more vulnerable to dismissal or pay cuts[24].

Part time workers now represent 23% of all employees in the UK[25]. Part time workers not only earn less but also have restricted employment rights. With this trend towards the casualisation of labour, estimates suggest that about a third of those in work at any one time are in jobs that will not last[26].

In 1986 the Government reduced the powers of Wages Councils which set enforceable minimum rates of pay in Britain. The 1986 Wages Act removed their right to set holiday entitlements, determine differential rates and set minimum rates for those under 21. The wages of young people in this age group have fallen since then[27]. The abolition of Wages Councils in August 1993 makes the position of low paid workers (most of whom are women) even more precarious.

(f) Social security benefits

The proportion of gross household income in the UK coming from social security benefits has risen from 12.6% in 1980/81 to 13.1% in 1992[28][29]. During the last 16 years those who are unemployed have had an increasing reliance on supplementary benefit and its replacement income support. There has also been a large increase in the numbers of single parents dependent on income support (see section 9.2 in the chapter on social security).

At a national level the Government is currently examining ways of reducing public expenditure. The main focus of attention is the social security budget which accounts for a third of all Government expenditure. Cuts to the social security budget are likely to hit Scots particularly hard because a higher proportion of household income in Scotland comes from benefits (see section 1.6 below). A suggested tax on invalidity benefit, for example, would affect three times as many Scots as those living in East Anglia which has the lowest level of claimants[30].

(g) Inequalities in income

Evidence from *Households Below Average Income* produced by the Department of Social Security points to increasing inequality in incomes[31]. Although overall the average income grew by around 28% before housing costs from 1979 to 1988/89, the rate of growth was much lower for those at the bottom end of the income scale[32]. For the bottom 10% of the population incomes only grew by an estimated 2% and for those in the bottom 10%-20% of the population by 5% before housing costs[33]. In 1979 the bottom half of the income distribution received 33% of total income but by 1988/89 this had fallen to 28% of total income[34]. In 1979 only 9% of the population had incomes below half of the contemporary average, but by 1988/89 this had risen to 22% of the population[35].

All these trends at the British and UK levels have played a part in determining who and how many live on low incomes. As we will see in the next section the impact of some of these trends has been more profound in Scotland, resulting in higher proportions of the population living on low incomes.

1.6 Scotland in Context

(a) Low incomes

Scotland has a higher proportion of the population living on low incomes than the UK average. Comparisons of average weekly household incomes show that more Scots have incomes at the lower end of the scale (Table 1.2).

In 1990/91, 32.4% of households in the UK had less than £175 per week but in Scotland a higher proportion (40.9%) had less than £175 per week[36].

Table 1.2 Average weekly household income, 1991

Households with weekly income	% Scotland	% UK
under £60	9.4	6.0
£60 and under £80	9.1	5.1
£80 and under £100	7.0	5.1
£100 and under £150	11.1	10.6
£150 and under £200	6.8	8.2
£200 and under £250	7.9	7.9
£250 and under £300	7.3	7.5
£300 or more	41.2	49.6

Note: Figures have been rounded and percentages may not add up to 100%.

Source: The Scottish Office, *Scottish Abstract of Statistics 1992*, Government Statistical Service, 1993, Table 10.13.

(b) Low pay

In April 1992, 21.2% of Scottish men working full time on adult rates earned less than £200 (gross) per week compared with only 18.7% of men in Britain as a whole. For Scottish women, 53.8% working full time at adult rates earned less than £200 (gross) weekly compared with 45.2% in Britain[37]. In 1992 the average gross weekly earnings of full time employees on adult rates was £324.6 in Scotland compared to £340.1 in Britain[38].

In 1992 the Scottish Low Pay Unit estimated that 45.1% of all employees fell below the low pay threshold[39]. In Scotland there is a significant gap between the highest and lowest pay. The low pay threshold developed by the Scottish Low Pay

Unit marks the lower limit of an acceptable living wage. Many low paid workers are paid at levels below this threshold. More full time workers in Scotland (32.0%) fell below the low pay threshold in 1992 than in Britain as a whole (27.1%). Over half of all women who work full time earned wages below the low pay threshold (52.2%)[40]. The situation for part time workers (most of whom are women) is even worse and three-quarters of part time workers earn less than the low pay threshold. Throughout Scotland there are wide variations in the number of workers on low pay according to analyses by the Scottish Low Pay Unit[41].

(c) Unemployment

Unemployment rates in Scotland have followed UK trends but at a higher level, until the early 1990s (Table 1.3). Unemployment rates within Scotland vary widely. In 1991 they ranged from 14.5% in the Western Isles and 12.1% in Strathclyde to 3.8% in Shetland and 4.1% in Grampian[42].

Table 1.3 Unemployment rates (percentages)

	1981	1983	1985	1987	1989	1991	1992	Jan 1993
UK	8.1	10.5	10.9	10.0	6.3	8.1	9.7	10.6
Scotland	9.9	12.3	12.9	13.0	9.3	8.7	9.5	9.9

Source: Central Statistical Office, *Regional Trends* No.28, HMSO, 1993, Table 7.15 and *Regional Trends*, No.27, HMSO, 1992, Table 7.16.

(d) Social security benefits

The proportion of household income derived from social security benefits is higher in Scotland (17.0%) than the UK average (13.1%)[43]. Spending on social security benefits is higher in Scotland than the UK average for sickness and invalidity benefit, and income support (Table 1.4).

Table 1.4 Estimated government expenditure on certain cash benefits, 1990/91

£ per head	Retirement pension	Sickness & invalidity	Unemployment	Disablement	Income support	Child benefit
UK	394.1	84.3	15.7	6.9	162.3	87.1
England	397.3	74.6	15.8	6.7	156.4	86.7
Wales	424.1	140.3	13.9	7.9	176.0	84.8
Scotland	372.6	132.0	14.9	6.9	177.8	83.8
N. Ireland	311.7	121.3	18.3	10.9	267.0	114.8

Source: Central Statistical Office, *Regional Trends*, No.28, HMSO, 1993, Table 8.6.

1.7 Household Expenditure

Data from successive Family Expenditure Surveys (FES) have shown that since the late 1970s the proportion of household expenditure spent on food has decreased substantially and there have also been decreases in the proportion spent on clothing and footwear, and motoring and travel fares. Those at the lower end of the income scale spend a higher proportion of their weekly budget on fuel, light and power, food, and household goods and services than those who are better off (Figure 1.2).

Figure 1.2 Expenditure of all households by decile groups of gross household income, 1992

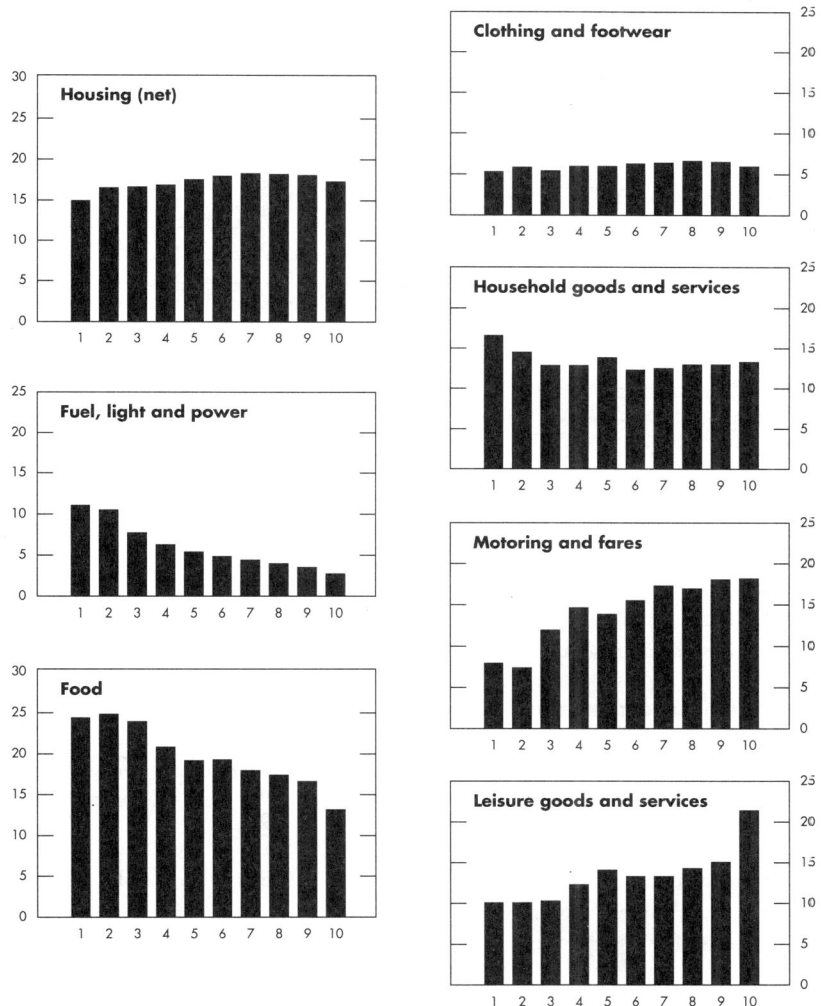

Decile groups of average weekly household income

Note: Percentages are expenditure on commodity or service group as a percentage of total household expenditure. Income bands are decile groups of the household income distribution (group 1 is the lowest 10% of the income distribution).
Source: Central Statistical Office, *Family Spending: A Report on the 1992 Family Expenditure Survey*, HMSO, 1993, Chart B.

They spend proportionately less on motoring and travel fares and on leisure goods and services.

Household expenditure in Scotland is much lower (£237.67 per week in 1992) than the UK average (£271.83) and is the third lowest of all the UK regions[44]. In addition, in 1992 Scotland had an average weekly disposable household income of £257 compared with the UK average of £280 per week[45]. The FES definition of disposable income is gross weekly cash income minus statutory deductions and payments of income tax and national insurance contributions. Scots spend less than the UK average for all commodities and services, except tobacco, and clothing and footwear (Table 1.5).

Table 1.5 Average weekly household expenditure (£)

Commodity or service	Scotland	UK
Housing (gross)	44.72	54.12
Housing (net)	35.92	47.36
Fuel, light and power	12.87	13.02
Food	45.87	47.66
Alcoholic drink	10.75	11.06
Tobacco	7.41	5.38
Clothing and footwear	17.20	16.39
Household goods	19.25	21.90
Household services	11.64	13.40
Personal goods and services	8.85	10.18
Motoring expenditure	27.71	35.66
Fares and other travel costs	4.96	7.20
Leisure goods	10.85	13.32
Leisure services	22.87	27.56
Miscellaneous	1.52	1.75
All expenditure groups	237.67	271.83

Source: Central Statistical Office, *Family Spending: A Report on the 1992 Family Expenditure Survey*, HMSO, 1993, Table 37.

1.8 Redressing Detriment

The evidence presented in the following chapters confirms that the poor are paying for their poverty in every sense. Not only do they pay proportionately more than other people for basic necessities like food and power, but in some cases they also pay more in actual money—when, for example, they cannot afford to bulk-buy or take advantage of special offers, or have to spend more on heating or credit repayments. In non-monetary terms the poor also pay for their poverty through inadequate nutrition, ill-health, low mobility, restricted opportunities and reduced life expectancy.

Consumer detriment for those on low incomes exists to some extent in every service sector. In some cases, for example in relation to food, health and energy consumption, consumer detriment is deeply ingrained and extensive. Only in relation to high street goods and services can it be argued that those on low incomes are only relatively disadvantaged (in this sector the real problem lies in access to the market).

The characteristics of consumer detriment outlined in section 1.9 below are merely symptoms of poverty. If the underlying causes of poverty in the UK are to be addressed at a national level, politicians must consider structural changes to economic and social policies. It is possible, however, to alleviate the problems faced by those on low incomes in the shorter term by implementing some of the solutions to consumer detriment suggested below—and throughout the book. These problems need to be tackled in a systematic way which allows those on low incomes opportunities to achieve a satisfactory quality of life while retaining their self-respect and independence.

1.9 Characteristics of Consumer Detriment

(a) Lack of capital

First and foremost, those on low incomes are at a disadvantage simply because they lack the financial resources available to everyone else. Lack of capital means that they cannot afford to spend large sums of money at any one time. This automatically excludes them from special offers that involve a large initial outlay, and they cannot buy in bulk to make savings. Budgeting on a low income often means budgeting on a day to day or a week to week basis. The savings that can be made by weekly or monthly shopping at a large supermarket cannot be enjoyed by those who can only afford to buy in small amounts on a daily basis. Being unable to pay outright for essential larger items like refrigerators or clothing leads those on low incomes to borrow money to pay for them and the types of credit available to those on low incomes are usually expensive to use.

Lack of money not only means that those on low incomes have to budget on a short term basis; it also means they may not be able to afford some things at all. Many consumer durables like freezers, refrigerators, cars, washing machines and economical heaters allow their owners to get better value for money but involve a large outlay. Low ownership of these items among those on low incomes reduces their opportunities to make savings by, for example, cutting out launderette charges and allowing travel to discount stores inaccessible by public transport.

Lack of capital and lack of capital equipment are the obvious outcomes of poverty. So long as people remain poor they cannot buy the consumer durables which would enable them to make savings. One solution is for the state to pay for essential items such as cookers, refrigerators and beds. As Angus Erskine shows in the chapter on social security, the Social Fund which is designed to help people with special one-off needs discriminates against the very poor. Those who cannot afford to repay the loan are not given one and, therefore, have to continue coping without basic necessities. Those who are too poor to repay a loan should be given a grant instead to pay for essentials.

Other schemes involving government assistance should be reassessed to ensure that those who are very poor can participate. As Bill Sheldrick explains in chapter 3, some people could not afford even the token contributions required to take advantage of Home Energy Efficiency Scheme insulation improvements, and the removal of the client contribution in October 1993 is to be welcomed.

Another way for those on low incomes to make the best use of what little money they have is to pool resources. There is potential for the development of more community ventures but they need to be properly supported and funded. For example, local authorities should continue to support and develop food co-operatives which can bring savings to those on low incomes and may help achieve dietary change.

Although, as Michael Adler and David McMillan point out in chapter 10, credit unions are not currently very significant for those on low incomes, there is still a need for the continued development of community-based credit unions which can be used by everyone, not just those in employment. The strategy for the growth of the credit union movement recently drawn up by the Credit Union Working Party[46] provides many recommendations that will help ensure that the benefits of credit unions will be available to more people[47].

(b) Access

A second characteristic of detriment is poor access to all types of goods and services. The principles of access include:

- *Physical access*—For example, is it possible to get to the local supermarket on foot? Is there a solicitor in the area? Is there a bus service to the nearest hospital? Is mains gas available in the area?

- *Cognitive access*—For instance, do you understand the terms of your credit agreement? Do you understand the options for treatment outlined by your doctor?

- *Cultural/social access*—For example, does the official speak your language? Do you lack confidence in dealing with professionals? Does the lawyer understand your cultural background?

Problems of access are encountered in every service sector. In chapter 8, for example, Keri Davies and Mark Gabbott identify lack of public transport as a cause of poor access to town centre shops and out-of-town stores. Also, some access difficulties are the result of the sparse provision of services; for instance, few lawyers have their offices in housing estates.

Solutions to problems of access are difficult to identify when poor access is the result of market led service provision. Retailers, lawyers and bus companies, for example, do not operate in areas where they would be commercially unsuccessful and it is, of course, unreasonable and unrealistic to expect them to do so. Mechanisms for improving access should, however, be sought by national and local government. Subsidising socially necessary bus services is one way in which local authorities can improve physical access. Public provision of services normally confined to the private sector can also address access problems. Publicly funded law centres, for example, can provide legal services in areas where there is little or no alternative source of legal advice.

Access problems caused by a language barrier or simply by professional jargon are more easily overcome. All service providers, but particularly those which rely heavily on professional jargon, should make a commitment to the use of plain language and where appropriate provide interpreters.

Barriers to access caused by lack of cultural understanding need longer term solutions. For example, more lawyers from ethnic minorities with an understanding of the community are needed to address problems of access faced by people from ethnic communities in relation to legal services[48].

Problems of access caused by the hierarchical nature of British society are firmly entrenched and difficult to address. Officials and professionals often seem intimidating to those who seek their help and bureaucracy may often exclude people from participation. Those in positions of authority should make every effort to allow those on low incomes to participate on equal terms. Schemes which enhance self-confidence should be widely promoted. A good example of an initiative of this kind is the development of the Patient Supporter scheme within the NHS, which Lisa Curtice mentions in chapter 5.

(c) Choice

Lack of choice is also a characteristic of detriment which affects those on low incomes. Choice is a vital weapon in ensuring that consumers get a good deal. In a free market, consumers can choose to buy another product or use another firm if they do not get what they want for their money. For many people, using another firm or buying another product may not be an option simply because they cannot afford to do so. In many cases where public services are involved there may be no choice at all; for example, there may only be one secondary school in the area or little choice of housing if you are a local authority tenant.

Lack of choice is as difficult to address as access when it depends on private sector provision. Where choice is dependent on the policies of private firms the needs of those on low incomes should be taken into account. Planning authorities should, for instance, consider their needs when approving sites for new supermarkets.

Increasing consumer choice is a central theme in the Citizen's Charter with the underlying belief that increased choice will lead to improved quality of service. In relation to public services like health and education, consumers may often find that exercising their right to choose is difficult if not impossible. Although parents can in theory choose which school their child is to attend, in practice there may be no choice at all because the school roll is already full or they cannot afford the travel fares to a more distant school.

For many on low incomes choice is restricted by price and there is often no option but to buy the cheapest product or service. This restriction is particularly detrimental where it affects health or quality of life. Being unable to buy economical heaters or healthy food simply because there is no option has serious consequences for well-being, as Bill Sheldrick and Damian Killeen demonstrate in chapters 3 and 4.

(d) Information and advice

Those on low incomes often cannot afford to pay for independent advice and information and are not aware of their rights or how to go about getting them fulfilled. Being unaware of their entitlement to benefits or to concessionary fares excludes people from take-up. Not knowing where to go for help and not knowing about entitlements puts those on low incomes at a big disadvantage.

The need for improved information and advice for those on low incomes is a common theme in the following chapters. Good information cannot, of course, compensate for lack of choice or poor access, but it can allow people to make informed decisions, and has the potential to substantially alleviate problems. Providers of goods and services should ensure that all the information they provide is appropriate, clear, up-to-date and in plain language. It is particularly important that consumers can have written information that they can take home to refer to or study.

Sources of independent advice and information tailored to the needs of those on low incomes also require development and expansion. Many of the authors of the following chapters argue the case for enhanced support for Citizens Advice Bureaux, Consumer Advice Centres and other centres providing specialist advice. Other sources of advice also need to be developed. For example, in chapter 2 Robina Goodlad and Nicholas Williams call for the role of housing authorities as providers of advice and information to be clarified and the adequacy of their service assessed.

There is no strategic overview of the provision of advice services in Scotland and a review of current provision is required. Identification of gaps in provision (both geographical and subject based) would allow a coherent strategy for the development of these services to be put into place. Any strategy for improving advice and information services must be accompanied by adequate funding.

(e) Representation and consultation

In general a lack of representation for, and consultation about, consumer interests can lead to detriment. Representation is essential whenever it is a replacement for choice. Those on low incomes particularly need to have their voice heard as they often have a very restricted ranges of choices open to them. Lack of strong consumer representation may be one of the reasons why some bus users, for example, have to put up with poor quality vehicles, erratic timetabling, lack of information and inappropriate scheduling and routing. The users of community care services also need a statutory body to represent their interests.

While users of some services may have a statutory representative who is consulted by service providers, other representatives may not be consulted at all. Even when consultation does take place it is important that not only representatives but consumers themselves are consulted and involved in decision making. Effective methods of consultation which involve both consumers and their representatives are needed. Consultation is the first step towards full participation by consumers in the decisions about the things that affect them. In the housing field, for instance, tenant liaison officers can help promote the interests of tenants and assist with preparing papers to be submitted to local authority committees.

(f) Discriminatory rules

A sixth characteristic of consumer detriment is the discriminatory rules operated by some service providers which in effect put those on low incomes at a disadvantage. Rules of this type include:

- the pricing policies of fuel companies which mean that the less fuel you use the more you pay per unit, chiefly because of uniform standing charges;

- the policies of retailers that result in higher prices for small packs and quantities;
- the interaction between benefits and income that traps many in poverty.

Rules which discriminate against those on low incomes should be rewritten as a matter of urgency. The rules which result in disincentives to work because of the interaction between benefits and wages need particular attention and must be reviewed.

1.10 Summary

In commissioning the chapters for this book we have provided a comprehensive overview of the disadvantages currently facing those on low incomes in Scotland. The book will help dispel myths about the ways in which people experience disadvantage and will provide an important reference for policy makers at all levels.

Although those on low incomes cannot participate equally or fairly under market conditions it should be recognised that as an integral part of the community they need and have the right to continuing protection and support. The extent of detriment identified throughout this book deserves serious attention and rapid action. Finding solutions to the problems experienced should be given a high priority by Government and local authorities. A wide-ranging review of the measures currently in place to support the poorest in Britain should be initiated without delay. This review would help inform the current debate on levels of benefit, rates of taxation and public spending. Although the solutions to consumer detriment identified here show a way forward which should be taken, more fundamental structural changes are needed to ensure that those who are poor do not remain in poverty.

References to Chapter 1

1. National Consumer Council, *Why the Poor Pay More*, MacMillan, 1977.
2. National Consumer Council, see reference 1.
3. Department of Social Security, *Households Below Average Income : a statistical analysis 1979-1988/89*, HMSO, 1992, Table A1.
4. Central Statistical Office, *Regional Trends*, No. 28, HMSO, 1993, Table 8.2.
5. Central Statistical Office, see reference 4, Table 8.1.
6. Central Statistical Office, *Family Spending: A Report on the 1992 Family Expenditure Survey*, HMSO, 1993, Chart B.
7. Scottish Low Pay Unit, *Payline*, No. 14, September 1993.
8. Scottish Low Pay Unit, see reference 7.
9. European Commission, *Final Report on the Second European Poverty Programme 1985-89*, European Commission COM(91) Final, 13 February 1991.
10. P. Townsend, *Poverty in the UK*, Penguin, 1979.
11. European Commission, *The European Poverty Programme Background Report*, European Commission, August 1991.
12. Central Statistical Office, *General Household Survey 1991*, HMSO, 1993, Table 2.1.
13. Central Statistical Office, see reference 12, Table 2.2.
14. Central Statistical Office, see reference 12, Table 2.1.
15. *The Independent*, 24.6.93.

16. *The Times*, 11.11.93.
17. Central Statistical Office, see reference 12, Table 2.9.
18. Central Statistical Office, see reference 12, Table 2.16.
19. Central Statistical Office, see reference 12, Table 2.18.
20. Central Statistical Office, see reference 12, Table 2.30.
21. Central Statistical Office, see reference 4, Table 7.15.
22. *The Guardian*, 17.9.93.
23. Central Statistical Office, see reference 12, Table 5.7.
24. M. Gillespie and U. Brown, 'Low pay and poverty - a programme for change', *Scottish Affairs*, Vol. 2, 1993, pp. 17-30.
25. M. Gillespie and U. Brown, see reference 24.
26. *The Times*, 26.5.93.
27. M. Gillespie and U. Brown, see reference 24.
28. Central Statistical Office, see reference 4, Table 8.1.
29. Central Statistical Office, see reference 6, Table 40.
30. *The Guardian*, 20.9.93.
31. Department of Social Security, see reference 3.
32. Department of Social Security, see reference 3.
33. Department of Social Security, see reference 3, Table A1.
34. Department of Social Security, see reference 3, Table A3.
35. Department of Social Security, see reference 3, Table F2. (AHC).
36. Central Statistical Office, see reference 4, Table 8.2.
37. Government Statistical Service, *Scottish Abstract of Statistics 1992*, The Scottish Office, 1993, Table 10.5.
38. Government Statistical Service, see reference 37, Table 10.6.
39. Scottish Low Pay Unit, *Payline*, No. 13, June/July 1993.
40. Scottish Low Pay Unit, see reference 39.
41. Scottish Low Pay Unit, see reference 7.
42. Government Statistical Service, see reference 37, Table 9.10a.
43. Central Statistical Office, see reference 6, Table 40.
44. Central Statistical Office, see reference 6, Chart E.
45. Central Statistical Office, see reference 6, Chart G.
46. The Credit Union Working Party which is funded by the Joseph Rowntree Foundation was convened by the National Consumer Council in 1992.
47. National Consumer Council, *Saving for Credit: The Future for Credit Unions in Britain*, NCC, 1994.
48. Scottish Consumer Council, *Access to Justice for Ethnic Minorities*, SCC, 1993.

Housing

by Robina Goodlad and Nicholas Williams

In 1977 those on low incomes often got better value for money for their housing than other people. In this chapter Robina Goodlad and Nicholas Williams explain how the situation has changed since then. In Scotland, home ownership has increased dramatically, largely through sales of public rented housing. Those on low incomes are still, however, largely dependent on rented housing. Rented housing in both the public and private sectors has declined in availability and quality. This trend has been accompanied by an increase in homelessness. Rising rents for those with homes mean that many on low incomes are finding bills harder to pay. While improvements in housing conditions have benefited some people on low incomes, many continue to live in poor quality housing.

2.1 Introduction

Housing is one of the largest items of expenditure low income consumers have to meet. The evidence that poorer people were disadvantaged in the housing system led governments earlier in the century to adopt a commitment to ensure decent housing for all, irrespective of income. By the late 1970s evidence had built up that government policy had achieved significant success. The National Consumer Council's report on consumer detriment, published in 1977[1], concluded that low income households often received better value for money than others. This was largely a result of high quality subsidised council housing; only tenants of furnished privately rented accommodation suffered to any significant degree from consumer detriment. Since 1977, however, there have been major changes in housing policy and a concerted attempt by government to change the role and significance of the public sector. It is appropriate, therefore, at this time to re-examine the housing situation of low income households to see whether their protected position has been maintained. This chapter looks at recent evidence for Scotland and evaluates the changes that have occurred over 14 years of Conservatism.

Throughout this chapter the term 'public renting' is used to include council, new town and Scottish Homes housing for rent; the 'private sector' is defined as including housing for owner occupation and renting from private landlords who may be individuals or companies; and the term 'housing associations' is used to include housing co-operatives which are, along with housing associations, non-profit voluntary associations registered with Scottish Homes and the Registrar of Friendly Societies.

The incoming Conservative Government of 1979 had very different views from its predecessors as to how housing should be provided and managed. Public sector involvement was to be minimised and a greater role given to the private sector and market forces. The general objectives were to increase the numbers of dwellings built or improved for a given level of public resources and to increase consumer choice. More specifically:

- owner occupation was to be extended to more households;

- public expenditure on housing was to be reduced and targeted more accurately at those in need;
- the role of local authorities as providers was to be reduced, partly through transfers of ownership, in practice mainly to housing associations and co-operatives, with majority consent from tenants;
- the private rented sector was to be revived;
- the role of housing associations was to be expanded[2].

All of the above apply to Britain as a whole. In Scotland the Tenants Rights, etc. (Scotland) Act 1980 and the Housing and Planning Act 1986 dealt largely with the expansion of home ownership, mainly through the mechanism of council house sales; and the Housing (Scotland) Act 1988 concentrated on attempting to revitalise the private rented sector, created a new framework for housing associations, and gave public sector tenants new rights to change their landlord.

Measures specific to Scotland included:

- the establishment of Scottish Homes, a quango with wide responsibilities and an important role in implementing government housing policy;
- with reference to low income households, an emphasis on area renewal of run-down public sector estates involving partnerships between the private sector and public sector agencies.

The Scottish context of historically low levels of owner occupation and high levels of public renting provided potentially great scope for these measures. Low income households were to benefit from these changes in a variety of ways.

- Council house sales through the Right-to-Buy would extend home ownership, and its benefits of investment and wealth accumulation, down the income scale. This right allowed tenants of public rented housing to buy their home at a price based on market value discounted according to the length of tenancy as a public sector tenant. More recently the Rent-to-Mortgage scheme allowed tenants to buy their home with the aid of a conventional loan which enabled the mortgage repayments to be broadly equivalent to the rental payments, and an additional interest-free loan, payable on resale.

- The shifting of subsidies from buildings to households would target limited resources where they are needed most, shield low income consumers from unaffordable housing costs and reduce public expenditure. This meant a reduction, for example, in the government grants paid to local authorities in support of the costs of running council housing; and any consequential rent rises would be cushioned through the housing benefit system which is targeted on low income tenants rather than all tenants generally. Tenants in the public, private and housing association sectors are entitled to apply for housing benefit which is payable to households according to a formula which takes account of income, and household characteristics and composition. The reference point for the system is broadly the income support system.

- A diminished role for council housing and an expanded role for the private rented sector and housing associations would increase quality and choice of rented housing, upon which most low income households depend.

To what extent have the Government's aims been achieved in Scotland, and more particularly how have low income households fared since the late 1970s? Has the quantity and quality of affordable rented housing, and choice within the rented sector, increased for low income households? Has the shift of subsidies from buildings to households resulted in a more accurate targeting of money to low income households? Have rents in the public and housing association sectors become more or less affordable for those with low or modest incomes from employment? What are the prospects for low income housing consumers in the last years of the century, and is there any cause for concern?

This chapter attempts to answer these questions drawing on evidence from a number of sources, including the Scottish House Condition Survey carried out by Scottish Homes in 1991[3], and official statistics from the General Household Survey[4] and the Family Expenditure Survey[5]. The evidence available is not, unfortunately, comprehensive, and in any case can be interpreted in different ways. We start by examining the nature and extent of tenure change, and go on to consider housing need, housing finance, and information and advice in the belief that tenure alone is not necessarily an indication of the housing conditions of low income consumers.

2.2 Tenure Change and its Effects

The Government can claim success in expanding home ownership in Scotland, a large part of the increase being due to purchases by sitting tenants from local authorities, New Town Development Corporations and the Scottish Special Housing Association (now Scottish Homes). This expansion has extended owner occupation down the income scale, but ownership has not been financially realistic for the poorest households, even with maximum discounts (up to 70% of market price for flats). Most sitting tenant purchasers have been drawn from the more affluent tenants[6]. Tenants are excluded from the Right-to-Buy and Rent-to-Mortgage schemes if their incomes are not considered big enough to cover repayments. For example, to take advantage of the Rent-to-Mortgage scheme tenants must have incomes above eligibility levels for housing benefit. The change in the housing stock, broken down by tenure, is shown in Table 2.1.

Table 2.1 Scottish housing stock by tenure (000s)

	Owner occupied	Rented privately	Housing association	Public rented
1979	699	200	11	1,073
1981	718	191	36	1,027
1983	781	174	41	1,001
1985	850	161	47	974
1987	922	147	54	943
1989	1,033	133	62	877
1992	1,142	117	71	815

Source: Scottish Office, *Statistical Bulletin*, HSG/1992/5, The Scottish Office, 1992.

Owner occupied dwellings have increased by 443,000 and now make up more than 50% of the stock. The growth of 60,000 in housing association stock has taken place as the public rented stock has shrunk by 258,000 dwellings (mainly as a result of sales to sitting tenants) and the private rented stock has declined by 83,000 dwellings, a decrease of 22% overall in rented housing. This raises questions about housing choice for poorer households.

A high quality public rented sector has in the past protected low income households from their weak position in the market. Between 1979 and 1992, the number of poor households in Scotland increased as a proportion and in absolute terms, largely as a consequence of high levels of unemployment. In the same period, public rented dwellings in Scotland fell by 25%, and furthermore 88% of these sales have been of houses, leading to an increasing proportion of flats in the remaining public sector stock. Over 50% of public rented properties in 1990 were flats (Table 2.2).

The more affluent tenants have been far more likely to buy their home. Scottish Office research already referred to has shown that buyers tend to have higher incomes than other local authority tenants but lower incomes than owner occupiers in general[7]. Evidence from early experience of the Rent-to-Mortgage scheme shows a very similar profile of purchasers, but slightly higher market values for the properties than under the Right-to-Buy[8]. In 1979, 51% of Scottish public sector tenants were in the lowest two income quintiles; in 1990 this had risen to 65%. By contrast, 27% of tenants were in the two highest income quintiles in 1979, and only 17% in 1990 (Table 2.3). A decreasing proportion of households in the upper income ranges are public sector tenants, mainly as a result of tenant purchases.

Attempts to revive the private rented sector through deregulation and targeted subsidies have not been effective so far, and hence the private sector stock available to rent has fallen. Housing associations have been given the task of building rented housing, with local authorities providing many fewer new units than the number sold under the Right-to-Buy. Housing associations have been active in urban and rural areas, and since 1988 have used private loans to supplement government funded grants from Scottish Homes. Associations such as Bield and Kirkcare have built new housing for older people, and in the inner cities community-based associations have transformed many older neighbourhoods and are now building new housing for rent, for shared ownership or for sale. In the peripheral estates new associations and co-operatives such as Calvay are taking over areas of run-down council housing for improvement. Although the housing associations have increased their total stock by more than 600%, this has not compensated for the loss of rented stock in the public and private rented categories.

Given the low levels of home ownership in Scotland in 1979 (about 35%) it could be argued that a declining stock of rented accommodation represents a healthy readjustment to the tenure balance. Movements between tenures, however, do not necessarily provide insight into the housing circumstances and choices available to particular groups such as those on the lowest incomes. The changes in tenure shown in Table 2.1 might be interpreted in a number of ways in relation to their effects on the poorest.

(a) An optimistic view

An optimistic interpretation emphasises that the growth in owner occupation, particularly through the Right-to-Buy, has allowed many lower income consumers

Table 2.2 Housing amenities and dwelling type by income and tenure, Scotland 1990

	%				
	Gross household income (quintiles*)				
	Lowest	2	3	4	Highest
Use of bath					
Exclusive	99	98	100	100	100
Shared	1	1	–	–	–
None	–	1	–	–	–
Type of home					
Detached	3	5	9	17	28
Semi	12	23	18	25	34
Terraced	13	16	26	24	14
Purpose built flat	68	47	40	32	19
Flat, other	3	9	7	2	3
Central Heating					
Yes	55	68	72	78	87

	Tenure					
	Owned outright	Owned with mortgage	Public rented	Housing association	Unf	Furn
Use of bath						
Exclusive	99	100	100	100	94	94
Shared	–	–	–	–	–	6
None	1	–	–	–	6	–
Type of home						
Detached	35	23	–	–	26	11
Semi	24	26	18	6	6	5
Terraced	15	22	30	11	17	–
Purpose built flat	20	24	51	79	44	58
Flat, other	5	5	2	4	7	26
Central heating						
Yes	80	87	70	53	33	55

Unf = Private rented unfurnished
Furn = Private rented furnished
* Lowest quintile = poorest 20%
  Highest quintile = richest 20%

Source: Central Statistical Office, *General Household Survey 1990, Scottish Data*, ESRC Data Archive, Essex, 1993 (authors' tabulation).

Table 2.3 Household income by tenure, Scotland 1979 and 1990

Tenure	Gross household income (quintiles*)						
	Lowest	2	3	4	Highest	%	(sample)
1979							
Public rented	28	23	23	19	8	100	(328)
Unfurnished rented	32	25	23	7	14	100	(44)
Furnished rented	8	31	38	8	15	100	(13)
Owned with mortgage	–	5	12	32	51	100	(126)
Owned outright	18	30	18	11	23	100	(73)
Rent free	5	20	20	35	20	100	(20)
1990							
Public rented	38	27	17	12	5	100	(255)
Housing association	45	31	17	–	7	100	(29)
Unfurnished rented	17	8	17	50	8	100	(12)
Furnished rented	7	36	36	14	7	100	(14)
Owned with mortgage	–	7	22	30	40	100	(215)
Owned outright	11	24	23	19	22	100	(108)
Rent free	17	34	8	34	8	100	(12)

*Lowest quintile = poorest 20%
Highest quintile = richest 20%
Source: Central Statistical Office, *Family Expenditure Survey 1990, Scottish Data*, ESRC Data Archive, Essex, 1993, (authors' tabulation).

to benefit from this popular tenure. The housing stock now contains a continuing, though diminishing, source of cheaper housing for owner occupation, so enhancing choice for consumers who wish to buy. The Right-to-Buy has improved the home ownership prospects of lower income consumers by making available an attractive and relatively cheap stock of good quality housing.

The loss of housing in the private rented sector is regrettable, but regret is tempered by the knowledge that this sector tends to provide the poorest quality housing. The growth of housing association stock compensates for over 70% of the loss in the private rented sector, and the housing concerned is in good condition and well managed. A particular success has been progress made in peripheral estates where transfers of stock and land have taken place. Scottish Homes and the private sector have funded improvements to areas of former council housing, and residents have played a big role in managing the improvements. The overall provision of rented housing is, an optimist might argue, still too great at over 40%. If rent levels for public rented housing have risen in real terms then the poorest continue to be protected through housing benefit.

(b) A pessimistic view

A more pessimistic interpretation is that the growth in owner occupation reflects the enhanced housing prospects of higher income public sector tenants who have been able to exercise the Right-to-Buy. For low income consumers there is not greater choice, but less—a declining prospect of an attractive council let. The growth in housing association housing, welcome as it is, does not fully compensate for the loss of private rented housing, let alone council housing. Furthermore, the condition of much of the unsold council stock in urban areas is unattractive and unacceptable, and rent rises have not been cushioned adequately by the housing benefit system for all low income households. The poorest households are now less well placed to exercise choice of decent, affordable rented housing. Those on low incomes who have achieved owner occupation are more vulnerable to mortgage arrears, and may not share the benefits of capital gains enjoyed by most home owners. The rise in homelessness reflects an increasingly polarised housing system, with the poorest suffering most.

Which of these interpretations of recent change is more accurate? What evidence supports or damages the arguments or is there some truth in both? The last section of this chapter draws conclusions on these issues after reviewing evidence about how well the housing needs of low income consumers are being met.

2.3 Housing Needs

(a) Homelessness

Homelessness is one indicator of the housing prospects of those on low incomes. The homeless statistics indicate an increasing difficulty with access to rented housing in Scotland. The number of applicant households under the homelessness legislation (Housing (Scotland) Act 1987) increased from 14,861 in 1980/81 to 39,500 in 1991/92; the numbers accepted by local authorities as homeless rose from 6,993 to 17,800[9]. The increase has arisen from social changes such as the rise in marital breakdown, economic changes such as rising unemployment making it difficult to pay housing costs, and legislative changes such as the withdrawal of benefit from 16 and 17 year olds. Local authorities were able to offer permanent accommodation to only around 9,000 households in 1991/92. Since homelessness bears predominantly on the poor, the figures indicate a situation of decreasing housing choice for the poorest households. The homelessness legislation is intended to secure accommodation for families with children and people who are vulnerable, for example through age or ill-health. Many single people qualify only for 'advice and assistance'. For some of these households, the concept of choosing between different landlords is meaningless since they face a situation of having no housing at all.

(b) Rented housing

Other indicators of need for rented housing are more difficult to interpret. Waiting lists are unreliable indicators of need without full information about the existing housing circumstances and characteristics of applicant households. In some parts of Scotland long waiting lists co-exist with vacant council housing, indicating a mismatch between the stock and applicants' aspirations. Elsewhere, though, the housing stock has barely kept pace with the rise in the number of households consequent upon the trend towards smaller household sizes. There is also evidence that within the general context of a reduced housing stock to rent, poorer households have been further disadvantaged.

Evidence suggests two important ways in which low income is associated with disadvantage in the public rented sector. First, research carried out in the early 1980s showed that low income applicants fared worse than higher income applicants in a number of respects, including waiting time and popularity of neighbourhood offered, in an allocations system which was not intended to discriminate in that way[10][11].

Second, evidence from the 1981 and 1991 Censuses confirm earlier findings that poor people—measured through indicators such as disability, age, unemployment and single parenthood—tend to be concentrated disproportionately in the less popular and least attractive council estates. The reasons for this unpopularity are complex, usually including some combination of poor design, isolated location, and the historical consequences of allocation policies. These are the estates in which houses and flats have sold least well under the Right-to-Buy.

The evidence points towards a group of poor and often younger households who have no choice, because of homelessness or the lack of priority they receive in the allocation process. They must accept tenancies in the least popular council estates, with better off tenants better placed to achieve tenancies in more attractive areas, where they may take advantage of their higher incomes and more attractive housing in exercising the Right-to-Buy.

(c) Physical conditions

The popularity of housing may not reflect its physical characteristics. High popularity may not indicate high physical standards, but the evidence from the General Household Survey of 1990 suggests it probably does[12].

Table 2.2 shows statistics for selected housing conditions by income and tenure for Scotland. As far as basic amenities are concerned, such as exclusive use of a bath, considerable progress has been made and even among the poorest households those lacking amenities are a small proportion of the total. The poorest households, however, are over-represented in flats rather than the more popular houses and fewer have central heating in their homes. Rented properties are more likely to be flats, and unfurnished private rented properties in particular are far more likely than others to lack central heating.

More detailed data on physical housing standards are available from the Scottish House Condition Survey carried out in 1991/92 by Scottish Homes[13]. Some 95,000 dwellings, 4.7% of the total stock, were Below the Tolerable Standard (BTS) set by Parliament; 22,000 of these dwellings were privately rented. Furthermore, BTS dwellings were more likely to be occupied by economically disadvantaged households. The most common reason for dwellings being considered BTS was not being free of damp and/or condensation. (See also section 3.5b in the chapter on energy and fuel consumption.)

These conditions were found to be more prevalent in the public rented sector than the owner occupied sector, and also were more likely to be experienced by poor households. The worst housing was to be found in the private rented sector, but considerable numbers of public sector houses suffered from dampness (128,000) and condensation (217,000). These dwellings were more likely to be tenanted by the poorer households, largely single parents, the unemployed and large families.

The conclusion that some low income households are suffering poor housing conditions as a consequence of their status as public sector tenants is at variance with the earlier National Consumer Council study for Great Britain which revealed that poor households were protected from consumer detriment in relation to housing by a high quality public sector[14]. The alteration in circumstances is a consequence of changes to public sector housing which have intensified since 1979. The most apparent change is the reduction in stock due to sales, mostly to sitting tenants. Other changes arise from the financial framework for public sector housing, and from social and economic change. These are considered in section 2.4 below.

(d) Special needs

Low income is often associated with other forms of disadvantage which have important housing implications. It may be more helpful to consider the housing circumstances and needs of single parent families, ethnic minorities, older people, single women, and people with health or disability problems, rather than low income consumers, since these groups are over-represented amongst the poorest members of Scottish society. In the period since 1979 the housing needs of some disadvantaged groups have received more recognition by central government, local government, and other housing providers than ever before. The development of community care policy has emphasised the need for suitable housing to complement social work services and health services.

Census results indicate continuing concentrations of some disadvantaged groups in areas of poor or unattractive housing, but consumers in all areas and in all tenures may need special care, or adaptations, at some point in their lives. New housing is not necessarily the solution to special needs, as many people prefer to stay in their own home. Housing authority *Housing Plans* show large shortfalls of special needs, especially 'very sheltered' housing for older people and housing for other community care target groups in many parts of Scotland[15]. Comparisons with 1979 are impossible since the perception of the need for special needs housing has developed since then in most authorities, and government targets or standards of provision for special needs groups have also changed, with the growing emphasis on community care policies[16].

(e) Need and low income

Some preliminary conclusions can now be drawn. The public sector in Scotland has shrunk and decreased in quality. It has a higher proportion than formerly of flats; it has higher levels of dampness and condensation than other tenures; and it has been selectively depleted of its better properties by sales to the more affluent sitting tenants. With the decline in the private rented sector, low income households have become increasingly concentrated in the shrinking public sector, and more particularly in the less popular parts of the public stock. In addition to their poverty, many low income households have to cope with problems of physical and social isolation and stigmatisation arising from their place of residence. Whether in urban or rural settings this might mean problems of access to doctors, chemists, relatives and friends, for example. However, not all low income consumers are to be found in public rented housing. Some of the worst conditions are experienced by low income residents in privately rented housing, and some owner occupied properties are a cause for concern.

The growing recognition of the special housing needs of some consumers has not yet been matched by sufficient provision.

Housing associations have been unable to make up the shortfall of socially rented accommodation, and the consequences, particularly in Scotland's cities, have included growing numbers of homeless households. The better quality estates of semi-detached and terraced properties have been subject to high levels of sales. For some of the poorest households, the public sector has changed from being a route to better housing to being a trap in bad housing. Housing problems such as dampness and condensation aggravate the general disadvantaged position of poor households by causing ill-health and increased heating bills (see section 3.5b in the chapter on energy and fuel consumption).

The picture is not entirely bleak, however. Council housing still provides good quality housing and environments for many tenants. The conditions in the worst estates in urban areas are not replicated elsewhere. For some tenants the route out of the worst conditions has been to join with neighbours in voting for a transfer of ownership of their homes to a housing association or co-operative. Funds for upgrading have been secured from Scottish Homes and through private loans, and tenants have played a large part in managing the improvement process. The four areas of Castlemilk (in Glasgow), Wester Hailes (in Edinburgh), Whitfield (in Dundee) and Ferguslie Park (in Paisley) have been transformed through a formal partnership between central government, local government, and the voluntary and private sectors. Housing associations have spread their influence in rural areas as well. They provide good quality and well managed housing, and have made a significant contribution to providing 'special needs' housing in some areas.

So the evidence suggests that there is some truth in both the optimistic and pessimistic accounts of how Scottish housing has changed and the impact on low income consumers. But this conclusion is incomplete without looking at the way in which the housing finance system has had an impact on consumers, and at how easily consumers can gain access to information and advice.

2.4 Housing Finance

Changes in housing finance since 1979 are mainly a result of policy changes at the UK level, and of social and economic change affecting individual households, rather than specifically Scottish policies or circumstances. For owner occupiers and potential owner occupiers the sources of mortgage finance are more numerous than in 1979, with banks as well as building societies taking advantage of deregulation measures in the 1980s. How to measure the level of subsidy applied to owner occupiers is a matter of controversy, but home ownership is generally accepted as having had very favourable tax treatment since at least the 1960s[17]. The effects of these subsidies are generally regressive; that is, the higher the consumer's income, the higher the tax relief obtained. Recent decisions to retain the ceiling (£30,000) on the amount of loan eligible for tax relief, and proposals to limit relief to the lowest (20 pence) tax band, may mark a new era of less favourable tax treatment, but do nothing to assist those whose incomes are so low that income tax is not a consideration.

Owner occupiers may also benefit from repair or improvement grants administered by local authorities within a Scottish legislative framework. Only the most expensive houses are excluded. Changes in England and Wales to target such grants more directly at low income consumers have not been made in Scotland, despite proposals to do so in 1985 and 1988[18][19]. The impact of these grants throughout Scotland is not well researched, but they have been used to good effect in improving the quality of housing in older areas of housing (sometimes in association with housing association activity); and increasingly they have been used to assist the improvement of poor quality former council housing in peripheral estates which has been transferred to co-operatives and housing associations. This type of improvement is more reliant, though, on grants provided by Scottish Homes.

For tenants, major changes have taken place which have meant higher rents in the public sector, deregulation of rent setting in the private sector and housing associations, and a reformed housing benefit system. The general effect has been to switch public funding from bricks and mortar subsidy to personal, means tested subsidy while keeping spending, on both together, at roughly the same level throughout the 1980s[20].

The 1988 reforms to housing benefit finally achieved the objective of creating a unified administrative system which treated public and private sector tenants alike. The reform was, however, accompanied by new eligibility criteria which reduced the Government's expenditure by £740 million in the UK in the first year—and this followed earlier cuts in the 1980s[21].

Despite this the scheme provides assistance with all housing costs for tenants on the lowest incomes. Two concerns remain, however. First, there is continuing evidence that a small proportion of tenants who are eligible for help do not apply[22]. Greater concern is often expressed, though, in relation to those whose income falls just above the full benefit levels.

For council tenants rent levels have risen in real terms. The 'standard rent' for a council house in Scotland was £7.67 per week in 1981/82. In 1992/93 it was £24.75, which represents a rise from 5.5% to 7.3% of average male earnings[23], and a higher rise if comparison were made with prices. Council tenants are increasingly unlikely to be in receipt of earnings at the average male earnings level. Rent levels have risen for a number of reasons (discussed below) and only partly, if at all, to fund improved management or maintenance. More significant has been the reduction in government subsidy to local authority housing revenue accounts. Only 29 authorities in Scotland received any subsidy in 1992/93; in 1979/80 all 56 did. In addition, central government gained powers in the mid-1980s to control the level of subsidy councils were allowed to provide from general funds, and this is now an insignificant element in council housing finance in Scotland.

Capital expenditure on council housing has been subject to close control since Exchequer subsidy was first made available in 1919. The nature of the control changed in 1977 from individual project control to control over total annual expenditure, made up partly through Right-to-Buy sales since 1980, and the remainder through borrowing. Very little capital expenditure is now devoted to new public sector house building; 960 new houses were completed in 1992 compared with 8,966 in 1981[24][25].

The changes for housing association tenants introduced in the Housing (Scotland) Act 1988 included two which had important implications for rent levels. First, housing associations are now required to fund a proportion of their new building or rehabilitation scheme costs with funds raised in the private sector as well as capital grants (which had formerly subsidised their activities to the extent that fair rents set by the Rent Officer could not cover loan charges). Second, associations are required to set rent levels themselves (in theory in negotiation with tenants) at levels which will repay the service charges on private loans and build up a fund to cover future maintenance and repair costs, as well as cover current management and maintenance costs.

The effect of these changes, and of the creation of new associations in deprived council estates, has been generally higher rents, and an increasingly 'benefit-dependent' group of new tenants[26]. The most systematic study so far carried out—by Kearns, Redmond and Malcolm—showed that almost two-thirds of new housing association tenants in Scotland are in the bottom quintile (lowest 20%) of the UK income distribution, and nine-tenths are in the bottom half[27]. The level of unemployment among new tenants after taking account of age and other factors was 24%, twice what might have been expected in the general population. Tenants on housing benefit were most likely to consider their rent difficult to afford. Also finding difficulty were those whose rent required an expenditure of more than 20% of their income. However, depending on the locality, housing association rents remain around the same or only a little more expensive than local authority rents. Moreover, there are no signs at present that the Government wishes to reduce Housing Association Grant in Scotland to the low levels anticipated in England and Wales and hence upward pressure on housing association rents will be less in Scotland.

Further evidence of these effects is found in the results from the Family Expenditure Survey shown in Table 2.4. This shows that over half (52%) of those in the lowest income quintile have nil housing costs, this group including outright owners and those who have the protective effect of housing benefit. A small but significant proportion (13%) of those on the lowest incomes of less than £86 are meeting housing costs of £15 or more. Those in the next income quintile, however, had significantly higher housing costs, 44% paying £15 or more. This is due to the sharp rate of benefit withdrawal.

A more sophisticated analysis of housing costs, incomes, and the incidence of subsidies in the Greater Glasgow area found that owner occupiers paid more than other consumers in housing costs but enjoyed the highest level of subsidy "no matter what definition of subsidy is adopted"[28]. The reliance on a poverty-based system of subsidy for renters means that many face a disincentive to increasing their income, whereas, for owner occupiers, an increased income means, broadly, higher subsidy. Although the very poorest households are largely protected from high housing costs, other slightly less poor households face severe affordability problems and many more affluent home owners receive subsidy that they do not need.

2.5 Advice, Information and Support

All consumers, whether they own or rent their homes or are looking for accommodation, require information. In some cases advice, counselling or advocacy may also be required. Low income consumers are more likely to require information and support because of their stronger likelihood of suffering disadvantages such as discrimination, disability and poor health which may require special attention in housing, or because their housing choices are reduced by their low income. They are also less likely to be able to afford to pay for information and advice services, in contrast with middle and high income consumers who use and pay for the services of lawyers, surveyors and other professionals involved in housing development, conveyancing and management.

Table 2.4 Housing costs by income group, Scotland 1990.

Housing costs weekly** £	Usual Gross Household Income (quintiles*) %					
	Lowest	2	3	4	Highest	All
Nil	52	35	21	18	19	29
0 - 4.99	15	7	2	0	2	5
5 - 9.99	10	5	2	1	0	4
10 - 14.99	10	9	5	2	2	5
15 - 19.99	9	20	16	12	5	12
20 - 49.99	4	21	37	46	33	28
50 - 99.99	0	3	15	20	30	14
100+	0	0	2	2	9	3
	100	100	100	100	100	100

* Lowest quintile = poorest 20%
  Highest quintile = richest 20%
**Mortgage payment or rent after rebate (n = 646).

Source: Central Statistical Office, *Family Expenditure Survey 1990, Scottish Data*, ESRC Data Archive, Essex, 1993 (authors' tabulation).

This can be illustrated with reference to four types of low income households.

- First, single young homeless people have very restricted housing choices, and without information and support may not gain access to available options.
- Second, public sector tenants, faced with a choice between a new landlord who offers the prospect of capital investment, and the council which can offer better legal tenancy rights but no investment, require help in weighing up the advantages and disadvantages of a change of tenure.
- Third, owner occupiers in mortgage arrears need to consider carefully the options open to them and may require information and support in doing so.
- Finally, older people whose housing no longer suits their needs or whose income no longer easily meets their housing costs require information on the variety of options which are now available to them in many parts of Scotland. Their vulnerability makes the provision of independent advice crucial and the work of Care and Repair schemes is a good example of what can be done to achieve improvements.

Little is known systematically about the adequacy of housing advice services in Scotland or how they have changed, but the importance of the issue has been recognised by the Secretary of State for Scotland in a request to Scottish Homes "to evaluate the quality and availability of housing information and advice and develop an appropriate strategy"[29]. The consultation paper produced as a first step in the process emphasises the great variety of provision in existence, and the special role of local authorities which 'most people' would see as 'the first port of call'[30]. The report identifies over 400 organisations providing housing information and advice at local, regional and national levels throughout Scotland, and the list is by no means comprehensive. It includes voluntary, statutory and professional organisations, but does not include the hundreds of lawyers, financial institutions, surveyors and consultants who provide housing advice.

The role of local housing authorities in providing information and advice to consumers or potential consumers in all tenures is generally considered to be crucial, and has been commended in official and professional reports on the role of housing authorities for many years. Yet few authorities provide or fund a wide-ranging service, and specific powers to provide some types of information and advice are unclear. Loughlin[31] argues that legal powers are adequate, but he shows that some local government solicitors disagree. A clarification of the law to establish that local housing authorities have powers to provide comprehensive advice services to consumers in all tenures would settle the issue, but would not require advice to be provided as a duty. Equally it would do nothing to ensure independent advice for council tenants or applicants aggrieved at how the council was handling their case.

Before considering in more detail the gaps in provision it is worth pointing out that "providing information and advice is not the same thing as meeting housing need ... advocacy cannot create additional affordable housing, and the work of housing advisers may help one needy group of people while preventing another group from gaining access to housing"[32]. However, advice and information can be seen as a right or entitlement which none should be barred from receiving on the grounds of low income, location, tenure or need. Three types of gap in provision can be identified.

(a) Uneven geographical coverage

Whether information and advice is available is partly a function of geography. In particular, low income consumers in many rural areas of Scotland have few voluntary organisations within easy reach, and their district councils rarely offer help 'on topics outside their role as public sector landlords'[33]. Research has shown, for example, large variations between housing authorities in the quality and type of advice offered under the terms of the homelessness legislation[34].

(b) Type of information and advice service

Information and support services vary from providing relatively simple facts, such as the eligibility of an applicant for council housing to, for example, providing practical assistance and representation in connection with a court case. In some areas a range of advocacy, counselling and practical assistance is available; in others simple requests for factual information may not be met. Again, the most varied provision seems to exist in the largest urban areas, but not necessarily in all neighbourhoods.

(c) Type of housing problem

It is possible to obtain information and advice about any type of housing problem or issue, providing money can be found to pay for it and the appropriate expertise can be found. For those on low incomes, information and advice is more easily available on some topics or problems than on others. In particular low income consumers are more likely to find it hard to obtain independent advice. If a council tenant has not had a repair done, where can advice be obtained? Since local housing authorities tend to concentrate on giving advice in relation to their own housing, where can a private sector tenant obtain advice on a repair not done? The answer in some parts of Scotland is 'nowhere'.

Although it is not clear how housing information and advice services have changed over the last decade or two it is possible to suggest how low income consumers could be served better:

- The role of housing authorities should be clarified and authorities should consider the adequacy of their own services and of grants to voluntary organisations in their area, particularly in rural and deprived areas.

- The role of the voluntary sector has been important and will continue to be if local authorities and central government continue to provide support, for example through the Urban Programme.

- Scottish Homes has an important new co-ordinating and development role which should be carried out in a way which takes account of the particular needs of low income consumers.

2.6 Conclusions

The Government's policy of expanding owner occupation in Scotland has been a success. Home ownership has expanded down the income scale, largely through public sector sales, and is now experienced by more households than ever before.

As far as rented housing is concerned, however, the record is less satisfactory. Most Right-to-Buy purchasers have come from the more affluent tenants and hence the rise of owner occupation has left the poorest households largely unaffected. They depend for good housing on an adequate supply of affordable, quality, rented accommodation. The 1988 housing legislation focused on rented housing with the objectives of revitalising the private rented sector and hence increasing consumer choice. The public sector has been rejected as a provider of housing, and the housing associations have been chosen as the major providers of subsidised rented housing. The traditional private rented sector has continued to decline overall, and much of the housing that does exist is in a poor condition. The public sector has also decreased in size and fallen in quality, and is increasingly the tenure of the poorest households. Homelessness has also been increasing.

Government policy can thus be seen as a success as far as owner occupation is concerned, but less satisfactory as regards rented housing upon which poor people depend. The major agencies for ensuring that low income consumers were well housed in the past—the local authorities—have been deprived of their housing provision function as a conscious act of policy, but the alternatives have not yet been able to replace them on a scale sufficient to ensure that all low income households are adequately housed.

Moreover, housing subsidies continue to be ill-directed and regressive despite attempts to move from bricks-and-mortar to means tested household subsidies. The major reasons for this are the continued existence of mortgage interest tax relief and the sharp rate of housing benefit reductions when income rises above full benefit level. Public expenditure on housing, therefore, continues to be inefficiently targeted and much is not used for the benefit of low income households. The poorest tenants are protected through housing benefit and pay little or no rent. Those with slightly higher incomes are suffering affordability problems due to rising rents, which have compounded the financial disincentives to increase earnings for those on low pay and in receipt of full or partial benefit.

While improvements have been made to the housing conditions of some low income consumers—for example, in housing association special needs developments, and in run-down council estates such as the four partnership areas of Castlemilk, Ferguslie Park, Wester Hailes and Whitfield—others have not shared in the improvements which have taken place more generally in the housing conditions of Scottish people. Indeed, as expectations have risen for most consumers, the opportunities of many of the poorest to achieve good housing have narrowed. The pessimistic interpretation outlined at the beginning of this chapter is the more persuasive, qualified to the extent that some significant improvements have been made. Policy measures are required which will improve the quality of existing rented stock more quickly and more widely, and deal with emerging problems such as the growing number of older people in poorer quality, owner occupied housing.

The evidence so far is that the 1988 legislation will not generate an effective increase in the private rented sector for low income households. The housing associations must, therefore, be given sufficient funding to make up the shortfall of rented housing on which the poor depend. The existing supply within the public sector needs substantial investment, and in this context the partnership schemes in the peripheral housing estates have potential. Increased choice among providers would be a bonus. Compulsory competitive tendering of housing management is intended to improve the services received by many poor households in public sector estates. The key to the housing chances of low income households, however, depends on investment to increase the quality of the rented stock, and its size in some areas. Much of this must come from public sources, and given current public expenditure constraints a more efficient targeting of existing expenditure is vital, including a phased withdrawal of at least some of the tax advantages of owner occupation. Overdependence on private sources will lead to high rents and the exclusion of those households just above benefit thresholds. A judicious balance of private and public capital, and household and bricks-and-mortar subsidies, is required if all low income households are to enjoy the improvements in housing standards enjoyed by those on higher incomes who have become home owners, or those on low incomes who happen to live in particular localities which have been targeted with expenditure.

References to Chapter 2

1. National Consumer Council, *Why the Poor Pay More*, MacMillan, 1977.
2. P. Kemp, 'Housing' in D. Marsh and R. Rhodes (eds), *Implementing Thatcherite Policies*, Open University Press, 1992, pp.65-80.
3. Scottish Homes, *Scottish House Condition Survey*, Survey Report, Scottish Homes, Edinburgh, 1993.
4. Central Statistical Office, *General Household Survey 1990*, Scottish Data, ESRC Data Archive, Essex, 1993.
5. Central Statistical Office, *Family Expenditure Survey 1990*, Scottish Data, ESRC Data Archive, Essex, 1993.

6. K. MacNee, *The Right to Buy in Scotland*, The Scottish Office, 1993.
7. K. MacNee, see reference 6.
8. H. Kay and J. Hardin, *The Rent to Mortgage Scheme in Scotland*, The Scottish Office Central Research Unit, Edinburgh, 1992.
9. Scottish Office, *Statistical Bulletin*, HSG/1992/6, The Scottish Office, 1992.
10. D. Clapham and K. Kintrea, 'Rationing, choice and constraint: the allocation of public housing in Glasgow', *Journal of Social Policy*, Vol.15, 1986, pp.51-67.
11. N. Williams, J. Sewel, and F. Twine 'Council house allocation and tenant incomes', *Area*, Vol.18, 1986, pp. 131-140.
12. Central Statistical Office, General Household Survey, see reference 4.
13. Scottish Homes, see reference 3.
14. National Consumer Council, see reference 1.
15. Scottish Homes, *Housing the Elderly in the 1990s: Discussion Paper*, Edinburgh, 1993.
16. Scottish Office Environment Department *Housing and Community Care : Circular ENV/8/1991*, Edinburgh, 1991.
17. K. Gibb and M. Munro, *Housing Finance in the UK: an Introduction*, Macmillan, 1991.
18. Scottish Development Department, *Home Improvement in Scotland—A New Approach*, Cmnd. 9677, HMSO, Edinburgh, 1985.
19. Scottish Development Department, *Private Housing Renewal—the Government's Proposals for Scotland* -SDD Consultation Paper, Edinburgh, 1988.
20. K. Gibb and M. Munro, see reference 17.
21. K. Gibb and M. Munro, see reference 17.
22. K. Gibb and M. Munro, see reference 17.
23. S. Wilcox, *Housing Finance Review 1992 : Papers in Housing Research 3*, Centre for Housing Management and Development, University of Wales, Cardiff, 1993.
24. Scottish Development Department, *Statistical Bulletin*, HSIU, No. 2, 1983.
25. Scottish Development Department, *Statistical Bulletin*, HSG/1993/3.
26. A. Kearns, D. Redmond and J. Malcolm, *The 'Ins' and 'Outs' of Renting : A Study of the Socio Economic Circumstances of Scottish Housing Association Tenants*, Centre for Housing Research, Glasgow, 1993.
27. A. Kearns, D. Redmond and J. Malcolm, see reference 26.
28. K. Hancock, C. Jones, M. Munro, M. Satsangi et al, *Housing Costs and Subsidies in Glasgow*, Joseph Rowntree Foundation, York, 1991.
29. Scottish Homes, *You Can't Ask a Leaflet Questions : Discussion Paper—Information and Advice*, Edinburgh, 1992.
30. Scottish Homes, see reference 29.
31. M. Loughlin, 'Housing advice, local government law and the enabling role', *Scottish Housing Law News*, Vol.14, 1991, pp. 21-5.
32. R. Goodlad, *The Housing Authority as Enabler*, Longman/Institute of Housing, 1993.
33. Scottish Homes, see reference 29.
34. G. Duguid, *Homelessness in Scotland—A Study of Policy and Practice*, Central Research Unit, The Scottish Office, 1990.

Energy and Fuel Consumption

by Bill Sheldrick

Everyone needs fuel for heating, lighting and cooking every day. Those on low incomes spend a much larger proportion of their income on fuel than those who are better off. As Bill Sheldrick explains in this chapter, paying for fuel is a big expense for many, including single parents with children under five and single pensioners. Those without good insulation, efficient heating systems and access to cheaper forms of fuel also face large bills. For Scots on low incomes in particular, the colder climate north of the border is an added disadvantage. Despite spending a lot on fuel many people still live in damp homes which are inadequately insulated and heated. The consequences of high bills and poor living conditions are debt, disconnection and ill health. The imposition of VAT on domestic fuel will further disadvantage those on low incomes unless they are fully compensated.

3.1 Introduction

As this chapter was being written, debate was engaged fully in the UK about some of the contents of the Government's March 1993 Budget. The particular item of concern was the Government's announced intention to end the zero rating of VAT on domestic fuel consumption, phasing in the proposed change over two years—with an initial VAT rate of 8% to apply from April 1994, rising to 17.5% in April 1995. Compensating pensioners and low income households for this VAT increase may cover the additional cost incurred by them as a result of VAT, but is not intended to redress any existing inability to afford to heat one's home adequately. With this VAT change, fuel consumption officially becomes a luxury good. For many low income households in Scotland this will not come as a surprise. Adequate warmth is already a luxury they cannot afford; it is only going to get more expensive.

The Government could only have increased the tax burden for an equivalent number of households if it had levied VAT on food or water. As noted during the parliamentary debate on the VAT proposal, "Everyone has to use gas and electricity. It is a basic necessity. It is not some optional extra"[1]. Even increasing the rate of income tax would not have touched as many households, because "Everyone will have to pay VAT on gas and electricity—even those who work but earn too little to pay income tax. Almost three quarters of pensioners pay no income tax, yet all of them will have to pay VAT on their gas and electricity bills"[2]. What was not disputed by any political party during this parliamentary debate was the regressive effect on low income consumers of levying VAT on domestic fuel consumption.

Yet, why all the fuss about VAT on domestic fuel consumption? Traditional supply and demand economics indicate that an equilibrium exists in the market place between the level of consumption and the price of goods or services such as fuel. When prices increase, whether as a result of fuel suppliers raising their tariffs or government levying VAT or for some other reason, then the demand for fuel will fall as the market adjusts. Those consumers who value their present level of consumption will accommodate the extra cost elsewhere within the household budget. Those who place a lower value on their fuel consumption will eliminate unnecessary consumption or will adopt more energy-conscious behaviour. Individual households may attempt to maintain their standards of living without incurring additional expenditure by investing in more energy-efficient appliances and insulation, or by switching to cheaper fuels or suppliers. Through these adjustments, so the theory goes, an equilibrium will be re-established within the market place between the price of fuel and the level of consumption for which consumers are willing to pay.

For many domestic consumers, and particularly low income households, the market may work, not because they do not value their consumption or are profligate and therefore have scope to cut back, or because they invest in energy efficiency, but through deprivation. This problem was highlighted explicitly in a letter from a consortium of consumer interest groups to the Chancellor of the Exchequer in response to the VAT proposal:

> "Your proposal to compensate low income householders will bring little comfort to the seven million who live in cold damp homes which they cannot afford to heat now, because of inadequate heating systems and poor thermal efficiency. Low income householders are beyond the reach of market forces and cannot respond to your price signal except by turning off their heating and going without"[3].

Responding to market signals requires scope to take action which may not be available for low income households.

As fuel prices rise, maintaining consumption at previous levels will result in higher costs for the householder. Within a limited or fixed income, these additional costs may not be able to be met without cutting back on other necessities. A 1992 survey found that a quarter of elderly people gave up other items to stay warm—mainly food[4]. One alternative to cutting back on other items is to continue as before, and live with the inevitable consequences of falling into debt with the fuel utilities and the threat of disconnection.

Another option for these households is to cut back on their fuel use, but reducing energy consumption when it is already inadequate may result in health problems or put people at risk from the cold. "Many elderly people will be so frightened by the prospect of rising bills that they will resort to self rationing. They will sit in the cold at risk to their health because of the fear of falling into debt"[5]. The 1992 survey among elderly people found 81% of room temperatures in the morning to be below World Health Organisation guidelines. A third of pensioners did not heat their bedrooms, the main reason cited being the lack of money[6].

This vicious circle can be broken through increasing energy efficiency standards in the home. Heating and insulation improvements, however, cost money regardless of their cost effectiveness or the length of the payback period. If access to the necessary capital to pay for the improvements is not available through savings, loans, or collateral then these options are not open to consumers. By their very definition, low income households are unlikely to have readily available capital, or the access to it, because they are viewed as poor risks for a loan. Despite the availability of a mandatory 90% grant for basic insulation improvements for eligible low income households, they may still experience difficulties in finding even token amounts from within their existing budgets. The client contributions of £10.70 for loft insulation and £7.50 for draughtproofing (and £16 when both are installed) required under the Home Energy Efficiency Scheme (HEES) have been found to limit the uptake of these basic insulation measures[7]; the Government abolished the need for the HEES client contribution in October 1993.

Switching fuels or suppliers to take advantage of cheaper tariffs may also be denied through the lack of capital to install the appropriate heating appliances, or through the lack of alternative suppliers or supply. Many rural areas are reliant upon expensive forms of heating because gas and sometimes electricity are not available via the national grid. Further, the regulatory regimes introduced with the privatisation of the gas and electricity industries prevent domestic consumers shopping round for a cheaper supplier for some time to come. With gas, separately negotiable contracts are only an option for consumers using over 2,500 therms per annum which is significantly more than most individual households would use. Franchise customers (effectively domestic consumers) are tied to Scottish Power and Scottish Hydro-Electric until 1998 for their electricity supply.

Energy is not only a commodity that is bought and sold subject to price, but also occupies a more fundamental role as a determinant of the quality of life. This chapter is concerned with the experiences of low income households in trading off energy consumption, the price of fuel, and the quality of life. It should come with a government health warning.

3.2 Fuel Expenditure

For most households, the energy debate is a misnomer. While much may be spoken about the subject of 'energy', it is not usually 'energy' per se that captures the domestic consumer's attention. Asking householders 'how many joules have you purchased of late?' is likely to be interpreted as an inquiry into a recent transaction at some high street jewellers. For low income households, the issue is not so much energy, but the price they have to pay for it.

How much fuel is purchased by a household will be, at least in part, a function of income but the relationship between the two is not linear; expenditure does not continue to grow in proportion to increases in income. Information from the Family Expenditure Survey reinforces this point. Households within lower income bands spend less on fuel than do those in higher income categories (see Table 3.1)[8].

Table 3.1 Weekly fuel expenditure by quintile of actual income distribution (1991 data)

	quintile*				
	1	2	3	4	5
Fuel expenditure per week	£9.45	£11.35	£11.97	£12.83	£15.67
Income per week	£66.35	£139.48	£229.45	£335.22	£605.26
% Fuel expenditure/ Total expenditure	13.05%	8.3%	5.7%	4.8%	4%

* Lowest quintile (1) = poorest 20%
Highest quintile (5) = richest 20%

Source: S. Hutton and G. Harmon, *Assessing the Impact of VAT on Fuel on Low Income Households: Analysis of Fuel Expenditure Data from 1991 Family Expenditure Survey*, GCC1058/4.93, Social Policy Research Unit, University of York, York, 1993.

However, the increase in fuel expenditure across income bands is nowhere near as great as the increase in income. In Table 3.1, the average income of the highest quintile (top 20% of the income distribution) is over nine times greater than that of the lowest, but the expenditure on fuel is only 66% more. There is a rapid levelling off of fuel expenditure as income increases.

The difference in fuel expenditure between the lowest and highest income categories narrows further when equivalent household income is used rather than actual income (that is, when household income is adjusted for the number of people in the household so that the lowest quintile, the bottom 20%, is not comprised solely of single person households)[9]. While the equivalent household income of the highest quintile is over five times that of the lowest quintile, the fuel expenditure among them is only 24% greater. Thus, despite an equivalent household income of over £400 more per week, the fuel expenditure among the highest quintile is only £2.65 greater than that of the lowest group (see Table 3.2). This narrowing of actual fuel expenditure across income bands led one assessment of the impact of VAT on domestic fuel consumption to conclude: "The effect on net income is very much the same on average across the whole distribution of (equivalent) income, indicating that expenditure on domestic fuel is associated more with household size than with income"[10].

Table 3.2 Weekly fuel expenditure by quintile of equivalent income distribution (1991 data)

	quintile*				
	1	2	3	4	5
Fuel expenditure per week	£11.13	£11.25	£12.62	£12.39	£13.78
Equivalent household income per week	£105.81	£165.58	£249.74	£336.43	£548.77
% Fuel expenditure/ Total expenditure	12.3%	9.8%	6.9%	5.1%	4.2%

* Lowest quintile (1) = poorest 20%
Highest quintile (5) = richest 20%

Source: S. Hutton and G. Harmon, *Assessing the Impact of VAT on Fuel on Low Income Households: Analysis of Fuel Expenditure Data from 1991 Family Expenditure Survey*, GCC1058/4.93, Social Policy Research Unit, University of York, York, 1993.

The effect of an increase in fuel prices on net household income may be similar across income bands, but fuel price increases have a disproportionate impact on low income households. Fuel expenditure represents a larger proportion of the household budget of low income groups than it does for higher income ones. In Table 3.1, fuel expenditure accounts for over 13% of all the weekly equivalent income of the lowest quintile group compared with only 4% of the weekly equivalent income of those in the highest quintile. The average UK household expenditure on fuel across all income groups is 4.7%[11].

This difference between actual fuel expenditure and the proportion of weekly income can be illustrated by a more detailed examination of the different households that make up the lowest quintile of equivalent income (see Table 3.3). Households with children (whether couples or single parents) spend on average £13 per week on fuel, while single householders and pensioners spend between £8 and £11 per week. The two households groups that spend the least per week on fuel (i.e. single pensioners and single people aged 25 to 60) move up to second and fourth in the rank ordering when ranked by proportion of income spent. Single parents with children under five and single pensioner households spend relatively more of their equivalent weekly income on fuel than do the other groups—16.42% and 16.36% respectively[12]; that is, they spend almost 3.5 times more of their income on fuel than the average UK household.

Table 3.3 Weekly fuel expenditure for different family types in lowest quintile of equivalent income (1991 data)

	Fuel expenditure	Equivalent weekly income	% Fuel expenditure of total expenditure
Couple with children	£13.96	£144.17	7.33%
Single parent	£13.80	£117.30	13.79%
Couple with children under five years	£13.57	£144.47	8.53%
Single parent with children under five years	£13.39	£112.23	16.42%
Pensioner couple	£10.94	£109.28	11.19%
Single pensioner	£8.84	£65.42	16.36%
Single person aged 25 to 60	£8.03	£56.31	11.98%

Source: S. Hutton and G. Harmon, *Assessing the Impact of VAT on Fuel on Low Income Households: Analysis of Fuel Expenditure Data from 1991 Family Expenditure Survey,* GCC1058/4.93, Social Policy Research Unit, University of York, York, 1993.

While low income households may spend less on fuel generally than better off households, what they do spend represents a greater proportion of their income. Any increase in fuel prices will have a greater impact on their income than that in more affluent households. The burden of the VAT increase was assessed to be more than seven times greater among the poorest 10% of households than it would be for the top 10% of income groups[13].

3.3 Insulation, Heating, and the Cost of Fuel

The previous section focused on the level of expenditure across different income groups. However, it is not merely the level of expenditure, or even its disproportionate nature, that is of concern, but the value for money that low income households receive for their expenditure on fuel.

Energy is not consumed for its own sake, but for the services it provides and the activities it allows. Within the domestic sector, a prime concern is warmth. When disaggregated by end use, over half (55.0%) of Scottish domestic sector energy consumption goes on space heating. Water heating (25.3%), cooking (7.9%), lighting and appliances (11.8%) consume the rest. The main fuel within the domestic sector is gas which represents over 50% of all energy consumption; electricity (28%), solid fuel (12%), and oil (7%) account for the rest of domestic consumption.

The predominance of space heating within the domestic sector explains, in part, the levelling off in fuel expenditure as income increases. Mean internal temperatures will rise, and fuel expenditure will increase, the more households use their heating. However, regardless of income, beyond a certain temperature range (generally between 18°C and 22°C, but very much dependent upon the level of activity of the individual), thermal discomfort begins to set in as the internal temperatures rise, and the heating is turned off. While higher income households may spend more on fuel on average than low income ones, what cannot be determined simply from the level of fuel expenditure or the amount of energy consumption is whether reasonable temperature standards are being achieved in a particular dwelling.

A household is not better or worse off simply because it uses more or less fuel than someone else. The relationships between demand temperatures in a home (the temperature households are striving to achieve through the use of heating rather than the actual or average temperatures achieved) and both the level of fuel expenditure and the level of energy consumption for heating a dwelling are illustrated in Figure 3.1 and Figure 3.2. Both graphs are based on the results of an energy audit of a dwelling in Glasgow, but assume variations in the heating appliances and the levels of insulation:

1. The Base Case: an unimproved dwelling with a gas fire in the lounge and reliant on direct-acting electric heating appliances elsewhere (the actual house did not have any installed heating other than the gas fire in the lounge);
2. Basic Insulation Improvements: assumes the house has received basic insulation measures funded under the Home Energy Efficiency Scheme i.e. draughtproofing of all windows and external doors, 150mm of loft insulation, and an 80mm hot water tank jacket;
3. Basic Insulation Plus Heating: assumes the installation of the basic insulation measures as set out above, as well as installing gas fires throughout the house, in keeping with the affordable warmth scheme proposed as one of initial three 'E-factor' pilot programmes[14];
4. Insulation Plus Heating: assumes cavity wall insulation is included along with the basic insulation and heating package as set out above;
5. Building Regulation Standard: assumes thermal standards of the dwelling comply with those set out in the 1991 Scottish Building Regulations for new dwellings and that the heating is provided by a modern gas central heating system.

Figure 3.1 Annual heating cost
(£ per annum by demand temperature)

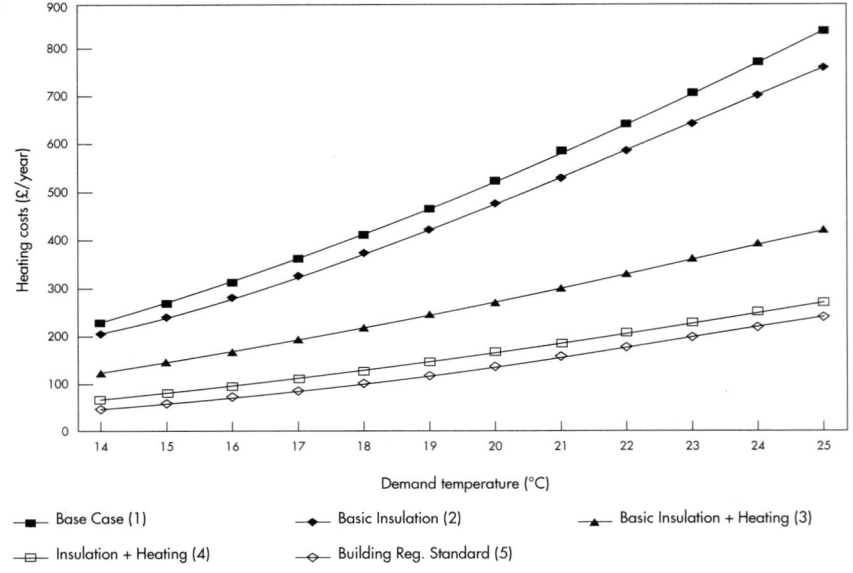

Figure 3.2 Annual heating consumption
(gigajoules per annum by demand temperature)

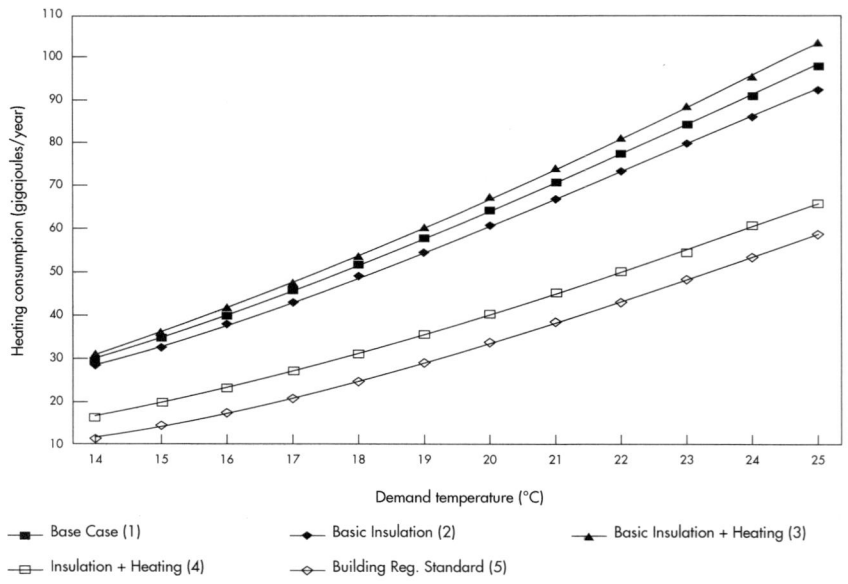

The cost of heating to any given demand temperature is dependent on factors such as the levels of insulation, the heating system, and the cost of fuel. As can be seen in Figure 3.1, the range can vary quite significantly. For a demand temperature of 21°C, the cost of heating ranged between £160 and £590 per year depending on the levels of insulation and the heating. As the insulation standards increase and the efficiency of the main heating improves, the cost of heating a dwelling to a particular temperature comes down (see Figure 3.1). With insulation to the thermal standards of the 1991 Scottish Building Regulations and a gas central heating system, it would be almost as cheap to heat the dwelling to a demand temperature of 25°C as it is to heat the existing, uninsulated dwelling to a demand temperature of only 14°C given the use of a gas fire in the lounge and direct-acting electric heating elsewhere in the house.

While improving the insulation and heating standards within a dwelling is one approach to realising lower heating costs for low income households, another is the use of fuel subsidies. In the past, heating additions have been paid, for example, for dwellings which are difficult to heat, estates with disproportionately expensive to use heating systems, and for central heating. The only subsidy at present is £6 per week under the Severe Weather Payment Scheme. Even if this subsidy was paid out every week of the year (i.e. £312 at 1993 rates), it would not reduce the cost of heating in the existing uninsulated Base Case House in Figure 3.1 by as much as insulating the house to the 1991 Scottish Building Regulation standards and installing gas central heating. The Severe Weather Payments, however, are not intended as a general subsidy, but as an exceptional needs payment. For the payments to be triggered, the average external air temperature has to fall to 0°C or below for seven consecutive days (at the designated monitoring station). Those eligible in Scotland for Severe Weather Payments, which does not include all low income households, are likely to receive such payments more regularly than claimants in England because of the generally colder Scottish climate. This subsidy, although useful, can only have a limited impact, as it is unlikely to amount to much more than £30 to £60 in any one year.

In energy terms, the house with the highest fuel costs in Figure 3.1—the existing Base Case House with its gas fire in the lounge and electric heating elsewhere—does not consume the most energy (see Figure 3.2). For a similar demand temperature, the energy consumption would be greater where gas fires were used throughout the house even after allowing for basic insulation measures (see the Basic Insulation Plus Heating Case in Figure 3.2). Gas fires are less efficient in their use of delivered energy than electric heaters but, importantly for low income households, are generally cheaper to run. Presently, they cost about a third of the price for 'a useful unit' of heat than do direct-acting electric heating appliances[15]. Thus, householders may be spending similar amounts on fuel or consuming similar amounts of energy but, depending on a dwelling's heating and insulation characteristics, living at widely different internal temperatures. Low income households tend to live in the dwellings that are both poorly insulated and reliant on heating that is expensive to use.

Analysis of ownership of insulation indicates that across all tenure groups there is a high presence of basic insulation measures (e.g. loft insulation) (see Figure 3.3). For the more significant measures, both in terms of insulation cost and the impact on reducing heat loss, there is a much lower market penetration (with the exception of double glazing amongst owner occupiers). Across all the tenure groups, private rented dwellings score lowest on all insulation measures. The presence of 'some' insulation does not imply that it meets a particular standard. Where more detailed information

Figure 3.3 Ownership of insulation in Scotland by type and tenure (1989)

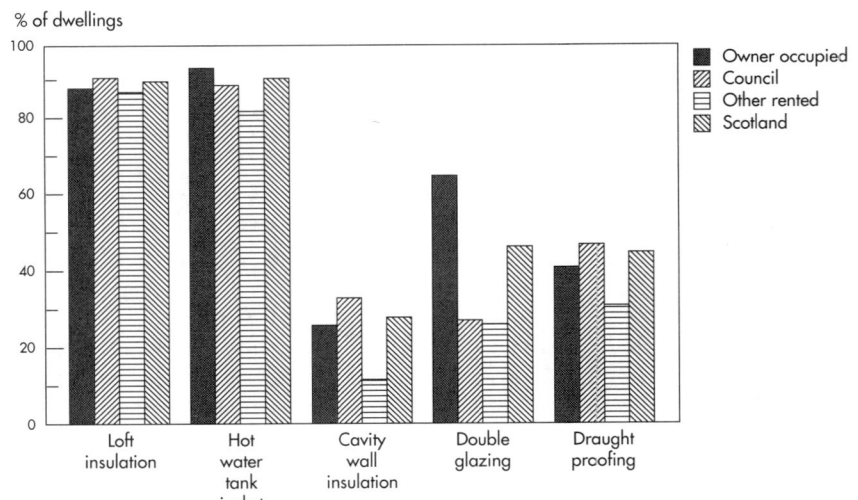

Source: Audits of Great Britain, *Home Audit,* Audits of Great Britain, London (unpublished), 1989 and 1990.

is available on the level of individual insulation measures the indication is that higher standards are found amongst owner occupiers[16].

Research has also found that dwellings with central heating were on average 2°C warmer than those without[17]. While the overall ownership of central heating in Scotland (at 74% of dwellings) compares well with statistics for Great Britain, it ranges between 35% in the private rented sector and 90% in the 'other' rented sector (i.e. housing associations) (see Figure 3.4). Where low income households have central

Figure 3.4 Ownership of central heating (March 1990)
Percentage of total dwelling stock

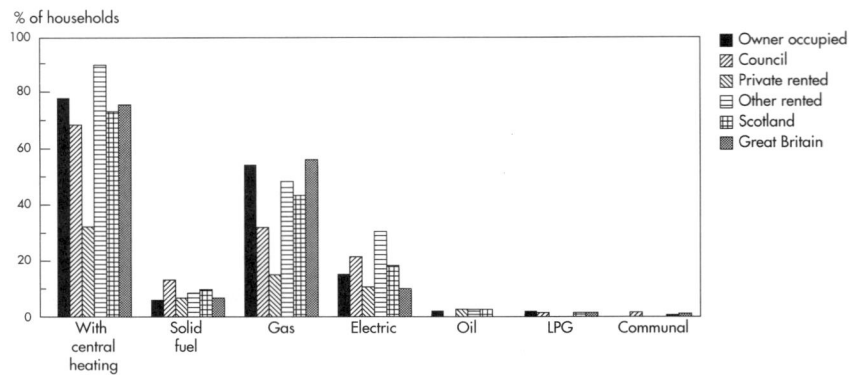

Source: Audits of Great Britain, *Home Audit,* Audits of Great Britain, London (unpublished), 1989 and 1990.

heating, however, it is less likely to be gas[18] and more likely to be electric,[19] which has significant cost implications for the householder.

In those dwellings without central heating, the main form of heating appliance varies with tenure. In the private rented sector, solid fuel and electric appliances are predominant. Almost 15% of privately rented houses without central heating are reliant on bottled gas. In the public sector, there is an equal split between individual gas, electric and solid fuel appliances. Owner occupiers are twice as likely to have gas fires compared with either electric or solid fuel appliances (see Figure 3.5) and, therefore, benefit from lower unit prices for fuel, as gas fires are cheaper to use than direct-acting electric or bottled gas heaters.

Figure 3.5 Use of heating appliances (March 1990)
Percentage of total dwelling stock

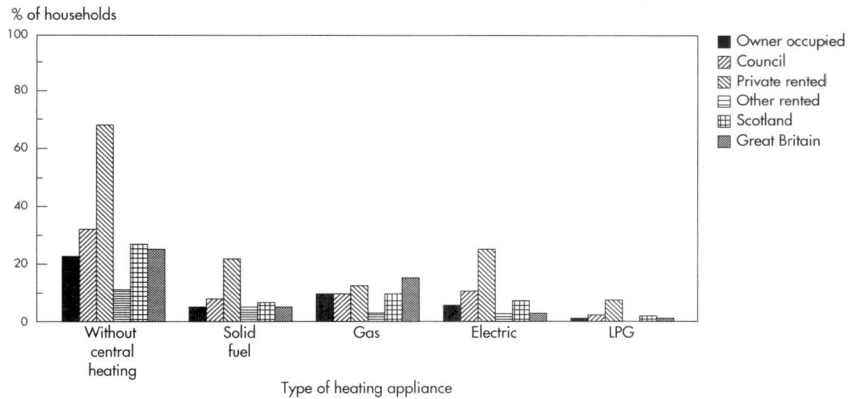

Source: Audits of Great Britain, *Home Audit*, Audits of Great Britain, London (unpublished), 1989 and 1990.

If low income households are living in generally poorer homes in terms of insulation standards, and are reliant on forms of heating which are more expensive to use, the logic is that their fuel expenditure should be greater than in more affluent households. As seen in the previous section, however, their fuel expenditure is less. Something in the equation has to give; for most low income households it will be their levels of comfort.

3.4 Cold Comfort

How much a household spends on fuel does not equate necessarily with the level of expenditure needed to achieve a reasonable temperature standard throughout a dwelling. The gap between the two can be quite large. This gap can be illustrated with data from energy audits and the monitoring of fuel expenditure and room temperatures in Easterhouse, Glasgow.

Easterhouse is one of Glasgow's four large peripheral estates and presently comprises about 13,000 dwellings. Much of the area, predominantly three and four storey tenements, was constructed during the late 1950s and early 1960s and pre-dates the inclusion of thermal standards within the Scottish Building Regulations after 1965. This is reflected in the lack of insulation in the unimproved dwellings. For example, the uninsulated external walls lose heat at between three and six times the rate of those constructed to the 1991 Scottish Building Regulation standards[20]. The poor insulation of the dwellings is compounded by the reliance upon heating appliances which are both inadequate and expensive to operate. Typically, the only installed heating in many of the homes is either a gas or an electric room heater in the lounge. Whole house heating, or even partial central heating, is rare except where refurbishment has taken place.

The provision of heating elsewhere in the house is left to the occupants to supply at their own expense. Where they do, the heating is likely to be by means of direct-acting electric appliances or others which are similarly expensive to use, such as bottled gas heaters. Less expensive alternatives such as gas fires or electric storage radiators are not an option without the household also incurring the installation and connection costs.

Details of the size and the construction of the walls, floors, roofs, and windows were surveyed in over 30 different dwellings in Easterhouse. By combining this information with data on the local climate, the type and use of space and water heating appliances, and fuel prices, the cost of heating a dwelling was estimated using an energy auditing programme based on the Building Research Establishment's BREDEM methodology[21].

The estimated annual heating and total fuel costs for different house sizes are summarised in Table 3.4. The heating costs range from £480 per annum to heat a one-apartment flat, to £1,600 for a five-apartment terraced house. These costs represent an average expenditure of between £9 and £31 per week, every week of the year, just to heat the house. When other fuel costs are added (water heating, cooking, lights and appliances and standing charges) the total annual fuel costs represent a mean expenditure of between £15 and £40 per week respectively.

From information published by the Energy Efficiency Office (EEO), an uninsulated, three-apartment flat in the UK should cost on average about £10 per

Table 3.4 Estimated Annual Fuel Costs

Dwelling	Whole house heating	Total fuel costs
5-apartment	£1200 - £1600	£1680 - £2070
4-apartment	£670 - £1180	£1140 - £1630
3-apartment	£590 - £1070	£910 - £1550
1-apartment	£480 - £640	£655 - £855

Source: B. Sheldrick, *Heating Costs in Easterhouse: an energy audit and fuel cost survey*, Heatwise Glasgow, Glasgow, 1988.

week to heat and a five-apartment house up to £17 per week (see Table 3.5)[22]. When the EEO figures are compared with the results from the Easterhouse energy audits, the cost of heating to the same temperature standard in Easterhouse is between:

- 13% and 50% more expensive for a one-apartment flat;
- 20% and 110% more expensive for a three-apartment flat;
- 35% and 82% more expensive for a five-apartment house.

Table 3.5 Comparative weekly heating fuel costs

	One Room Flat	Two Bedroom Flat	Four Bedroom House
Energy Efficiency Office estimates	£8	£10	£17
Easterhouse energy audit estimates: 'as existing'	£9 to £12	£12 to £21	£23 to £31
% Difference	+ 13% to 50%	+ 20% to 110%	+ 35% to 82%

Source: B. Sheldrick, *Heating Costs in Easterhouse: An energy audit and fuel cost survey*, Heatwise Glasgow, Glasgow, 1988.

What emerges from these audits is that, wherever one lives in Easterhouse, to heat a house to reasonable temperatures is expensive and, in certain instances, exceptionally so.

A significant difference between the EEO fuel cost estimates and those estimated for Easterhouse is that many of the dwellings in Easterhouse have worse than average insulation characteristics, have to rely on more expensive forms of heating, and are located in an area with a colder than average climate than assumed by the EEO. Easterhouse is about 10% colder than the UK average, but then all Scottish climatic regions are colder than the UK average[23] and will, therefore, require more fuel to heat a given building to a specific temperature standard.

The question is whether people in Easterhouse actually are spending up to £2,000 per year on fuel. When the dwellings were surveyed, fuel bill details were noted where they were available, or, with the permission of the householder, obtained from the fuel utilities. Actual expenditure on fuel was not as high as that estimated, but some households were spending in excess of £1,000 a year.

In Figure 3.6, the actual mean weekly household expenditure on fuel in 1988/89 is compared with the estimated fuel costs for 16 of the 30 households surveyed where access to their past fuel bills was available. While actual household expenditure varied quite considerably, the majority of those sampled were found to be spending:

- more than the Scottish average household expenditure on fuel despite many of those surveyed living in smaller than average sized flats;

- more than the historic DHSS 'notional fuel element' of £8.80 contained within the welfare benefit scale rates at the point at which it ended in April 1988.

Figure 3.6 Comparison of actual and estimated expenditure on fuel

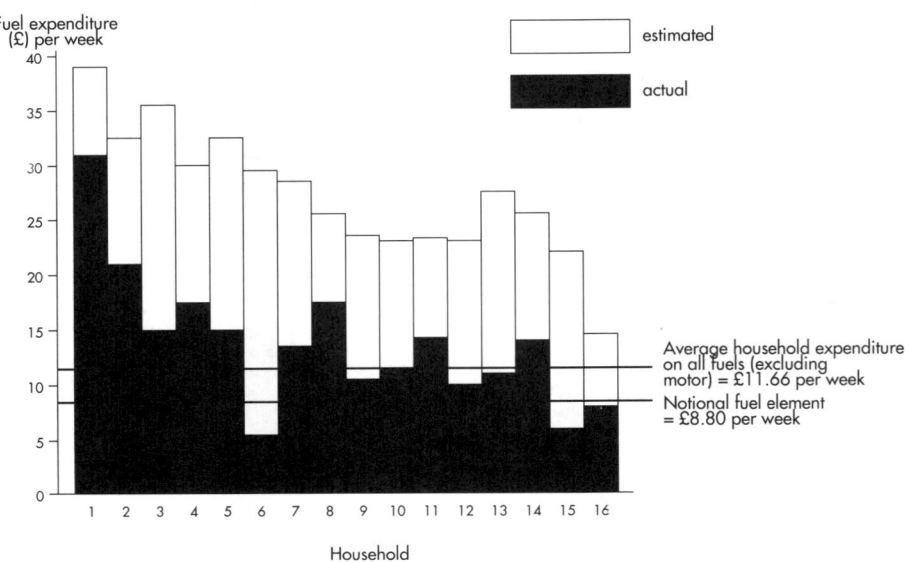

House size and construction
No.1–3   5-apartment brick terrace house
4–5   4-apartment Wilson block flats
6–7   3-apartment Wilson block flats
8   4-apartment brick built flats
9–15   3-apartment brick built flats
16   1-apartment brick built flat

Source: B. Sheldrick, *Heating Costs in Easterhouse: an energy audit and fuel cost survey*, Heatwise Glasgow, Glasgow, 1988.

Approximately 70% of the population of Easterhouse are reliant for their income on state benefits, such as unemployment benefits, pensions or invalidity benefits. Among those households surveyed, they were not only spending proportionately more of their incomes on fuel than better off households, but were also spending more than average in cash terms as well.

The actual fuel expenditure illustrated in Figure 3.6 refers only to the cost of the fuel consumed over the year and the related standing charges, but this total can underestimate the amount individual households may be paying to the fuel utilities. Many households in Easterhouse are on 'fuel direct', an arrangement whereby money is deducted from an individual's welfare benefit entitlement and paid directly to the fuel utility to cover past debts. Over 50,000 income support recipients in Scotland have had such deductions made from their benefit in each of the last three years, which represents around 10% of all income support recipients in Scotland, and is twice the UK average[24].

The estimated fuel costs above were calculated using a range of assumptions that may, or may not, hold true for individual households. In poorly insulated dwellings with heating appliances which are expensive to operate, the difference between the estimated and actual expenditure is likely to be reflected in the temperature standards. For the energy audits, it was assumed that households would heat their homes to a reasonable standard with a demand temperature of 21°C in the lounge and 18°C elsewhere in the house. These temperatures were chosen for two reasons. First, for a modern central heating system to carry the British Standard kitemark (an indication of quality) they have to be able to deliver these temperatures when the external air temperature is -1°C. Secondly, the EEO has noted: "These temperatures are commonly found in well-heated houses. The elderly, sick, disabled or very young children may need slightly higher temperatures"[25]. On the basis of these findings, few dwellings in Easterhouse are likely to be considered well heated.

A comparison between the assumed temperature standards and actual living conditions can be illustrated with actual temperatures monitored between October 1991 and May 1992 in an uninsulated three-apartment flat in Easterhouse. The only installed heating in this flat was a two-bar, direct-acting electric heater in the lounge. Temperatures of 18°C or more, identified as a minimum comfort level in the living room between the hours of 0800 and 2300 in adequately heated homes[26], were achieved in the lounge for just over a fifth of the heating season, and this was the warmest room in the house. The rest of the house (the two bedrooms, hall, kitchen and bathroom) was considerably colder. Temperatures of:

- 16°C or more, identified as the seven-day mean internal temperature in an adequately heated house[27], were achieved for less than a fifth of the heating season;

- 12°C or less, the point that appears to be significant medically in terms of cardiovascular changes and protection from hypothermia[28], were recorded for a third of the heating season.

The fuel bill for the occupants of this house totalled £760 for the year (i.e. on average £14.60 per week although, on occasions during the winter, their fuel expenditure rose to over £20 per week). Despite spending more than average on fuel (in Scotland, £12.87 per week in 1992)[29], what was spent was not only insufficient to maintain a reasonable temperature standard in their home, but left them medically at risk from the cold for significant periods of the winter.

The temperature profile for the year for this dwelling indicates that the major determinant of the mean internal temperature was not the use of the heating or the level of fuel expenditure, but the external air temperature. The temperatures in both the lounge and the bedrooms correlated closely with the external air temperature (see Figure 3.7a). In an insulated and well heated house, the use of heating compensates for the fall in external temperature (see Figure 3.7b) to maintain reasonable internal temperatures.

Despite the expensive heating, the poor insulation, and the low internal temperatures, this house complies with the Tolerable Standard which statutorily

Figure 3.7a Unimproved flat - temperature & costs
November 1991 - November 1992

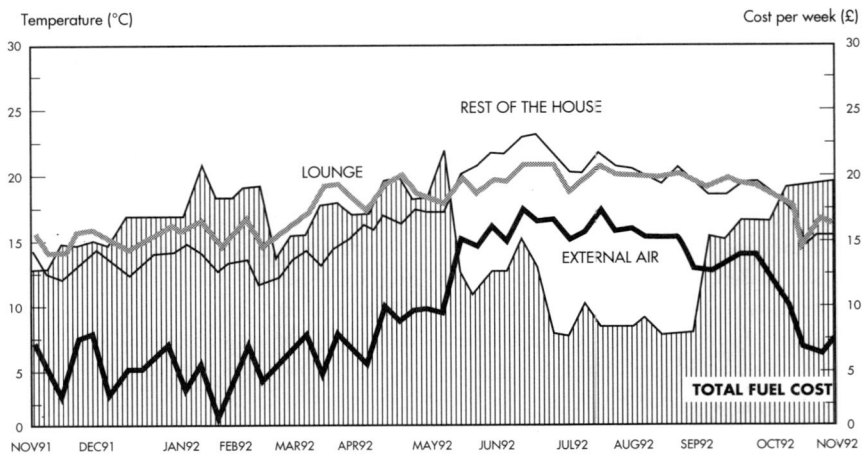

Average temperatures: external air 9.4°C, lounge 17.5°C, rest of house 16.4°C. Average fuel costs: £14.60.

Source: B. Sheldrick, *Beyond Draughtproofing*, Heatwise Glasgow, Glasgow, forthcoming.

Figure 3.7b Improved flat - temperature & costs
November 1991 - November 1992

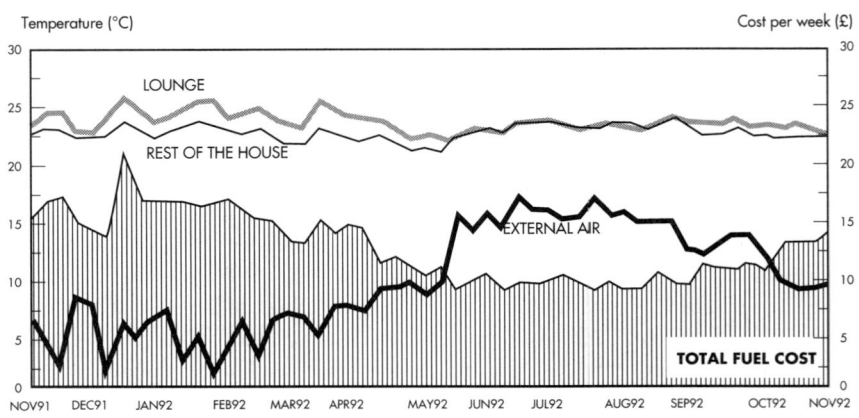

Average temperatures: external air 9.6°C, lounge 23.8°C, rest of house 22.8°C. Average fuel costs: £12.60.

Source: B. Sheldrick, *Beyond Draughtproofing*, Heatwise Glasgow, Glasgow, forthcoming.

defines the minimum acceptable standards for a dwelling to be deemed fit to live in. Under the Tolerable Standard, a dwelling must have an adequate provision for heating. However, rather than define 'adequacy' in terms of performance criteria or temperature standards, the Scottish Office guidance on the subject indicates that the presence of a socket or a point into which to plug a heater is sufficient[30]. Thus, a dwelling needs neither an actual heating system nor insulation to comply with the Tolerable Standard.

An alternative definition of a 'house' is a place independent of external weather conditions[31]. The house monitored in Easterhouse and referred to above would fail this definition. This unimproved house is neither an isolated nor an extreme case. Given the 'spec-built' nature of much of Easterhouse, and the other post war peripheral estates in Scotland, the results of the Easterhouse energy audits results have a wider applicability for a significant number of Scottish dwellings. Under the alternative definition of a 'house', many dwellings in Scotland, given their insulation and heating characteristics, would fail the criterion of being independent of the external weather.

3.5 Other Costs

The previous sections examined separately the disproportionate level of fuel expenditure among low income households, the cost of fuel in poorly insulated dwellings with inappropriate heating appliances, and the issue of inadequate heating and cold homes. These issues are not, however, unconnected. Research has found that there is a very significant overlap between those living in poorly insulated, badly heated homes and those on low income[32]. Thus, the people who already spend a disproportionate amount on fuel, and those that are least likely to be able to spend more, are also those most likely to live in dwellings that require above average levels of expenditure to obtain reasonable temperatures.

The problems do not stop there as they are not confined to technical considerations or financial transactions alone. The interaction between income, heating and insulation, and the cost of fuel touch upon a household's living environment and its health, as well as its wallet. Many of the issues are well documented elsewhere[33][34][35][36], so the following is intended as a brief overview of the associated issues.

(a) Fuel debt and disconnection

For the lowest income groups, spending in excess of 10% of income on fuel is the norm[37]. This situation results in pressure on the household budget, and problems when income is insufficient to pay the bills. Glasgow City Council has found that the largest household debt in the city after rent arrears is that owed to the fuel utilities[38]. This indebtedness can be seen in the presence of 'power card meters', the number of people on 'fuel direct' and, when all else fails, the number of people who are disconnected by the utilities.

The installation of modern prepayment meters (e.g. Scottish Hydro's card meter and Scottish Power's Powercard Register) has become a common response to avoid disconnection (and pay off past arrears). UK statistics indicate that households opting for prepayment meters or 'fuel direct' have increased from 189,000 in 1977 to 615,000 in 1990[39]. These facilities have helped people to budget their fuel bills and pay off their arrears, and have resulted in lower disconnection rates, but at a cost. They have also shifted the nature of the problem. Instead of the utility cutting off the consumer, households now disconnect themselves[40][41]. However, it would appear that for many self-disconnection is more acceptable than disconnection by the utility, since the interruption in supply is shorter and there are no reconnection charges or demands for deposits. Yet, ironically, the very people who are having difficulty paying their fuel bills and have accumulated a fuel debt may also have to pay more for their fuel. The utilities add an extra amount to the standing charge for providing a prepayment meter.

When it comes to debt and the installation of powercard meters, the utilities are in a position of strength. They are not bound by all the same laws governing other creditors when recovering money owed to them, and they have the ultimate sanction—disconnection. Loss of gas supply can mean no space or water heating or cooking. Loss of electricity supply cuts off lights and appliances as well. Both are traumatic for the household, and result not only in hardship, but in people resorting to dangerous practices such as illegal reconnection and the use of inappropriate methods to heat and light their home.

(b) Condensation and mould growth

Condensation and mould growth problems are the result of the imbalance in the house between the use of heating, the levels of insulation, and the ventilation rate[42]. Where this imbalance occurs, the results can range from a bit of condensation on the window pane through to rooms with the walls covered in black mould. It is not only a visual problem or one of smell. Where it keeps recurring, so that wallpaper or paint does not stay on the wall, or clothes, bed linen or other furnishings have to be replaced, it is dispiriting and demoralising for the household. What may start as a superficial problem can also give rise to structural problems with the building fabric.

It does not help when the occupants are told that they are fault because they are using bottled gas or paraffin heaters because it is all they can afford; or that they are drying clothes indoors because the climate does not allow them to dry them outdoors; or that they boil food without lids on the pans. Being advised to open the windows and turn up the heating is less than useful advice when the household has problems paying for its present fuel consumption.

As already noted, many homes in Scotland have less than adequate insulation or are reliant on inappropriate heating. The preliminary results from the Scottish House Condition Survey found that 423,000 dwellings (i.e. 1 in 5 of the total housing stock) suffer from the problem of dampness, serious condensation and mould growth[43]. (For further information on house conditions, see section 2.3c in the chapter on housing.)

Not all of the dwellings with dampness, condensation and mould growth fail the Tolerable Standard. Unlike the English Fitness Standard, where a house is deemed unfit for occupation on the grounds of dampness prejudicial to health, the Scottish Tolerable Standard only encompasses rising or penetrating damp. Changing the Scottish legislation to match that of the English would increase significantly the number of dwellings deemed unfit for occupation. Condensation and mould growth would then come under the Scottish Tolerable Standard, as they now do in England, and increase the opportunity for legal redress for those suffering the consequences of living in damp housing.

(c) Health

The cost implications of living in cold, damp and mouldy houses are not only paid for through the fuel bills or problems with the building fabric. Research findings have found linkages between living in damp and mouldy homes and the incidence of respiratory and gastric illnesses, particularly in the very young and elderly[44]. Also, the problems are not confined to physical well-being, but affect mental health as well. (For more information on the link between health and living conditions, see section 5.1 in the chapter on health and welfare services.) They may even lead to death. Statistics indicate an increase in winter mortality which is not necessarily experienced in countries with higher heating and insulation standards. In Scotland, 2,000 more people die on average in the first and last quarters of the year (i.e. the heating season) than do in the spring and summer quarters[45].

(d) Cold rooms

Nominally, a dwelling may comprise three or four apartments, but how many rooms are usable in the winter? Inadequate room temperatures throughout the house during the winter lead households to congregate in one warm room, to the point where the elderly may sleep in their lounges because of the low temperatures in unheated bedrooms. Although this strategy is adopted to stay warm and to economise on fuel expenditure, it is not necessarily cheap. It can cost more to heat one room than to heat the whole of an insulated house to a higher temperature standard with an appropriate heating system[46].

3.6 Conclusions

No other ostensibly technical issue provides the same indication of social, economic and environmental welfare in the house that 'energy' does. Energy is not only about gas, electricity, or solid fuel. It is not only a commodity that is bought and sold at a price. It is not only about the consumption of kilowatt hours, therms, or gigajoules. It is not only about the type of heating or the levels of insulation. In the home, energy use is about warmth, comfort, and the quality of life.

The adequate use of energy in the home is about achieving minimum acceptable standards. Too many low income households are denied these standards, and the benefits that come from them. This is not to imply that low income households are not using energy or not spending money on fuel. As has been seen, low income households can spend well above average on fuel and still not realise reasonable temperature standards. It can cost more to heat one room badly in a poorly insulated, inappropriately heated dwelling than to heat the whole of a house to reasonable temperatures in an insulated dwelling with an appropriate heating system.

When the balance between energy consumption and the price of fuel is wrong, the ramifications impact on housing conditions, the health of the occupants, and their disposable income. These impacts are evidenced in high fuel bills, the extent of cold homes, the incidence of condensation and mould growth in dwellings, the levels of fuel debt, and the rates of disconnection. All of these indicators are too high.

It is not enough to install new heating systems and expect the problems of paying for fuel to go away. The heating may still not be affordable without addressing the levels of insulation as well, or people may not use the system properly through lack of knowledge[47] or fear of running up bills they cannot afford to pay. Basic insulation measures are a start but, given the magnitude of the problem in much of the Scottish housing stock, they too are insufficient on their own. To overcome the problem of homes that are hard to heat and expensive to heat, there needs to be a comprehensive approach that combines insulation of the building fabric with installing appropriate forms of whole house heating. Also, these improvements must be followed up with customised energy advice packages to ensure that households understand how to operate their heating system effectively and obtain value for money from their fuel expenditure.

Homes can be made warm, dry and affordable to heat, even for low income households. As seen above, we know what to do. Unfortunately, too often we do not act on our knowledge.

References and footnotes to Chapter 3

1. House of Commons Official Report, *Parliamentary Debates,* Vol. 224, Col.504, HMSO, London, 10 May 1993.
2. House of Commons Official Report, see reference 1.
3. Quoted in House of Commons Official Report, *Parliamentary Debates,* Vol. 227, Col. 535, HMSO, London, 10 May 1993.
4. Institute of Gerontology, *Cold Comfort,* Age Concern, London, 1993.
5. House of Commons Official Report, see reference 1, Col. 570.
6. Institute of Gerontology, see reference 4.
7. Neighbourhood Energy Action, *Home Energy Efficiency Scheme - the first fifteen months,* NEA, Newcastle upon Tyne, 1992.
8. S. Hutton and G. Harmon, *Assessing the Impact of VAT on Fuel on Low Income Households: Analysis of Fuel Expenditure and Data from 1991 Family Expenditure Survey,* GCCI058/4.93, Social Policy Research Unit, University of York, York, 1993.
9. S. Hutton and G. Harmon, see reference 8.
10. H. Sutherland and G. Redmond, *The Impact of the 1993 Budget on the Distribution of Household Incomes,* Microsimulation Unit, Department of Applied Economics, University of Cambridge, Cambridge, 1993.
11. S. Hutton and G. Harmon, see reference 8.
12. S. Hutton and G. Harmon, see reference 8.
13. H. Sutherland and G. Redmond, see reference 10.
14. Office of Gas Supply, *Gas and Energy Efficiency: The E-factor,* Ofgas, London, 1992.
15. The term 'useful unit' takes into account the energy content of a unit of fuel, the efficiency of the heating appliances, and the cost of fuel, allowing different fuels to be compared directly in terms of the cost of heating.
16. B. Sheldrick, *Energy Efficiency in the Scottish Domestic Sector,* Scottish Energy Study Task 4, Scottish Enterprise, Glasgow, forthcoming.
17. Building Research Energy Conservation Unit, *Energy Efficiency and Affordable Warmth: a workshop manual,* GIR7, Energy Efficiency Office, London, 1991.
18. S. Hutton and G. Harmon, see reference 8.
19. B. Boardman, *Fuel Poverty: From Cold Homes to Affordable Warmth,* Belhaven Press, London, 1991.
20. B. Sheldrick, *Heating Costs in Easterhouse: an energy audit and fuel cost survey,* Heatwise Glasgow, Glasgow, 1988.
21. B. Anderson et al, *BREDEM - BRE Domestic Energy Model: background, philosophy and description,* Building Research Establishment, Garston, 1985.
22. Energy Efficiency Office, *Cutting Home Energy Costs,* Energy Efficiency Office, London, 1986.

23. Building Research Establishment, *Energy Assessments of Dwellings using BREDEM Worksheet*, IP 13/88, Building Research Establishment, Garston, 1988.
24. House of Commons Official Records, *Parliamentary Debates*, Vol. 215, Col. 72 wa, HMSO, London, 30 November 1992.
25. Energy Efficiency Office, *Guide to Home Heating Costs*, Energy Efficiency Office, London, 1985.
26. G. Raw, 'What is Adequate Heating', in G. Raw, S. Hutton, D. Ward and G. Ward, *Adequate and Affordable Heating for the Elderly at Home*, CR30/87, Building Research Establishment, London, 1987, pp. 1-11.
27. G. Raw, see reference 26.
28. G. Raw, see reference 26.
29. Central Statistical Office, Family Spending: A Report on the 1992 Family Expenditure Survey, HMSO, 1993.
30. Scottish Development Department, *The New Scottish Housing Handbook*, Bulletin No. 2, SDD, Edinburgh, 1969.
31. T. Markus, *Homes for the Future*, paper presented at Warm Homes - Social Needs and Business Opportunities Conference, April 20-21 1993, Glasgow (forthcoming).
32. B. Boardman, see reference 19.
33. B. Boardman, see reference 19.
34. C. Porteous and T. Markus, *Condensation: Causes and Cures*, Right to Warmth, Glasgow, 1991.
35. S. Hunt, *Unhealthy Housing*, Right to Warmth, Glasgow, 1991.
36. R. Harrison, *Paying For Fuel*, Right to Warmth, Glasgow, 1992.
37. B. Boardman, see reference 19.
38. Glasgow City Council, *Elis Fisher Award Submission*, City Housing, Glasgow, 1993.
39. B. Boardman, see reference 19.
40. R. Harrison, *Powercards and Card Meters*, Right to Warmth, Glasgow, 1993.
41. Birmingham Settlement, Community Energy Research and Bristol Energy Centre, *Hidden Disconnected*, Birmingham Settlement, Birmingham, 1993.
42. C. Porteous and T. Markus, see reference 34.
43. Scottish Homes, *Scottish House Condition Survey: preliminary results*, Scottish Homes, Edinburgh, 1993.
44. S. Hunt, see reference 35.
45. House of Commons Official Report, *Parliamentary Debates*, Vol. 220, Col. 719 wa, HMSO, London, 11 March 1993.
46. B. Sheldrick, *Warm, Dry and Affordable to Heat: interim report on the monitoring of the Easthall project: March 1990 to May 1991*, Heatwise Glasgow, Glasgow, 1992.
47. Heatwise Glasgow, *Castlemilk Energy Advice Demonstration Project Report*, Heatwise Glasgow, Glasgow, 1992.

Food And Nutrition

by Damian Killeen

Food is a basic necessity. Damian Killeen shows here that those on low incomes sometimes cannot afford to eat enough and that inadequate intake of some nutrients and overdependence on some substances such as fats and sugars lead to ill-health for many Scots. Despite awareness of healthy eating recommendations, those on low incomes cannot afford to respond to the advice. Idealised low cost healthy diets are not cheap enough for some and in general take no account of special dietary needs or realistic eating behaviour. For many people, choice is restricted and access to affordable, good quality food is difficult or expensive in terms of travel fares. Damian Killeen argues that initiatives to tackle food poverty will have little impact unless income support levels are raised.

4.1 Introduction

Immediately following the Second World War many parents reserved their egg rations for their children. Some of today's single parents also deny themselves egg, except as an occasional ingredient of other dishes, so their children can have what they regard as a wholesome diet[1]. It is tempting to conclude from this example that little about the domestic food economy has changed for those on low incomes in the past 50 years. But in the late 1940s and early 1950s there was a common diet for the whole nation; food supply was controlled firstly by rationing and later by retail price maintenance, and a national food policy contributed to ensuring that the population avoided many of the diet related health disorders such as heart and bowel disorders, bad teeth and obesity which are currently the cause of considerable concern. While post war families may have said, as do many low income households today, that they often did not get to eat what they liked and that they often did not like what they had to eat, the circumstances of post war Britain offered consumers a framework of regulation which aimed to ensure a relatively equitable distribution of nutritious food.

By comparison, today's parents who attempt to provide for their families on a low income must deal with a different set of dietary expectations and food cultures which are widely disseminated in society through education, advertisement and peer group pressures; they must judge the nutritional value and health implications of the food available to them against a variety of, sometimes competing, claims and they must use their limited purchasing power to secure what they require in a largely unregulated market. Whatever their personal food preferences or however extensive their knowledge of concepts such as 'healthy eating', these parents must also adapt to the practicalities of increasingly centralised shopping facilities and to the emphasis placed by producers and retailers on frozen and chilled foods which bring with them specific storage requirements. Finally, they must provide for their households within the constraints of their cash flow and the nature and quality of their domestic equipment and living circumstances. These constraints apply, of course, to everyone but in this chapter an attempt is made to establish whether those on low incomes are disproportionately disadvantaged in terms of the food they eat and their nutritional standards.

The term 'consumer' has a very particular significance with respect to food. Not only does the purchaser look for factors such as availability, choice, suitability to purpose, safety and value for money which apply to all consumer products but other, more personal, factors also come into play.

Consumer detriment with regard to food involves more than just the usual questions of availability, quality, price and value for money. Detriment can also be demonstrated by the impact of retail practices and low income on the physical and emotional health of individuals. Difficulties in accessing ready supplies of affordable food can also contribute to the deprivation of whole communities.

4.2 Low Income, Inadequate Nutrition and Poor Health

It is a long time since the overall availability of foodstuffs has been a factor in determining nutritional standards or the nation's health. Indeed it is an irony of the debate on nutrition and health that the major concerns are less for food shortages than for the adverse health effects of over-nutrition (malnutrition in the sense of eating too much of some nutrients, for example, saturated fat) such as obesity, cardiovascular disease, dental caries and bowel disorders.[2] It is suggested by most informed commentators that as a population our major health problems stem from eating too much of the 'wrong' foods rather than from eating insufficient food, although it has been demonstrated that women at *all* levels of income are falling short of the target levels for some basic vitamins and minerals[3]. It is unlikely that the reason for contemporary malnutrition will be the same for affluent sections of society as it is for those living in poverty, who not only may have elements of over-nutrition in their diets from high consumption levels of fat and sugar but may also suffer under-nutrition in having inadequate intakes of, say, Vitamin C or dietary fibre. It is not the case that all dietary related problems are due to over-nutrition and low income households continue to be at risk because they do not have access to a supply of affordable, nutritious food.

The connection between poor health and poverty is indisputable. In his Report for 1991-1992 the Director of Public Health for Greater Glasgow stated:

> "Health status in both sexes is clearly related to indicators of both material and social deprivation even after standardising for a wide range of lifestyle and demographic factors. Material deprivation has a slightly greater impact on health than social deprivation, but both forms of deprivation appear to be more important than lifestyle factors"[4].

(For more detail on the link between health and deprivation see section 5.1a in the chapter on health and welfare services.)

Developments in public health over the last century have increasingly isolated the role of poverty and poor diet in causing poor health[5]. Developing scientific opinion was divided between those who placed the blame for malnutrition on the 'fecklessness' of the urban poor—who appeared resistant to all attempts to improve their cooking skills—and responded with the introduction of 'domestic science' into the school curriculum in 1897, and those who attempted to place food consumption behaviour into the wider context of economic and social conditions. In 1936, following a detailed study of the eating habits of people at different levels of income, John Boyd Orr of the Rowett Research Institute in Aberdeen concluded that "...a diet completely adequate for health, according to modern standards, is reached at an income level above that of fifty per cent of the population..."[6].

Government encouragement for education on the relationship between nutrition and health has continued since the war, including the publication by the Department of Health and Social Security in 1978 of *Eating for Health*, a set of guidelines for healthy eating in the UK. However, since the war, the inability or unwillingness of governments to reduce inequalities of income in order to increase the access of low income households to a wider range of affordable, quality foods has been a constant theme in the debates about poverty and health.

The British Government's failure to grasp the nettle of the relationship between poverty, poor nutrition and poor health standards was crystallised for many by the failure of the Health Education Authority to publish a report on *Food Patterns Amongst Lower Income Groups in the UK* prepared for them by Isobel Cole-Hamilton in 1988. After presenting an accumulation of evidence of the links between low income, poor diet and poor health, Cole-Hamilton concluded:

> "The real problem for most people with low incomes is, clearly, that they have insufficient money available to them to lead what could even be described as a 'modest-but-adequate' lifestyle. Until this intolerable situation is confronted head on and incomes rise sufficiently, the problems of food poverty in Britain will never go away"[7].

The next year, by contrast, the Health Education Authority published *Diet, Nutrition, and 'Healthy Eating' in Low Income Groups* which made no recommendations on income and argued for 'a new healthy eating resource' (i.e. an information pack). This was despite its acknowledgement that "...there is a core of people for whom further information on healthy eating will have little or no interest, given the overriding importance of their other concerns"[8]. Successive reports, such as the *Poverty and Nutrition Survey* conducted for the National Children's Home, have shown that it is lack of money, not ignorance, which determines what people eat[9].

What both Cole-Hamilton and the Health Education Authority agreed on, nevertheless, was that low income households are more efficient in selecting nutritious items of food than the more affluent and that knowledge of current dietary guidelines was fairly high across *all* socio-economic groups. When choosing food, the paramount concerns of most purchasers were price, ease and speed of preparation, and family acceptability. 'Healthiness' was often pushed down the list of priorities by these more immediate concerns. This is the reality of 'home economics' in low income households against which proposals for addressing the poverty/diet/health connection must be assessed.

4.3 What Do Low Income Households Eat ?

An underlying weakness of all arguments about the relationship between poverty, health and diet is the absence of comprehensive, reliable research into the subject. The *National Food Survey*, while providing a measure of changes in food consumption in the population as a whole, is not regarded as a satisfactory indicator of consumption for specific groups such as low income households. There are concerns that these households are more reluctant to participate in the survey and that the behaviour of those who do take part changes in survey weeks with the purchase of more food than normal. There are also whole groups such as homeless people and those in insecure housing who are excluded from the survey. Before 1993 the survey has not included food purchased for consumption outside the home, such as snacks, pub food or takeaways which can play an important part in nutrition for people with very limited cooking facilities such as homeless families in bed and breakfast accommodation. For these households and for many others in overcrowded and deprived conditions these types of food are regarded as essential items rather than luxuries. Finally, the way in which conclusions are drawn from the survey tends to mask the specific food consumption behaviour of low income households.

Nevertheless, despite the requests from consumer representatives and others on its Consumer Panel, the Ministry of Agriculture, Fisheries and Food, which is responsible for monitoring the nation's food consumption, has consistently refused to undertake specific work on the consumption of food by low income households. In addition, the Ministry also dismisses the accumulation of smaller, localised pieces of relevant research as unrepresentative of any more general trend.

However, in the absence of a national survey, it is notable that there is a broad consistency among the findings of the surveys which have been undertaken. Findings from the Scottish Heart Health Study (SHHS) show that, overall, men and women in manual occupations have a poorer quality diet than those in non-manual occupations. This is compatible with the view that poor diet may be a contributory factor in higher mortality rates for coronary heart disease[10]. Other findings from SHHS demonstrate the different food sources from which nutrition is derived by men and women and by different social classes. Men, for instance, drink more alcohol than women and eat less fruit. Meat products such as pies and sausages (as distinct from carcass meat) and hard margarines are responsible for most of the differences in total fat and saturated fat intake between the social class groups. Key differences occur in the percentage of vitamin C and fibre from fruit juice, fresh fruit, green vegetables and potatoes.

The Scottish Heart and Health Study bore out the findings of a survey of 440 low income individuals in Renfrew in 1986–1987 which was based on a self-administered questionnaire[11]. This also demonstrated the effects of hardship on food consumption, with 48% of the total sample indicating that food was one of the first items to be cut when money was short, and 41% of all surveyed (76% of the unemployed respondents) stating that they did not have, or just about had, enough money for food all week. In addition to the gender differences in diet this study also highlighted age differences; young people aged 16–20 clearly ate the least nutritious diet and were least well informed about 'healthy eating'. This finding raises serious issues for the future and further research is required to determine whether young people eat less nutritious diets because of unemployment, poverty and low income or because they care less than older people about their health.

More recent reports have demonstrated the inability of low income households, families with children and also young single people to feed themselves satisfactorily on incomes at or below income support levels and have described the coping strategies which these households adopt[12][13]. These include parents failing to feed themselves adequately in order to ensure a reasonable supply of food for their children.

Typically, in order to stop feeling hungry and to have something 'tasty' to eat, low income households will purchase higher proportions of foods which are high in fats, such as cheap sausages, or in sugars, such as biscuits and sweets. Although it has been established that low income consumers are more efficient purchasers of nutrients per pence than higher income groups, these nutrients are accompanied by elements which present greater health risks to lower income groups. This is not because low income consumers are ignorant of 'healthy eating' considerations but because they cannot afford to meet all their needs in a 'healthy' way within their budgets.

4.4 Influences on Food Choice in Low Income Households

With the health and welfare of themselves and their families so significantly at stake, those on low incomes have to make their purchasing decisions in the framework of both the dominant cultures of food consumption in Britain, the sometimes contradictory advice on the health consequences of food choices, the marketing efforts of food retailers, and the constraints of income versus the demands of other expenditures. A wide range of influences on food choice are addressed in the National Consumer Council's publication *Your Food: Whose Choice*[14].

However, while government, retailers and health educators have launched numerous programmes to alter patterns of food consumption, they have done so without any comprehensive understanding of how food choices are made. To meet this significant gap in current knowledge, the Economic and Social Research Council has recently launched a multi-disciplinary research programme which will address the question 'Why do people eat what they do?' This will investigate

> "...the immediate influences on food choices, (including the physio-pharmacological, psychological, social, cultural and economic) and the wider context shaping the general environment of the individual (including public attitudes and economic, social, legislative and political considerations)."

In the absence of detailed research it is only possible to suggest some of the factors which will play a part in determining food choice.

- Consumers have different food requirements; these may be cultural, as in the case of ethnic minorities or those who wish to sustain a particular diet for religious or ethical reasons, or they may be related to special needs associated with personal health.

- Consumers may be affected by ideas such 'as a traditional diet', based on what they were fed as children, which make them more resistant to dietary change such as a change to wholemeal bread.

- As most parents know, children can develop some very fixed ideas about what they will or will not eat.

- Consumers are influenced by the messages of both food marketers and the health educators; it is not surprising, given the balance of resources spent on these two sets of messages, that many consumers are attracted towards high added value, more profitable food products. It would, for example, be an exceptionally progressive retailer who promoted the sale of porridge oats at the expense of the shelves of other breakfast cereals.

- Consumers are influenced by the availability, accessibility and price of food products; these factors, in turn, are affected not only by pure free market considerations but also by regulatory factors influencing price and by political arrangements such as the Common Agricultural Policy. Low income households are no more immune to these and other influences than the average household and in some cases, such as in relation to price and accessibility, are more vulnerable.

4.5 Welfare Benefits and Food Poverty

A key factor influencing low income households as consumers of food is the amount of money they can afford to spend. Especially for those dependent on state benefits, this is a particularly controversial issue. No government in recent years has been willing to identify a specific allocation for food within the overall benefit level. The concept of 'choice' is regularly used to suggest that it is not government's business to intervene in benefit recipients' decisions about the allocation of their resources. Nor, since the inception of the welfare state, have benefit rates been based on any consensus of the nutritional and other needs of individuals and, thereby, the likely cost of an acceptable diet. While such a consensus, which would have to take account of the different needs of men and women, workers and the unemployed, children and elderly people, would be difficult to achieve it would be more equitable than the present situation in which the Government can claim that benefits are sufficient to meet needs without there being any requirement on them to prove its case.

The debate on the appropriateness of the food element in welfare benefits goes back to 1948 when the National Assistance Board (NAB) set the 'assistance scales'. When the Department of Health and Social Services reviewed nutritional standards in 1979, it developed a measure of 'Recommended Daily Amounts of Food Energy and Nutrients for People in the UK' (RDAs). These are based on the principle of minimum levels below which signs of deficiency might be expected. Within the supplementary benefit system there was a limited facility for benefits levels to be adjusted (by means of the Diet Addition) to take account of varying dietary needs. This was abandoned with the introduction of income support in 1988, although the Government claimed that dietary allowances had been included in the calculation of the special premiums which were made available to people in specific groups.

As the scientific understanding of dietary requirements developed in the 1980s a series of reports began to show that basic nutritional standards could not be sustained on the amounts allowed for in current welfare payments[15].

4.6 The Cost of a Healthy Diet

There have been a number of attempts in recent years to develop basic guidelines for a healthy diet (most particularly, the Dietary Reference Values (DRVs) recommended by the Department of Health in its 1991 report)[16]. These and other guidelines have also been used to develop 'healthy' and low-cost diets. The cost of these diets has varied. Some of these results have been used to develop the argument that a 'healthy' diet is cheaper than a 'non-healthy' diet. However, as these diets ignore meals, snacks, sweets and drinks taken outside the house, they represent a rather idealised vision of the realities of food consumption by all groups, including those on low incomes, and they also ignore the fact that families on low incomes would be required to change drastically their current eating habits.

As a contribution to the debate on healthy, affordable diets for low income households, the Ministry of Agriculture, Fisheries and Food (MAFF) was prompted by its Consumer Panel to investigate claims that a healthy diet would cost more than present 'unhealthy' diets[17]. First, MAFF set a target energy intake of 1,859 kilocalories per day, the average energy intake of British adults. Using the *National Food Survey* as a basis and altering the amount of individual food items consumed by no more than double or a half of the norm, MAFF was able to identify a 'healthy' diet which costs slightly less than the typical British diet. Second, MAFF devised a diet which would take account of the new DRVs for fats, saturated fats, sugars and fibre. Again, MAFF claimed that this healthier diet is also cheaper than normal consumption.

Third, MAFF set out to devise a diet which would meet DRVs within a cost constraint of £10.00 per week (Table 4.1). This was achieved by shifting consumption even further towards items which are high in dietary fibre and away from animal proteins. The resulting 'MAFF £10.00 diet' has attracted considerable comment, not least because it has been suggested that the Department of Social Security is happy with the outcome.

Table 4.1 MAFF £10.00 per person low cost diet

Type of Food	Grams	Equivalent Helping
Cheese	28	Under 2 slices of processed cheese
Carcass meat	140	About 6 chicken wings
Other meat products	119	About 6 rashers bacon
Fish	91	About 3 fish fingers
Egg	35	About an egg a week
Whole milk (full fat)		2.03 pints
Skimmed milk		1.26 pints
Butter/margarine	133	Enough for 9 slices of bread
Other fats/oils	119	8 tablespoonfuls
Sugar	203	41 teaspoonfuls
Jam	28	Dessertspoonful
Potatoes	1,239	7 baked potatoes
Fresh green vegetables	322	Lettuce/½ cabbage
Other fresh vegetables	462	Large cauliflower or 4 onions
Canned beans	343	Medium tin beans
Frozen vegetables	399	Pack frozen carrots
Other processed vegetables	387	Small tin of peas
Fresh fruit	595	3-4 apples
Fruit juice	161	Under ¾ of a glass of juice
Other fruit products	154	1.5 portions of tinned fruit salad
Cakes, buns, biscuits	63	7 rich tea biscuits
Breakfast cereal	259	7 medium sized portions of cornflakes
Wholemeal bread	336	14 slices of small loaf (2 per day)
Other bread	1,043	43 slices of small white loaf (6 per day)
Other cereal products	497	7 portions of cooked pasta
Beverages	112	Several cups per day tea/coffee

Based on: Ministry of Agriculture, Fisheries and Food, The Cost of Alternative Diets, MAFF, CP (92), 9/3.

One member of the MAFF Consumer Panel has claimed that

"...it would be hard to argue that MAFF's low cost diet was realistic. To follow it low income households would have to cut out meat entirely, more than double their consumption of tinned fruit and frozen vegetables (an implicit assumption that they cannot afford enough fresh fruit and vegetables), double their consumption of breakfast cereals (in order, presumably, to achieve fibre and fortified vitamins), eat five times more wholemeal bread than at present, and eat more white bread. Of the eight slices of bread to be eaten each day, only three would have even a thin spread of margarine and butter; the rest would be eaten dry. Yoghurts and other dairy products are completely excluded. Expecting poor consumers to eat a totally different diet from the rest of the population is discriminatory. And as one commentator said, they better not watch any television, especially if they have kids' "[18].

In order to test out the acceptability of the MAFF £10.00 diet to low income households the Poverty and Health Working Group of the Strathclyde Poverty Alliance conducted focus group discussions with the members of local community health initiatives in Drumchapel in Glasgow and Ferguslie Park in Paisley. Some common points emerged which have a practical relevance to the lives of people living in conditions of poverty and which illustrate the difficulties in devising low income diets.

In each case, the participants estimated that they would be able to purchase the required items at a cost close to that suggested by MAFF but only if retailers were prepared to sell small quantities, such as four eggs rather than six, without increasing the price. This was particularly true with regard to fresh vegetables which would have to be bought in particularly small quantities if there was to be any variety in the diet. Participants were concerned that the diet made no allowances for people with special dietary needs such as diabetics. Women who travel away from their home area by bus or taxi to gain access to cheaper shops were concerned that, without the necessary storage facilities at home, the cost of travel several times a week would outweigh any other benefits. Several participants commented on the dependence on tinned and processed foods compared with fresh food in the MAFF diet and on the absence of a specific reference to pulses as a source of protein.

When it came to the question of the acceptability of the MAFF diet, either from the point of view of the women who are required to stretch it to cover breakfasts, lunches and a main meal every day of the week, or from the perspective of the families who are expected to eat it, the attitude of the focus group participants was unanimous. The diet might sustain life, but the meals it provides did not represent what the women believed they could realistically offer to their families; the quantities were too small and, most importantly, the MAFF diet lacks the potential for variety. Finally, the participants were concerned at the gap between the expectations which MAFF appears to have of their eating requirements and those of wider society.

When focus group participants spoke about their actual practice with regard to food, it became clear that there were occasions when they had to cope on even less than what is provided for in the MAFF diet, even though food is a priority for them and their families. When circumstances are tight, these women are prepared to feed their families first and worry about other bills later. The 1991 *Poverty and Nutrition Survey* conducted by the National Children's Home found that the average amount spent on food per person by the low income households was under £10.00 per week[19]. This represented 35% of total household expenditure compared with 12.4% spent on food by the average household. Despite this major commitment of resources, two-thirds of the children and over half the parents were eating nutritionally poor or very poor diets although there was a widespread awareness of the requirements for a healthy diet. Lack of income was identified as the principal reason for these poor diets and for the fact that both parents and children periodically had to go without food or to go short.

All the available evidence suggests that the greatest inhibitor to low income consumers having adequate nutritious food is shortage of money. The findings already quoted demonstrate that a healthy diet is impossible to maintain on expenditure of less than £10.00 per head per week and that many households cannot afford to spend even this amount. The 'healthy' diets devised by government are unrealistic in terms of the realities of life on low incomes and they are discriminatory in that they require people in poverty to adopt consumption patterns which are alien to the majority of the population. How then, with their limited resources, do low income households fare when it comes to exercising their role as consumers.

4.7 Access and Choice

One of the common complaints of the residents of Scotland's peripheral estates is the lack or shortage of supermarkets. Because of their isolation from the variety which is available in city centres, these consumers are either subject to the stocking and pricing policies of semi-monopoly providers in the local shopping centre or they are virtually excluded from access to a supermarket by the cost, time and effort involved in travelling by public transport—often with small children in tow. These problems are compounded for low income households living in rural and remote areas.

It is generally recognised that there has been a significant shift in food retailing from the local shop to large superstores which now account for 70% of all food sales in Scotland. The near monopolies enjoyed by the major players in the food retail industry put them in a particularly powerful position with regard not only to their own sales but also to developments in food technology and production. The operation of these multiples also has a distorting effect on shopping provision and choice by contributing to the closure of smaller, more local stores and—via the production of 'own-brand' goods, advertising and marketing—plays a significant part in influencing—for good or bad—consumer attitudes towards food. The power of the major retailers is well illustrated by their attempts to encourage the Government to outlaw the introduction into Britain of warehouse clubs, such as Costco, which enable their members, for an initial fee, to buy food at even cheaper prices[20].

However, the needs of low income households will not be met simply by placing supermarkets within everybody's reach. In order to gain the best advantage from what the superstores have to offer, purchasers need to be able to buy in larger packs and quantities and to store food appropriately. For many low income households cash flow is a constant problem and most food is purchased on a daily basis. Many low income households do not own freezers or refrigerators and, in the case of those who live in bed and breakfast accommodation or hostels and the homeless, have few or no storage facilities. For disabled or elderly people even the prospect of a relatively short journey to a supermarket, as compared with a corner shop, can make the supermarket inaccessible.

Anyone who is accustomed to supermarket or high street shopping will be faced with a startling contrast if they visit the shopping centres of peripheral housing estates in Scotland. Invariably, they will find a proportion, sometimes as high as a third or more, of the shop units unused. In some cases they will be struck by the poor quality of goods on display and the emphasis on processed rather than fresh products. The problems faced by local shopkeepers are, inevitably, reflected in the prices of goods.

One local food poverty group, for example, found that a tin of branded spaghetti, which could be bought for as little as 18p in the town centre was on sale in their local shops at prices between 35p and 79p. This pattern held true for a wide range of items including bread, milk, sugar, tea and margarine[21].

Local shops and shopping centres in Scotland's peripheral estates tend to focus, for understandable reasons, on offering consumers inexpensive goods, but this is often achieved at the expense of choice. Stores will carry a relatively small number of items but very few of these will be fresh or wholefood produce. Recent research shows 'healthy' items are often expensive and not so attractive in comparison with other goods, and that fruit and vegetables, when they are available, are often not of the best quality[22]. Taken together these amount to a major disincentive to low income shoppers to purchase nutritious and affordable food. One further feature which is largely absent in Scotland but which is common elsewhere in the UK is street market trading in cheap, wholesome, fresh produce at competitive and popular prices.

4.8 Planning, Regulation and Food Poverty

It is evident that the shift from local, small scale retailing outlets to large stores located away from the traditional high street has been accompanied by increased disadvantage for a number of groups including the elderly, large young families, those who are unemployed, or sick and infirm, carers and those without cars. This move has not been made without protest from communities and the authorities which represent them. Nevertheless, a feeling has been generated that in responding to demand from the majority of consumers where mass marketing is likely to be profitable, retailers are neglecting the demand from low income consumers, and that demand-led provision is a juggernaut which has no need to respond in any more than a superficial way to the needs of minority and special interest groups.

There was once a view in government planning circles that "...the existence of any planning system constitutes an acceptance of the principle that the market will not of itself inevitably arrive at a satisfactory conclusion..."[23]. The increasing marginalisation of low income consumers is evidence of the contemporary relevance of this view. There has been a growing awareness of the limits of laissez-faire market policies to retailing, with voices being raised in favour of a return to more locally based planning controls on retail developments[24].

Such an approach runs completely contrary to the trend of current liberal economic thinking in which the operation of the free market is the dominant factor. It is also worth noting that in Europe the food market is less 'free' than the market for some other commodities and services. There is an extensive framework of regulation and controls affecting the details of the production, importation, distribution and marketing of foodstuffs in the shape of the Common Agricultural Policy (CAP).

It is estimated that the cost through the CAP is an average of £17.00 per week per household in Britain. The poor of Britain, along with the rest of us, are paying what is, in effect, a food tax in order to keep farmers in work, and, as with other forms of indirect taxation, the poor pay proportionately more. With such a major intervention in place to protect producers, arguments against protections for disadvantaged consumers are difficult to maintain. In the interests of social equity there is a case for ensuring that planning law and economic regulation protect not only the producers of food but also the consumers, especially those disadvantaged consumers who are exposed to serious dangers of ill-health and a discriminatory lifestyle.

4.9 Responses to Food Poverty

The problem of food poverty, or consumer detriment with regard to food in low income households, is not universally recognised. There is still a tendency, not confined to government ministers, to blame the poor household management skills of people living in poverty for their failure to provide their families with a wholesome, healthy diet. For example, one commentator stated:

> "The families which organise their slender resources successfully display *moral* characteristics; perseverance and a willingness to go without in the short term in order to stay out of debt, carefulness, fortitude and, especially in the case of many of the wives, personal sacrifice and sustained commitment. Managing is a mix of skills, moral commitments and habits"[25].

The many reports into the effects of food poverty in low income households demonstrate that these personal qualities are in good supply in those who sacrifice their own welfare for that of their children. But no amount of moral commitment will balance the books when income is insufficient to provide a nutritious and acceptable diet, nor will it defeat the physiological effects of living on a poor diet for extended periods, especially during pregnancy, infancy and childhood. Other initiatives will be required if the problem of food poverty is to be tackled effectively. These will include self-help measures but also needed will be greater market controls and a more interventionist role for government.

(a) Community initiatives

Community responses to food poverty are generally of three kinds. First, there is a wide range of initiatives directed mainly though not exclusively at women, which aim to increase awareness of food and health issues for households on low incomes and to promote healthy eating. Many of these initiatives adopt an empowerment model which is designed to enable local communities to challenge local policies and practices which affect them directly. These local groups conduct 'shopping basket' surveys of the prices of food available to them in their areas—possibly in comparison with others. In addition to highlighting local prices these groups will also raise public awareness about local planning decisions affecting the siting of retail outlets and will press for improved transport services which will increase the range of shopping which they can access at a reasonable price. Typically, this type of local initiative will have been started by a community health worker or community nutritionist whose principal concern is to promote dietary change but who recognises that this depends on economic change as well as on education.

Second, a number of community groups have taken the initiative in becoming practically involved in the provision of affordable, quality food to low income households by setting up food co-operatives. These are membership organisations, with a minimal membership fee, which bulk-buy food items and pass on the savings to all members. Most of their work, including the purchase of food and the repackaging and resale to members, is undertaken by volunteers. In some areas there are food co-operative development agencies which assist local groups with setting up, training, hygiene and, particularly, financial management. There is no central source of information on the extent of food co-operative provision in Scotland, but recent research in Strathclyde has identified 50 which are directly funded by the

Regional Council[26]. An unknown number of additional food co-operatives in Strathclyde are funded by district councils and other agencies. Some of these are managed by local community groups, while others are managed by other member based organisations such as unemployed workers' centres.

There is no doubt that food co-operatives are appreciated by their members as a source of affordable food. Some also have an emphasis on healthy eating and are a more reliable source of fruit and fresh vegetables than local shops. There are, however, a number of management problems which limit their effectiveness. The reliance on volunteers limits times of opening and the range of services which can be offered, and dependency on the local 'cash and carry' warehouse also constrains the co-operatives' ability to provide choice.

Food co-operatives have been supported by local authorities as community businesses which will enable local communities to meet their needs. However, it has to be acknowledged that the scale of their activity in Scotland is minimal. Some are extremely successful on a local scale, with the majority of local households in membership. However, membership ranges from as low as ten to more than 500. Considering that they are situated in areas which contain many hundreds, even thousands, of low income households, it cannot be claimed that they make a substantial impact on the scale of food poverty. There is also a problem for local authorities in promoting their expansion in that they have the potential to be in direct competition with local retailers. The more effective the food co-operatives become, the more acute a problem this is for the council which has to achieve both social and economic objectives. There has been no systematic study of their impact on health and nutrition but anecdotal evidence from food co-operative workers suggests that members have been encouraged to buy less familiar foods such as kiwi fruit and that the consumption of fresh vegetables and fruit in their areas has increased simply because they have introduced a reliable supply.

A third type of development, still in its early stages, is the community food store. This type of initiative, currently being developed in conjunction with the Co-operative Wholesale Society by Community Enterprise Strathclyde, aims to give community groups greater access to economies of scale by enabling a network of local community managed retail outlets to purchase from one major distributor further back in the wholesale chain. The local outlets, in addition to running conventional, small supermarkets, would also provide a base for a number of services directed towards people with special needs such as elderly or disabled people who require to have their food delivered to them. These shops could also be the base for local groups with an interest in promoting healthy eating.

(b) Market initiatives

The food industry is itself affected by problems of overproduction and waste. A recent response to this problem, currently being promoted by the Institute of Grocery Distributors and shortly to be launched in Scotland, is the scheme Provision which is designed to make surpluses from participating companies available to residents of hostels and users of other charitably operated schemes such as soup kitchens and day centres. This can be seen as a development of the current practice of some chains, such as Marks and Spencer, of making surplus items available to charities at the end of trading. Provision, however, will operate on a much larger scale with surpluses delivered to central warehousing and distribution centres.

Provision has been keen to establish that it will operate within the existing framework of datemarking and all the other microbiological controls which affect food. There are concerns, however, that without substantial capital investment in storage and food handling facilities the participating charities might have difficulty in achieving the standards expected of the trade. But over and above these practical concerns there is controversy over the principle which is being established by this type of initiative. If the issue is to respond to food poverty, it is claimed, the dumping of surpluses will not affect the underlying issue of inadequate income. If the underlying problem is the handling of surpluses, is it appropriate that the poor should be used to resolve the problem?

Of all the objections to the Provision scheme the most substantial is that it creates the risk of the institutionalisation of the use of food surpluses as an alternative to welfare payments. While the present scheme will be limited to licensed charitable operators, the structure of the scheme, once established, could soon be adapted to distribution by a much wider welfare network. Tim Lang of Parents for Safe Food and a long-time food campaigner has compared the initiative with Third World Food Aid policies, which, he says, are now discredited because they do nothing to enable people to feed themselves in the long term[27]. He also observes that other Food Bank and Second Harvest schemes elsewhere in Europe and America have done nothing substantial to address underlying problems of poverty; instead they have become useful tax dodges for companies which can make a charitable concern out of waste distribution and they provide an element of conscience salving for executives whose other activities actually disadvantage the poor.

The food retail market does not operate in favour of Scotland's low income households. Indeed it can be claimed that to a significant extent the food retailing business has abandoned the poor, moved up-market, closed local shops, left the inner city and peripheral estates and moved out of town for car owners; and that it has encouraged value-adding, 'non-food' foods and one-stop shopping, and has contributed to the de-skilling of cooking. It would be possible, though perhaps not so highly profitable, for food retailers to refocus their attention on ensuring a supply of affordable, quality food of a highly nutritious nature to all by reversing some of these trends.

Supermarket chains are prominent in the health education field, supporting the production of healthy and low budget eating guides, but are they prepared to take the logic of this position forward and to use their power in the market place to promote the cheaper production and wider consumption of items such as wholemeal bread? Are they prepared to use the scale of their operations to ensure that it is the fresh food items which are discounted in store promotions rather than the cans of processed foods? If the food industry shares any responsibility for the health of the nation, which it is in such a powerful position to influence, then it should begin to consider ways in which satisfactory supplies of food to low income households could be restored.

(c) Government initiatives

The Scottish Office has become very concerned about the relationship between poor diet and ill-health in Scotland and has set in train a process which is intended to identify appropriate nutritional standards for Scotland. Also, in a recent White Paper, *Scotland's Health - A Challenge To Us All*, the Scottish Office has made the connection between these concerns and socio-economic deprivation:

"There is a particular need to encourage people living in deprived areas to adopt a healthier diet. These are the areas where diet is worst, with consumption of fresh fruit and vegetables being particularly low, and they are also the areas where the incidence of coronary heart disease is highest... proposed discussions with food retailers will include consideration of the availability and promotion of nutritious foods in areas where the range of outlets and choice, for example, of fruit and vegetables is often limited"[28].

To this extent the Scottish Office has begun to address the issue of consumer detriment with regard to food alongside its concern to emphasise the health promotion argument of individual responsibility for healthy eating. (See also section 5.1e in the chapter on health and welfare services). Whilst this is welcome, it is a matter of considerable concern that, at least by default, the Scottish Office appears to share the views of the Ministry of Agriculture, Fisheries and Food with respect to the adequacy of welfare benefits, as no mention is made in *Scotland's Health - A Challenge To Us All* of the problems which low income households experience in paying for food. If the Scottish Office seriously expects Scottish income support recipients to adopt the MAFF £10.00 diet as their contribution to national dietary change and the reduction of coronary heart disease, something more substantial than a health promotion exercise will be required to achieve the change. Instead, the Scottish Office should pay attention to the body of research, such as that published by the National Children's Home, which shows clearly that, given extra money, it is exactly those more healthy items, such as fruit and vegetables, which most low income householders would buy for their families.

4.10 Conclusions

The fact that there is a link between deprivation, poor diet and poor health is widely accepted. The precise nature of this linkage and what should be done to address it are matters of deep controversy. However, commonsense, which tells us that we only get what we pay for, supports the argument that low income households have an inferior choice of products; and the organisation of the food retail market leads to low income households being disadvantaged in terms of accessibility and price. The impact of this detriment on the health of people living in low income households and the cost of this impact on public spending through the health service is significant for everyone.

Scotland, along with the rest of Western Europe, has long moved away from the situation in which people were largely self-sufficient in food and there are no good arguments for claiming that we should return to those conditions. But it could also be argued that the majority of our population has become too alienated from the process of food production, making it unlikely that people grow their own produce, cook their own food or control the content of the food they consume.

We are not short of food, so rationing is not the answer. Instead our problems are ones of inequitable distribution of food and inequalities of income with which to buy it. The idea that the market is able to, or indeed would wish to, correct this imbalance of its own accord is not supported by the evidence of the steady shift away from poorer consumers towards a car owning, added-value shopping culture. The only alternative to the current free for all is an increased role for intervention in market activities by national and local government.

At the root of the problem, however, is the lack of control by individuals and communities over the basic necessities of food and other goods and services. Here there is a significant role for the education of individuals, not only in healthy eating and in cooking but also in the systems by which food is produced and distributed. There is also a role for the empowerment of communities to resist practices which reduce their quality of life and to establish alternative systems of more localised food production which create employment and which meet local needs. To succeed, this requires a framework of law and regulation which balances monetary values against social values and which asserts the needs of the individuals against those of corporations.

There is no simple set of legislative changes which can be proposed which will automatically result in equalising the position of low income consumers of food. The matter is complex and change will require the cooperation of many agencies and the private sector. What would assist is the establishment by government of a National Food Commission with powers to regulate the market in food, including the promotion of more small scale and localised measures managed both by communities and by entrepreneurs. Such a Commission could draw on both the Industry and Home and Health Departments of the Scottish Office as well as representation from the public, private and voluntary sectors.

More immediately, however, there is a case for challenging the current level of income support in terms of the access it allows low income households to an adequate supply of affordable quality food. The Retail Price Index, to which benefits increases are linked, does not adequately reflect the changes in the cost of living which are experienced by low income households. Food poverty is largely a question of income and even the current market would find more effective ways of delivering food to low income households if they had more money to spend.

References to Chapter 4

1. Oral Communication to author, 1993.
2. The Faculty of Public Health of the Royal College of Physicians, *UK Levels of Health*, 2nd Report, 1992.
3. T. Lobstein, *The Nutrition of Women on Low Incomes*, The Food Commission, 1991.
4. Greater Glasgow Health Board, *The Annual Report of the Director of Public Health, 1991/92*.
5. T.C. Smout, *A Century of the Scottish People 1830–1950*, Collins, 1986.
6. J. Boyd Orr, *Food, Health and Income*, London, 1936.
7. I. Cole-Hamilton, *Review of Food Patterns Amongst Lower Income Groups in the UK*. A report to the Health Education Authority (unpublished), 1988.
8. Health Education Authority, *Diet, Nutrition and 'Healthy Eating' in Low Income Groups*, 1989.
9. National Children's Home, *Poverty and Nutrition Survey*, 1991.
10. C. Bolton-Smith, A. L. Woodward and H. Tunstall-Pedoe, 'Nutrient intakes of different social classes: results from the Scottish Heart Health Study', *British Journal of Nutrition*, Vol. 6, No.5, 1991, pp. 321-335.
11. J. Millburn, A. Clarke and F. Smith, *Nae Bread*, Health Education Department, Argyll & Clyde Health Board, 1988.
12. *Excluding Youth*, Bridges Project and Edinburgh Centre for Social Welfare Research, University of Edinburgh, 1991.
13. National Children's Home, see reference 9.

14. National Consumer Council, *Your Food: Whose Choice,* HMSO, 1993.
15. S. Stitt, *Poor Income, Poor Health,* Newcastle upon Tyne Polytechnic, 1991.
16. Department of Health, *Dietary Reference Values for Food Energy and Nutrients for the United Kingdom,* HMSO, 1991.
17. S. Leather, *Less Money, Less Choice,* in National Consumer Council, *Your Food: Whose Choice,* HMSO, 1993.
18. S. Leather, *The Politics of Right and Wrong Food,* in the report of L.A.Y.H. Network Day Food and Low Income Initiatives, Friday 2nd October 1992, Health Promotion Unit, Princess Royal Community Health Centre.
19. National Children's Home, see reference 9.
20. *The Independent,* 2 August 1993.
21. *Food for Thought,* Ferguslie Women's Food Poverty Group, 1992.
22. A. Sooman, S. Macintyre and A. Anderson, 'Scotland's health: a more difficult challenge for some? The price and availability of healthy foods in socially contrasting localities in the west of Scotland'. *Health Bulletin,* Vol 51, (5), September, 1993, pp.276-284.
23. Department of the Environment, *Development Control Policy - Retailing,* HMSO, London, 1984.
24. T. Westlake and K. Dagleish, 'Disadvantaged consumers - can planning respond?', *Planning Outlook,* Vol. 3, No.2, 1990.
25. D. C. Anderson, *The Unmentionable Face of Poverty in the Nineties* (the moral dimension of social policy), Social Affairs Unit, 1990.
26. *Food, Poverty and Health* - a report of a Community Conference held in November, 1992, Glasgow Healthy City Project.
27. *Food, Poverty and Health,* see reference 26.
28. Scottish Office, *Scotland's Health - A Challenge To Us All.* A Policy Statement from the Scottish Office, HMSO, 1992.

5 Health and Welfare Services

by Lisa Curtice

Scotland has a notoriously poor health record and those on low incomes not only experience worse health than those who are better off but also have a reduced life expectancy. The clear link between deprivation and ill-health is reinforced by environmental factors, poorer access to health services, charges for care or prescriptions and a lower quality service. Improved services for those who are disadvantaged depend, in part, on increased user involvement in the planning and delivery of services. Lisa Curtice explains why inequalities in health are difficult to redress and why implementing equity policies is a first step that needs to be taken by service providers.

5.1 The Challenge of Health in Scotland

(a) Health variations and deprivation

The health status of people in Scotland gives cause for serious concern. Among developed countries Scotland has the highest death rates from heart disease and cancer, and Scottish women have the world's highest death rates from lung cancer[1]. More people die prematurely in some parts of Scotland than in any areas of England and Wales[2][3]. There are also marked differences in health experiences within Scotland. The health of people living in the west of Scotland is significantly worse than that of people living in the east. For example, you are likely to die three and a half years earlier if you live in Glasgow than if you live in Edinburgh[4].

The greater part of the health differences within Scotland, and between Scotland and England and Wales, is explained by the socio-economic conditions in which people live; by disadvantage not geography. Carstairs and Morris comprehensively analysed deaths and health events in Scotland, such as discharge from hospital, cancer and reports of temporary and permanent sickness, according to area of residence. They gave people in each area a deprivation score based on selected census variables (i.e. overcrowding, male unemployment, low social class and car ownership). When the scores are analysed by postcode sector they consistently show more deprivation in the west of Scotland and relatively greater affluence in the east. The western Health Boards, particularly Greater Glasgow, have the highest deprivation.

Although they are not an exact mirror image, patterns of death and illness are strongly associated with these patterns of deprivation. Death rates at ages 0-64 in the deprived areas are more than double those in the most affluent and the gap is even wider for deaths between the ages of 25 and 44. There is lower mortality in eastern Health Boards compared with western Health Boards at all levels of deprivation[5].

(b) Explaining health inequalities

Carstairs and Morris conclude that these differences are because, in the west of Scotland, more people are living—and dying—in deprived areas. A higher proportion of people living in Scotland have experience of extreme deprivation in comparison with England and Wales. The deprivation scores (based on the 1981 census) show that 18% of Scots were experiencing levels of deprivation which corresponded with the living conditions of, at most, 5% of people in England and Wales[6]. Similar conclusions about the reasons for health differences between areas have been reached by Townsend et al. for the northern region of England and by Blaxter considering data on health and lifestyles for England, Wales and Scotland[7][8].

The Health and Lifestyle data, derived from a survey of 9,000 adults throughout Britain, make it possible to look at different patterns of health experience. Blaxter identifies four separate dimensions of health: fitness/unfitness; the presence/absence of disease and impairment; illness or its absence, and 'pyscho-social health', which includes symptoms such as depression, worry and sleep disturbance. She found that in every region of Britain the health of both men and women in manual occupational groups was worse than the health of those in non-manual groups on all four health dimensions. The most important reason for this seems to be the lower income of people in manual occupations; low income was found to be particularly strongly associated with the dimensions of disease/disability, illness and pyscho-social health[9].

Living on a low income matters not only because it stops people obtaining basic necessities which are essential to health, such as warmth and food, but also because it increases the likelihood of exposure to health hazards such as poor housing and pollution[10]. The impact of damp housing, for example, on physical and mental health has been demonstrated by a study undertaken in Glasgow, Edinburgh and London[11]. Poverty also restricts social life and, if people are isolated from social support, this can leave them feeling powerless. On the other hand, access to social networks as well as to resources, such as health care and leisure facilities, may protect against illness and promote health. The Dumfries and Galloway health survey carried out in 1989 on a 1% sample of Health Board residents found, however, that only 40% of respondents were active members of clubs, social organisations or churches[12].

Wilkinson's work has shown that differences in life expectancy between countries are associated with income distribution rather than absolute levels of income[13]. Countries which have the narrowest social inequalities have the least health inequality[14]. Relative deprivation may, therefore, be the key to the mechanisms by which socio-economic differences influence health and the relevance of this to Scotland is demonstrated by the finding of Carstairs and Morris that all districts contain at least one affluent and one deprived area[15].

Macintyre and colleagues have identified some features of the local social and physical environment which help to explain how socio-economic circumstances influence health. They compared two contrasting areas in Glasgow city, a 'better' area in the north-west and a 'worse' area in the south-west. They suggest that health differences between people who live in different types of area are not wholly explained by the characteristics of the people living there. They show that poorer areas may systematically provide less opportunity for health-promoting activities. The poorer area they studied had fewer shops, buses, taxis and trains, despite the fact that 75% of households in that area had no car compared to 53% in the other area. Although there were several favourable aspects of the quality of general practitioner care in the poorer area, there were proportionally fewer doctors[16].

There was also evidence in the Health and Lifestyle survey that environmental influences may multiply the effects of socio-economic disadvantage on health. Wider differences in health appeared in manufacturing and industrial areas, as compared with more environmentally advantaged areas[17]. A weaker statistical relationship is generally found between poor health and material deprivation in rural areas. Further research has suggested, however, that this is because the comparisons are not taking account of the different types of rural area: in fact those living in the most deprived types of rural areas suffer as much as those in similar deprived urban areas[18].

Health-related behaviours are also associated with deprivation, the most important of these being smoking. Each year 10,600 Scots die as a result of smoking and more Scottish women die of lung cancer than of breast cancer; 80% to 90% of lung cancers in men and women are caused by smoking[19]. One in six of all deaths in Scotland is directly attributable to smoking[20]. There is a clear correlation between levels of smoking and deprivation. For example, Monklands and Glasgow city, two of the most deprived areas in Scotland, have the highest levels of smoking and the highest deaths from lung cancer[21].

While smoking has declined since the 1950s, smoking rates in women are now strongly class-related because the rate of decline has been higher among women in professional households (Table 5.1).

Table 5.1 Change in patterns of women smokers 1972-1990

	Social Class	
	Professional	Semi-skilled and Unskilled
Per cent women smoking		
1972	33	42
1990	16	36
Change 1972-1990	–17	–6

Source H. Graham, 'Women's smoking: government targets and social trends', *Health Visitor*, Vol.66, No.3, 1993, pp.80-82.

Graham has studied the reasons why women on low incomes are more likely to smoke. It appears that smoking among women on low income is linked to their caring responsibilities and is part of a coping strategy when living in poverty[22]. Graham suggests that policies to increase the social resources available to women living in hardship are needed to reduce smoking use. These include improved housing conditions, one-to-one support, access to more child care and adequate benefit levels.

Socio-economic factors also influence children's health behaviours. The Scottish Health Behaviour in Schoolchildren Study, last conducted in 1990, showed that consumption of healthy and unhealthy foods is linked to father's occupational group and smoking behaviour to the child's available spending money which is higher in lower occupational groups[23].

(c) Experiencing health inequalities

People's perceptions of their own health are also related to their socio-economic circumstances. In the Dumfries and Galloway health survey, those on low incomes (defined as less than £5,000 per year) perceived themselves to be in poorer health compared with other income groups[24]. Also, unpublished data from the Health and Lifestyle survey carried out for Borders Health Board by the Research Unit in Health and Behavioural Change show that people in manual occupations are significantly less likely than those in non-manual occupations to define their health as 'very good'[25].

People living in disadvantaged circumstances identify how material, environmental and social disadvantages affect their health. For example, a woman from Edinburgh writes of how cold and dampness affects her family's health;

> "Living with cold and dampness causes so many unnecessary problems. My kids can go to bed at night full of beans, the next thing you're woken at 2:30 in the morning with someone crying and the noise of someone fighting so hard to breathe"[26].

A young mother from Wester Hailes in Edinburgh stated simply "If you've no money you cannae buy things and do things." In another discussion group in the same area a man commented that, because of the many problems that he and his neighbours faced daily, it was impossible to get on with "the three basic things in life: work, rest and play"[27].

Stott and Pill have studied a group of working class mothers over a period of five years to understand how they tackle change in health-related behaviours. They show that a variety of social pressures can constrain health-related choices: smoking, diet and exercise patterns, for example, can be a reaction to a particular combination of social circumstances.

> "Well I think it's the fact that we don't do any sports at all now. I think it did help, not just physically, I think your mental well-being is helped a lot developing and socialising and meeting other people .... [So why give it up?] I played a lot earlier than my husband and then we'd join up and play as a team and it was lack of time and with working nights and then 2 days a week and then there was the housework."[28].

People on low income are not necessarily less interested in lifestyle change but they may face more obstacles in starting or maintaining it.

(d) Healthy public policies

'Healthy public policies' are policies which address health, and particularly health inequalities, through action in all relevant sectors. Healthy public policies in Scotland would include action on employment, housing, low income, income inequalities and the support services available to people locally.

Regulation, or what is sometimes called 'health protection' is necessary to promote health in the most vulnerable. Environmental hazards in the workplace and neighbourhood are more likely to affect the poor and least likely to receive political attention. Measures which reduce the risks to which the most vulnerable are excessively exposed—such as tobacco, accidents and pollution—would, therefore, be expected to contribute to equalising health chances. Health promotion measures of this type include a ban on tobacco advertising, traffic regulation and the implementation of workplace safety[29].

Health promotion strategies aimed at the whole population run the risk of increasing health inequalities because those sections of the population with greater access to resources are more likely to be able to respond. The strategy of designing health promotion programmes in settings such as the neighbourhood or workplace offers the possibility of overcoming some of the barriers to uptake of health-promoting opportunities. For example, the health-promoting school and the health-promoting hospital are methods of using and developing existing social resources and networks to improve the circumstances of people's everyday lives.

(e) The Framework for health policy in Scotland

A general framework for developments in the National Health Service (NHS) in Scotland has been set out in *Framework for Action,* published by the Scottish Office. In 1992, on the same day that *The Health of the Nation* was published in England, the Scottish Office issued a policy statement on health in Scotland, *Scotland's Health: A Challenge To Us All*, which set national priorities for health in Scotland and targets to be achieved. The national priorities (Table 5.2) are to be achieved through a partnership effort. A special Health Board, the Health Education Board for Scotland (HEBS), takes responsibility for translating national policy into health education programmes in Scotland. HEBS was established on 1 April 1991 and has defined a role for itself within the wider context of health promotion. Its programmes will be organised in key settings and sectors—schools, health service, workplace, voluntary sector, community and general public.

Table 5.2 Scotland's health priorities

Health Conditions	*Lifestyles*
* coronary heart disease	* smoking
* cancers	* alcohol misuse
* HIV/AIDS	* drug misuse
* accidents	* diet
* dental and oral health	* exercise

Scotland's Health: A Challenge To Us All acknowledges the influence of many sectors on health. A new interdepartmental committee within the Scottish Office has been set up at ministerial level. However, the main emphasis is on behavioural change, which it is hoped will be brought about largely through health education. Paragraph 38 under the heading 'other influences' states that, while "health varies according to socioeconomic standing and wealth", the reasons for these variations are complex,

"... and certainly there is no general agreement on what are the most important factors. What is clear is that smoking rates and diet, which have a direct impact on health, vary according to socioeconomic standing"[30].

Scottish health policy is, therefore, a microcosm of the dilemmas facing the development of healthy public policies throughout the world. Multi-sectoral policy responses are needed to promote health because the determinants of health lie largely outside the health sector. Many of the policy areas covered in other chapters of this book are essential to the creation of a healthier Scotland.

5.2 Health Services

(a) Matching resources to needs

Equity should be a target of an effective and efficient health service. Resource allocation between and within Health Boards is the first stage in this process. The White Paper on the NHS, *Working for Patients*, simplified the system by which the Government allocates resources to health authorities[31]. Since 1990 allocations have been based on the resident population, weighted for demographic structure and health need. Costs for patients treated elsewhere have to be paid for directly.

In Scotland the formula by which resources for current expenditure are distributed between the 15 Health Boards is called the Scottish Health Authorities Revenue Equalisation formula (SHARE). SHARE reflects differences in need by adjusting resources according to the age and sex structure of the population and any additional burden of illness, as measured by Standardised Mortality Ratios, which are used to calculate death rates. Under SHARE, the shift in resources currently underway should redress the imbalance which has existed hitherto towards more urban Health Boards. A resource allocation formula, however, is unlikely to be able to reflect problems in specific Boards, such as the additional costs that may exist in providing services in areas where the population is sparse. The transfer from Health Boards to local authorities of responsibilities and resources to provide community care (see section 5.3) may bring problems in matching resources to needs, since poorer local authorities will have to find resources to meet the needs of costly populations of elderly people.

For resources to be targeted effectively, between and within Health Boards, there need to be ways of measuring need, information about the costs of providing care and research to show the effects of targeting resources in different ways to meet needs. It has been proposed that the use of more direct measures of health need would enable resources to be targeted more effectively. For example, self-assessed health is a valid measure of acute ill-health and a measure of chronic ill-health is available from the 1991 Census[32]. The new contract for general practitioners, also introduced in 1990, attempted to reflect the additional costs of treating patients living in areas of social deprivation. The deprivation formula is, in fact, more a measure of additional general practitioner workload than of social deprivation[33] and has been criticised for putting GPs on peripheral estates at a relative disadvantage as compared to those in inner city areas[34]. General practitioners working in deprived areas serving patients with multiple problems and a high burden of chronic illness may not be helped to give enough time to their patients by a payment system based on list size[35]. Hopton, considering research based in Scotland, has pointed out the need for GPs to have information on health needs in their practice populations as a basis for costing the relationship of social deprivation to specific health needs and service use[36].

(b) Purchasing for health

The development of an internal market in the NHS, where Health Boards and a small number of GP fundholders purchase health services on behalf of their populations, has separated the functions of purchasing and providing services. The long term challenge for purchasers is ultimately to try to achieve improvements in the health status of their populations (health gain). In conjunction with national policy, purchasers have opportunities to implement strategies to address local health needs. There is an increasing body of experience to provide options for practical health equity strategies[37]. For example, a case study of the needs of older people with visual impairment and disability demonstrated: a considerable need not currently met by existing services; restricted access because of the way services were organised; and imbalance of resources towards the acute sector[38].

Contracts are the means by which knowledge of user needs is translated into specifications for services. Discussions with providers will be needed to avoid fragmentation of services and to help specify service requirements to meet the needs of priority groups. The British Paediatric Association has, for example, produced professional guidelines for purchasers of child health services. The Association points out that providing a seamless service for children in need, as defined under the Children Act, will require joint planning with local authorities for long term health gain[39]. The tendering process can be used to encourage the provision of services which are appropriate to the needs of groups who might otherwise fall through the net, such as the homeless who are a heterogeneous group and need provision for special health needs like alcoholism and mental illness[40]. Experience suggests that attainable and measurable standards must be specified in contracts if services are to meet the needs of, for example, ethnic minorities and groups with special needs[41].

The relationships between the various partners in the public health effort are critical for effective public health strategies in the new market situation. It has traditionally been public health departments that have considered the health needs of the population and they may take the lead in assessing health needs. However, the strategic and advisory role of public health departments is not necessarily safeguarded by the reforms. Equity strategies may founder due to the continued dominance of acute high technology medicine which may prevent radical shifts of emphasis in favour of community services and primary care. Relationships with local authorities are the cornerstone of integrated health strategies. The Healthy Cities Project in Glasgow is a partnership between Glasgow District Council, Strathclyde Regional Council and Greater Glasgow Health Board, as well as the universities of Glasgow and Strathclyde. On this basis it has been able to support the development of community health development projects in deprived areas as well as the development of a women's health policy for Glasgow[42]. Hogg has suggested an independent base is needed for these and other health-promotion activities[43]. A radical option for the future is for local authorities to purchase for health need[44]. Another route would be to return to the position before 1974 when public health was part of the local authority. The implications of the proposed reorganisation of local authorities in Scotland for social health policy and provision are yet to be assessed.

The development of joint planning is discussed further in section 5.3 on community care. For low income consumers the key issue will be whether the current changes are making any measurable impacts on inequalities and whether the system is succeeding in meeting needs. For many low income consumers health and social needs are inextricably linked. The extent to which Health Boards and local authorities succeed in co-operating to identify and meet needs will, therefore, be important in determining whether poor people fall through the gap between health and social provision.

(c) Providing accessible and effective services

Whitehead has reviewed the literature produced since the *Black Report* on 'Health inequalities'. From this she identifies three issues, in addition to resource allocation, by which the fairness of health service provision may be assessed. These are access, quality and uptake[45].

Access depends on the distribution and delivery of services as well as on the resources available to particular user groups. A study of GP surgeries in Aberdeen showed how the location of surgeries, combined with the pattern of car ownership, served to make GPs least accessible to those living on the peripheral housing estates[46]. Another example comes from Glasgow's east end where, in the early 1980s, three health centres were opened in an area where there had previously been some 31 surgeries. Robertson studied the effects of the change on user access and found that the time necessary to reach a GP had increased for at least 70% of the population in the area. She concluded that, while the health centres might have had better facilities, more priority should have been given to population access when deciding on the sites, since distance was likely to be a barrier to use in an area where people were poor and car ownership was very low[47].

There is evidence that health care charges result in reductions in the use of care so that, while they may result in revenue savings, they conflict with the objectives of a health service which is efficient and equitable. Increases in prescription charges between 1979 and 1985 by 490% in real terms resulted in a fall of 33% in the rate of non-exempt prescriptions dispensed. Sixty-six per cent of the savings made were due to reductions in use and there is no reason to presume that unnecessary use was most affected[48]. The 1990 dental contract may result in exclusions from care on grounds of income as dentists find themselves unable to provide NHS services within the budget allocated. A two-tier system has already been reported to have emerged in the Highlands where 55 of the 58 NHS dentists joined to offer patients a private paying plan and salaried Health Board dentists treat those not insured[49]. An increase from two part time to three full time dentists was required to meet the increased number of adults in the Highlands seeking even emergency care[50]. The British Dental Association reports that only 57% of dentists are willing to accept new NHS patients. In 1993 *The Scotsman* also reported that dentists in Kilmarnock, Stranraer and Dunfermline were jointly refusing new NHS patients[51]. Continued central support for children's dentistry will be essential as it is a loss-making service.

There is some evidence that people living in the most deprived areas experience services which are poorer in quality. Lower social class patients have been found to be less likely to receive specialist referrals[52] and to receive less information voluntarily from GPs[53]. Less information and explanation are likely to affect these patients' uptake of services and treatment. Reasons for differences in the outcomes of treatment for different groups are complex, although differences in quality of care may be a contributory factor.

Use of preventive services is, in any case, less among lower occupational class groups. In a survey conducted for Argyll and Clyde Health Board one-third of people in social classes III, IV and V reported having a dental check-up in the past six months compared to two-thirds in social classes I and II[54]. Stott and Pill studied why some people attend health checks in general practice and others do not. They found that people who attended for screening had more formal education than those who did not and they were also more likely to think that their health was under their own control[55].

(d) The user perspective

The NHS Management Executive has pointed out the opportunities and benefits of incorporating local consultation in the needs assessment process[56]. Approaches for encouraging the participation of local voices have been developed by multi-agency initiatives working with disadvantaged groups. In a small area of Drumchapel in Glasgow, for example, local residents took an active part in drawing up a local community health profile and have made a video tape of their experiences. The survey took place in one street of 109 households where only 15% of residents were in work of any kind and over one-third of those in employment were on housing benefit. The most common household was single parent, headed by a woman. Sixty-six per cent of respondents identified a need for more local support for people experiencing emotional difficulties[57]. The three most commonly mentioned options for providing support were self-help groups, a place to go and someone to talk to, and individual counselling.

Measuring consumer satisfaction is increasingly used in assessing the quality of services. Many studies have shown that general questions tend to elicit high levels of satisfaction but that more dissatisfaction is uncovered in response to specific questions. A study of the criteria used by consumers to assess satisfaction with general practice, dentist and hospital care found that the most important issues for consumers were the competence of the professionals and the nature and quality of the relationship between the patient and the professional[58]. Consumer satisfaction surveys are likely to under-represent dissatisfaction among lower income groups. People of high socio-economic status are less likely to report themselves satisfied with any aspect of health care, whereas, in national surveys, unemployed people are much more likely to say that they are satisfied with the running of the NHS[59].

It is not sufficient to consider the inputs of health services in relation to deprivation. Assessment of the effectiveness of health services also depends on our ability to measure and evaluate the outputs of expenditure. Only assessments of health service performance which take into account progress towards health targets and improvements in the quality of services delivered to the population can resolve arguments as to the point at which efficiency savings (cuts) are being made at the expense of effectiveness.

5.3 Community Care

(a) Resources for change

The implementation of the community care legislation requires a major transfer of resources from Health Boards to local authorities so that the social needs of long-stay patients can be met in the community rather than in hospitals[60]. Don Cruickshank, the former NHS Chief Executive in Scotland, estimated that, over the next decade, well over £100 million should transfer from health to local authority budgets to make this policy viable[61]. Nonetheless, the limitations imposed by available resources provide the context in which reforms are being implemented. Need for health and social care must now be assessed and key issues for consumers will be how far quality of service, as against financial pressure, determines decisions and to what extent it is possible to respect the choices of individual consumers.

In England one of the issues affecting low income elderly consumers is the provision of nursing care in the community. In Scotland there is a need to develop more low dependency care. Only 38% of the total provision for the elderly in Scotland is in residential care compared to 66% in England. An expansion in low dependency provision is likely to strain the DSS resources received by local authorities[62]. Historically Scotland has a stronger legacy of institutional care, for the mentally ill as well as for the elderly. As a result community care services are less well developed and the involvement of the private sector in a mixed economy of care has been slow[63].

(b) Co-operation between agencies

The success of community care for vulnerable groups is dependent on co-ordination between agencies. A vision for equitable implementation of care in the community includes joint commissioning of services by Health Boards and local authorities and even joint resource management to ensure targeting of resources to identified needs[64]. Joint planning is underdeveloped in Scotland, in comparison with England and Wales[65]. Joint Liaison Committees between Health Boards and local authorities were voluntary in Scotland before the care in the community legislation and support finance to provide an incentive for collaboration was introduced later and was more discretionary.

Researchers from the Social Work Research Centre at Stirling University have carried out a study of the initial planning agreements and community care plans drawn up in Scotland. They found great variation in the extent to which initial planning agreements represented agreed objectives between the agencies. The initial care plans did not consistently address the minor care groups, for example HIV/Aids and drugs/alcohol. There was little information on the resources available to meet needs. The authors point out that there are likely to be difficulties in reconciling the priorities of different agencies. For example, the Health Board priority might be elderly people on long-stay wards, while the local authority priority might be the social care needs of a younger population. Given the low baseline of joint working, the authors of this study conclude that real progress had been made to produce six joint care plans in Scotland by 1992. Scottish local authorities and Health Boards may produce their own community care plans, but they then have to issue joint planning agreements. Lothian has involved a wide range of partners in planning and its joint plan encompasses the widest range of services including, for example, transport, welfare rights, housing, education, leisure and environment[66].

(c) The Assessment of health and social needs

Initial planning agreements had provided little detail on how Health Boards and local authorities were planning to organise the process of assessment, which now has to be separated from the process of providing services. In late 1992 Buglass reviewed the progress being made in each local authority in Scotland in preparation for the introduction of assessment and care management. She notes that it is authorities with relatively small populations (Dumfries and Galloway, Orkney and the Western Isles) that have opted for the most integrated model of implementation. They have decided that these processes will be carried out by the most appropriate worker from a joint health and social work team. There was concern in some social work departments that the pressure on health services to reduce continuing care beds quickly may make it difficult to implement assessments in an orderly way. Agreements with the local authority are also terminated when hospital units acquire trust status. Thus agencies face considerable uncertainties as they try to implement many profound changes in practice[67].

(d) The Role of community health services

Disadvantaged consumers depend in particular on community health services which provide an important link in ensuring the effective delivery of many other services. Haggard notes that effective community health services are crucial for: early and effective hospital discharge; the support of patients with complex needs in the community; and community care for the frail elderly and chronic sick. The risks of fragmentation during the processes of the reforms are acute since community nurses are affected on many levels by the changes in hospital, community, GP and local authority services[68].

Strategies are, therefore, required to ensure the effective management of community health services in the mixed economy of care. Constantinides and Gordon have illustrated the implications of different options by describing three different organisational models[69]. They suggest that a service which is hospital-led (as when a hospital and a community unit make a joint bid for status as a self-governing trust) may work well in providing an integrated service for patients covered by that agreement. Hospital-led services may, however, weaken the local base of community nurses and decrease their preventive role with vulnerable groups, such as the frail elderly. An alternative scenario is primary-care-led services. This provides exciting possibilities for long term integration but is hampered by variability in the capacity of practices. This is particularly the case in deprived areas, where attempts to fulfil this role are fraught with the risks of developing parallel services, notably through practice nurses. A third model is where community services are locality-based. This offers good possibilities for meeting local needs and taking part in inter-agency working, although geographical service boundaries and differences in professional objectives create obstacles.

(e) Consumer costs

Underlying the philosophy of care in the community is the presumption that the quality of life for priority groups, such as people with mental health problems, will be improved by their being integrated into the community. However, as argued earlier, people need a variety of resources if they are to be able to enjoy the benefits of being part of an everyday social environment. In a study of 11 projects that were providing supported accommodation for people with mental health problems in Scotland during 1988/89 virtually all the residents interviewed complained that their personal allowance (then £10 a week) was very restrictive: "You are told you can come and go as you please, but you're at a situation where you can't really, you're on such a low income" and "I haven't got any money to go anywhere so I just stay in the bed."

The majority of these projects were based in the voluntary sector, funded through DSS residential care allowance. The author questions a policy which speaks of community integration but does not allow people enough money to clothe themselves, buy personal items and go out[70].

Monitoring is important to check that policies intended to target care more effectively do so in practice. Between 1980 and 1985 there was a slight increase in the provision of home care among households containing an elderly person (from 8.7% to 9.3% according to the General Household Survey). This represented a spreading of the service more widely and was not accompanied by more efficient targeting on those most in need[71].

5.4 Consumer Participation and Advocacy

The *Patient's Charter* sets out entitlements for patients in Scotland which include a say in how a Health Board proposes to improve the health of its local population: "Health Boards will seek your views on: the problems on which you and your community most want help and what action should be taken to help local people"[72].

Hospitals and health services in Scotland should now publicise the name, address and telephone number of staff responsible for dealing with complaints. Patients are entitled to be kept fully informed of the receipt, progress, likely timetable for resolving, and explanation of the outcome of any complaint and also what to do if they are not satisfied. The first annual survey to ascertain user views on their experiences of the NHS in Scotland was commissioned by the NHS Management Executive in 1992. It found high levels of satisfaction with access, information and user involvement, but users of accident and emergency and maternity services were least satisfied with NHS performance on these criteria. Three per cent of users wanted to complain about NHS services but only 1% did so; three-quarters did not know who to complain to and most complainants remain unsatisfied[73]. The Management Executive in Scotland is currently piloting 'patient's supporter' schemes as a way of helping patients to speak up and to ask for more information about their care.

Strategies to increase the involvement of users and carers in the planning and delivery of services are particularly important in the process of making services accessible and appropriate to disadvantaged consumers. There is now considerable experience in how to achieve appropriate feedback[74]. For example, user panels and carers' forums provide opportunities for obtaining ongoing involvement. Work to encourage the participation of the most disempowered groups may result in useful training recommendations for other parts of the consultative and management process. Training for people with learning difficulties, for example, showed that professionals as well as users could benefit from learning effective meeting skills[75]. Advocacy is also an appropriate approach to represent the rights of people with learning difficulties. In addition, Scotland is currently witnessing a growth in patient-led activity through local Patients' Associations and the national Scotland Patients Association.

While considerable opportunities for user involvement are present and it is the duty of Health Boards to assess local health needs, clear structures to encourage user participation are generally lacking. The process of decision making is understandably not clear to the public[76]. Grampian Healthcare has appointed a community liaison manager with the role of meeting local groups and explaining and discussing decisions with them. In the 1980s Jones noted the resource limitations which may have prevented many Local Health Councils in Scotland from undertaking consumer research, and Community Health Councils in England and Wales have expressed considerable concerns at the lack of provision in the NHS reforms for an effective consumer voice[77][78]. The Scottish Council for Voluntary Organisations found evidence of considerable effort to involve voluntary organisations in community care planning, but large organisations had been more successfully involved than smaller groups[79]. The need for this public accountability is illustrated by the record of NHS trusts across the UK as a whole. While required by legislation to hold public meetings within their first year, 50% of first-wave trusts and 60% of second-wave trusts did not do so. Almost half of second-wave trusts did not permit the attendance of community health representatives at board meetings[80].

Feedback and participation are also relevant to approaches taken to monitoring and evaluation. The Social Work Services Group of the Scottish Office has produced a handbook on monitoring and evaluation for voluntary organisations, based on research with 26 projects[81]. Voluntary organisations provide direct care in the community and under the community care arrangements and the government review of voluntary sector funding will be required to demonstrate that they have methods for obtaining and responding to feedback from users. This study found that most projects were able to improve their direct service to users and links to other agencies as a result of their evaluation and monitoring work.

5.5 Conclusions

Research has defended and amplified the conclusions drawn by the *Black Report*, published in 1980, about the causal relationships between poverty and ill-health[82]. Yet, behavioural remedies, where the cost of change is borne primarily by the individual, continue to predominate over structural ones in official policy. One explanation for the failure to adopt integrated policies at national level to tackle the links between ill-health and poverty is that economic goals have dominated social policy goals and the issue of poverty has been marginalised as a consequence[83]. This fragmentation within thinking and policy making is part of the explanation why relationships between poverty or deprivation and health have been cited in official policies as too complex to be the basis for direct policies and planned programmes[84].

Poverty is a form of social exclusion. It may be defined as an enforced way of life in which people do not have the necessary resources to meet their basic needs, to take part in the ordinary social life of their neighbourhood and to fulfil their normal social obligations. Access to these prerequisites to participation in society is part of the rights of social citizenship[85]. A person's health and social needs cannot be seen in isolation. Whether you have a job, live in warm, dry, accommodation, and have enough time and money to get out and meet people and do something you enjoy will also make a difference to your health.

To achieve the greatest health and social gain for their populations Health Boards and local authorities could do no better than to prioritise equity objectives in their strategies and it can be argued that tackling inequalities will have productive social benefits.

Equity policies will enable people who are currently not able to take a full part in society to take a much more active social role. Development of the resources needed for health will create more social resources. The mechanisms underlying health equity policies allow improved social resources to lead to health gains which in turn lead to increased social participation and further health gains.

Health and social services play only a small part in redressing inequalities in health but inequalities in access to health and social care represent a further component of disadvantage which must be redressed. Where preventive care and health promotion activity is delivered in such a way as to be less available to low income consumers, this represents a further limitation on the social resources available to help people maintain a healthy life and a sense of well-being. A crucial test of the current reforms in health and social services is whether they can deliver services which are equitable as well as efficient.

References to Chapter 5

1. Scottish Office, *Scotland's Health: A Challenge to Us All, A Policy Statement*, HMSO, 1992.
2. V. Carstairs and R. Morris, *Deprivation and Health in Scotland*, Aberdeen University Press, 1991.
3. P. Townsend, P. Phillimore and A. Beattie, *Health and Deprivation: Inequality and the North*, Croom Helm, 1987.
4. G. Watt and R. Ecob, `Mortality in Glasgow and Edinburgh: a paradigm of inequality in health', *Journal of Epidemiology and Community Health*, Vol.46, 1992, pp.498-505.
5. V. Carstairs and R. Morris, see reference 2.
6. V. Carstairs and R. Morris, see reference 2.
7. P. Townsend, P. Phillimore and A. Beattie, see reference 3.
8. M. Blaxter, *Health and Lifestyles*, Routledge, 1990.
9. M. Blaxter, see reference 8.
10. C. Blackburn, `Wealth and the nation's health', *Health Visitor*, Vol.66, No.7, 1993, pp.254-256.
11. S. Platt, C. Martin, S. Hunt and C. Lewis, `Damp housing, mould growth and symptomatic health state', *British Medical Journal*, Vol.298, 1989, pp.1673-1678.
12. Dumfries and Galloway Health Board, *The Picture of Health: Dumfries and Galloway Health and Lifestyle Survey*, Dumfries and Galloway Health Board, 1990.
13. R. Wilkinson, `Income distribution and life expectancy', *British Medical Journal*, Vol.304, 1992, pp. 165-168.
14. R. Wilkinson, `National mortality rates: the impact of inequality?', *American Journal of Public Health*, Vol.82, No.8, 1992, pp. 1082-1084.
15. V. Carstairs and R. Morris, see reference 2.
16. S. Macintyre, S. MacIver and A. Sooman, `Area, class and health: should we be focusing on places or people?', *Journal of Social Policy*, Vol.22, No.2, 1993, pp.213-234.
17. M. Blaxter, see reference 8.
18. P. Phillimore and R. Reading, `A rural advantage? Urban-rural health differences in Northern England', *Journal of Public Health Medicine*, Vol.14, No.3, 1992, pp.290-299.
19. Scottish Office, see reference 1.
20. Chief Medical Officer, The Scottish Office, *Health in Scotland 1991*, HMSO, 1992.
21. V. Carstairs and R. Morris, see reference 2.
22. H. Graham, `Women smoking in the United Kingdom: the implications for health promotion', *Health Promotion*, Vol.3, No.4, 1988, pp. 371-383.

23. C. Currie, J. Todd, and K. Wijkmans, *Health Behaviours of Scottish Schoolchildren: Report No.2, Family, Peer, School and Socioeconomic Influence*, Research Unit in Health and Behavioural Change and Health Education Board for Scotland, 1993.
24. Dumfries and Galloway Health Board, see reference 12.
25. C. Crosswaite and C. Currie, *Borders Health Board: Health and Lifestyle Survey Report*, Research Unit in Health and Behavioural Change, University of Edinburgh, 1993.
26. J. Crofton, *Housing and Health in Scotland*, Public Health Alliance, Scotland, 1993.
27. L. Curtice, K. Backett and S. Cunningham-Burley, *Living a Healthy Life in Wester Hailes*, Research Unit in Health and Behavioural Change, University of Edinburgh, 1993.
28. N. Stott and R. Pill, *Making Changes*, Department of General Practice, University of Wales College of Medicine, 1990.
29. B. Jacobson, A. Smith and M. Whitehead (eds), *The Nation's Health*, Independent Multidisciplinary Committee, King Edward's Hospital Fund for London, 1991.
30. Scottish Office, see reference 1.
31. Secretaries of State for Health, *Working for Patients*, HMSO, 1989.
32. N. Mays, S. Chinn and K. Mui Ho, 'Interregional variations in measures of health from the Health and Lifestyle Survey and their relation with indicators of health care need in England', *Journal of Epidemiology and Community Health*, Vol.46, 1992, pp.38-47.
33. R. Talbot, 'Underprivileged areas and health care planning: implications of use of Jarman indicators of urban deprivation', *British Medical Journal*, Vol.302, 1991, pp.383-386.
34. M. Senior, 'Deprivation payments to GPs: not what the doctor ordered', *Environment and Planning: Government and Policy*, Vol.9, 1991, pp. 79-94.
35. A. Hastings and A. Rashid, 'General practice in deprived areas; problems and solutions', *British Journal of General Practice*, Vol.43, 1993, pp. 47-48.
36. J. Hopton, J. Howie and A. Porter, 'Social indicators of health needs for general practice: a simpler approach', *British Journal of General Practice*, Vol.42, 1992, pp.236-240.
37. G. Dahlgren and M. Whitehead, *Policies and Strategies to Promote Equity in Health*, WHO Regional Office for Europe, 1992.
38. U. Harris, J. Popay and R. Leventhall, 'The vision thing', *Health Service Journal*, 18 February 1993, pp. 20-21.
39. L. Polnay, H. Bingham and R. Tamhne, 'Contracting for child health services in the community', *Archives of Disease in Childhood*, Vol.68, 1993, pp.517-520.
40. P. Wall, 'Health and homelessness', *Health Service Journal*, 11 April 1991, pp.16-17.
41. S. Mohammed, *User-Sensitive Purchasing*, King's Fund Centre, 1993.
42. Glasgow Healthy City Project, *The Health of the City: A Shared Concern*, Glasgow Healthy City Project, 1992.
43. C. Hogg, *Healthy Change*, Socialist Health Association, 1991.
44. G. Wistow, 'Democratic deficit', *Community Care*, 30 September 1993, p.29.

6 Education

by Sheila Riddell

Children who belong to low income families become educationally disadvantaged at an early age and continue to be disadvantaged throughout their school careers. In this chapter, Sheila Riddell shows how children from poor homes do less well than their middle class neighbours both in terms of the progress they make while at school and their final levels of achievement on leaving. Some equalisation of attainment levels has taken place in some Scottish schools in the last 16 years but current government policies may hinder this process. Recent initiatives to promote parental choice and plans to reorganise funding arrangements have as yet uncertain implications for the quality of education delivered to children of low income families.

6.1 Introduction

Shortly after its election to power in 1979, the Conservative Party made clear that education would be at the forefront of its policy agenda, on the grounds that there were strong links between the state of education and the economic and moral health of the nation. During the post war period, politicians on both sides of the House emphasised the principle of equality of access to education for all. Kenneth Baker signalled a break with this consensus when, introducing the Education Reform Bill for England and Wales at the 1987 Conservative Party Conference, he declared: "the pursuit of egalitarianism is now over".

Official documents now emphasise parental choice and professional accountability rather than equality. For instance, the *Citizens' Charter* identifies the following as central themes in government policy:
- "a sustained new programme for improving quality;
- an emphasis on choice, wherever possible between competing providers, as the best spur to quality improvement;
- the citizen's right to be told what service standards are and to be assured of action when service is unacceptable; and
- the need for public services to give value for money within a tax bill the nation can afford"[1].

One of the central assumptions of these policies is that everyone is equally capable of making free choices in the market place, so that unequal educational outcomes may be attributed to parents making wrong choices for their children rather than to any fault in the system. This paper explores the context in which choices are made, highlighting unequal patterns of educational outcomes and questioning the implications of the focus on choice and accountability for socially and economically disadvantaged groups.

The following questions are addressed in this chapter. Is there evidence of pupils from low income families experiencing educational disadvantage? If so, how big is the gap between more and less advantaged social groups and how has it changed over time? Do low income consumers experience poorer quality education than others and, if so, what are the factors which cause this to happen? What effect is the current emphasis on parental choice likely to have on existing patterns of educational disadvantage?

Section 6.2 summarises research findings on the relationship between educational outcomes and social class, and discusses other factors associated with low income and educational disadvantage, including ethnicity and membership of a single parent family. This is followed by a consideration of the extent to which schools must accept responsibility for the poorer educational outcomes of children from low income families or whether wider social factors, including the cultural and material resources of the home, should be blamed. Much recent research suggests that, although social background is the major factor associated with educational outcome, the school attended by the child affects progress and, therefore, does make a difference to the final level of educational attainment. In view of this, an attempt is made in section 6.4 to identify factors in schools which appear to foster or hinder pupil progress. (The distinction between educational outcome and progress is important; the former indicates an absolute level of achievement whereas the latter measures the extent to which the pupil has grown from the point of entry to the point of departure.) As noted above, a key aspect of recent government policy has been the introduction of market forces into the social policy domain, and the final section assesses the present and future implications of this for education. Throughout this chapter, the focus is on Scottish data but reference is also made to the wider UK and international context where appropriate. The terms 'socio-economic status' and 'social class' are used as surrogate measures of low income.

6.2 Educational Outcomes of Children from Low Income Families in Scotland

(a) Social class and educational disadvantage

Before discussing the relationship between social class and educational disadvantage in greater detail, it is important to consider the definition of 'social class' which is used throughout this paper. The measure of social circumstances normally employed by educational researchers is social class rather than income level, although there is a very strong association between these two variables. The former is often measured according to the Registrar General's Classification of Occupations, based on both income level and social status of jobs. With the growth of unemployment, and the expansion of the service sector of the economy, coupled with the collapse of the manufacturing sector, a simple working/middle class split is now less valid as an accurate description of social circumstances within the Scottish context. Paterson argued that socio-economic status, based on a measure of parents' occupation and education, is a more helpful concept than social class, since it reflects the material and cultural resources to which a child has access within the home[2]. In this paper, some of the studies cited use the term 'socio-economic status', based on measures of parents' occupational and educational status. Others use the more traditional measure of social class based on the Registrar General's Classification of Occupations. In referring to particular studies, the terminology adopted by the author has been used.

Despite efforts by Scottish education authorities to equalise provision, there continues to be a strong association between children's social circumstances and their level of educational attainment. Bondi looked at Scottish primary school pupils' scores on reading and aptitude tests, which were found to be correlated with socio-economic status at primary 3, with an even stronger correlation emerging at primary 7[3]. As pupils progress through secondary school, the relationship between socio-economic status and attainment becomes even more marked. The Scottish Young People's Surveys conducted by the Centre for Educational Sociology at the University of Edinburgh produced data throughout the 1980s which showed that the gap in attainment in fourth year between young people whose fathers were in professional occupations (class I or II as measured by the Registrar General's Classification of Occupations) and pupils whose families were in semi-skilled and unskilled manual occupations (classes IV and V) was on average about three awards at levels 1 - 3 of the Ordinary or Standard Grade. (Standard Grade is awarded at levels 1 - 7, with levels 1 - 3 being equivalent to 'O' Grades A - C. These have traditionally been regarded as 'pass' grades, although this terminology is no longer used within Standard Grade.)

The proportion of young people gaining a place in higher education has increased, but is still less than a quarter of the age group. In 1991, 18% of school leavers embarked on a full time higher education course; 11% went into other forms of full time education; 32% gained full time employment; and 24% entered a youth training scheme[4]. In the following section, examination passes and participation in higher education are used as benchmarks of relative achievement between young people from more and less privileged backgrounds, although it is recognised that these are not the only measures of successful education. Nonetheless, the attainment of a degree-level qualification is likely to lead to better paid and more secure employment and thus may be seen as a passport to higher social status. As pupils move through the later stages of secondary education and into higher education, the negative effect of lower material resources, measured by fathers' occupational status, becomes increasingly clearly marked at each transition point. Figure 6.1 shows that a higher proportion of pupils from social classes I and II stay on after the compulsory school leaving age (approximately 75% of pupils from social classes I and II compared with 40% of pupils from social classes IV and V). Of those who remain, a higher proportion of middle class pupils pass three or more Highers. (Figure 6.2 shows that the proportions are approximately 60% of those in social classes I and II compared with 40% of those in social classes IV and V). Even among those who succeed in attaining the minimum level of entry to higher education, working class pupils are less likely to apply (90% of those qualified in social classes I and II compared with 65% of those in social classes IV and V - see Figure 6.3), although, having applied, working class pupils are as likely as middle class pupils to be accepted. Figure 6.4 illustrates the way in which, at each point of transition, working class pupils are lost to the system. Paterson reminding us of the enduring nature of social class divisions in education, noted that in 1978, of young people moving into higher education, 30% were from families in the Registrar General's classes I and II, compared with 6% of young people in social classes IV or V[5]. In 1988, the figures were 30% and 3% respectively. During this period, entrance to full time higher education in Scotland (degree and non-degree courses) had increased from 21,540 in 1978 to 27,158 in 1988[6].

Level of parental education is often used as a surrogate measure of cultural resources within the family and Paterson demonstrated an independent effect of higher levels of parental education on the likelihood of pupils staying on after the statutory leaving age, passing three or more Highers and applying for a place in higher education[7]. There is evidence that cultural resources may be able to compensate for material

Figure 6.1 Proportion staying on to end of fifth year or after, by Registrar General's class of father's occupation.

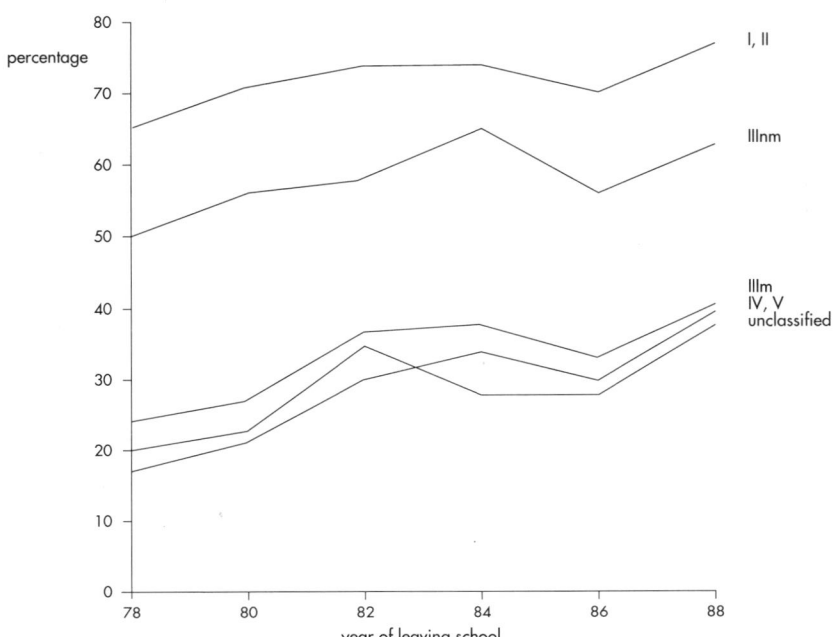

From: L. Paterson, 'Social origins of under-achievement amongst school leavers' in H. Maguiness (ed.), *Educational Opportunity: The Challenge of Under-achievement and Social Deprivation*, Local Government Centre, Paisley College, 1992.

Widest 95% confidence interval: ± 2%

deprivation[8]. Thus, if parents have low status occupations but higher levels of education, their ability to offer academic support to their children is likely to mitigate some of the negative effects of lower occupational status and lower income.

It is important to note that socio-economic status is not only associated with the attainment level which children have reached at a particular time, but also with the amount of progress they make between one stage of schooling and another. Paterson reported data from Fife in the mid-80s which shows that, after controlling for prior academic attainment, pupils with fathers of higher occupational and educational status were likely to do better than those of lower socio-economic status[9]. Membership of a higher socio-economic status group assists pupils in two distinct ways. First, as has been noted in the preceding paragraphs, pupils of lower socio-economic status are more likely to leave education than their more privileged peers at each point of transition. Second, children from higher socio-economic status families make better progress than those of similar measured ability but lower socio-economic status. However, although quantitative work reveals the clear and enduring

EDUCATION

Figure 6.2 Proportion passing 3 or more Highers among those who stay on by Registrar General's class of father's occupation.

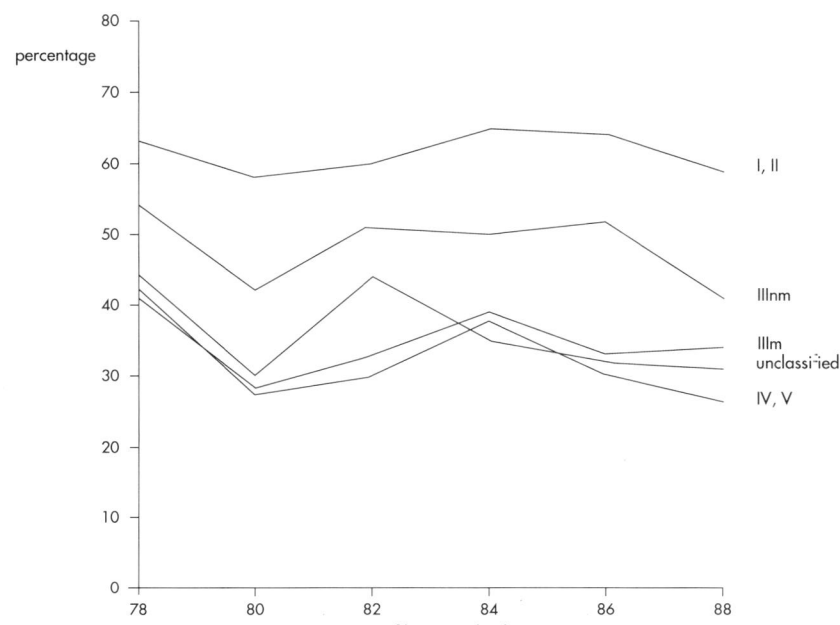

From: L. Paterson, 'Social origins of under-achievement amongst school leavers' in H. Maguiness (ed.), *Educational Opportunity: The Challenge of Under-achievement and Social Deprivation*. Local Government Centre, Paisley College, 1992.

Widest 95% confidence interval: ± 7%

link between social class and educational outcome, it is unable to reveal the mechanisms and processes which produce given outcomes. For insight into the effect of school and family processes, we need to refer to the findings of qualitative investigations.

A number of ethnographic studies carried out in England and Wales have revealed the nature of the processes which are likely to reproduce social class disadvantage. For instance, Sharp and Green discussed the way in which primary teachers in progressive schools made judgements about children's 'readiness' for certain tasks which tended to favour those from middle class backgrounds[10]. Children's use of spoken language, for instance, was often used by the teacher as an indication that they were ready to begin reading. In the secondary context, Willis, in his study of a group of 'lads' in a north of England industrial town, described the way in which they emerged from school ready and willing to take up hard manual labour, treating with contempt those who applied themselves to academic work[11]. Willis depicted the lads as not merely dupes of the system, but as having some insight into the selective processes in operation and as actively embracing their destiny, glorifying manual toil

Figure 6.3 Proportion applying to any higher education amongst those with three or more Highers, by Registrar General's class of father's occupation.

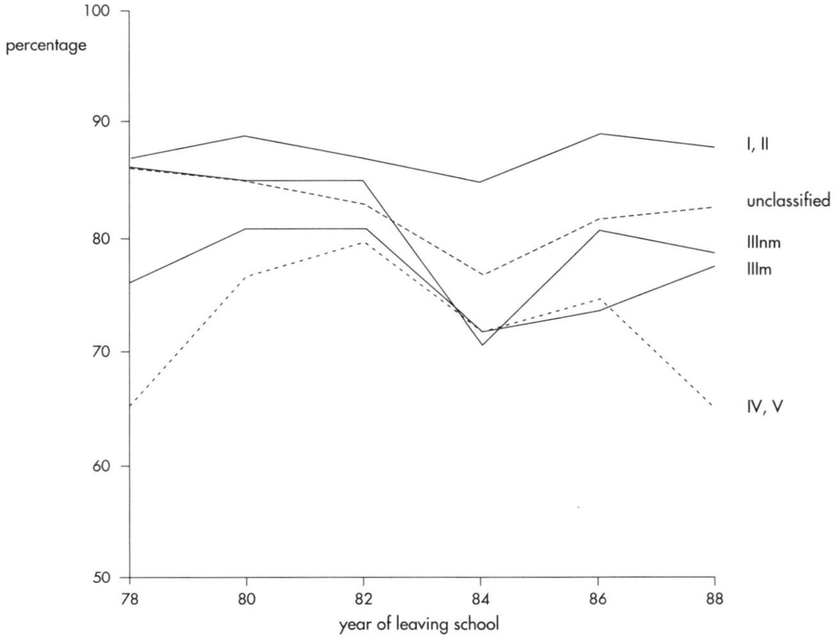

[Line graph showing percentage (50-100) on y-axis against year of leaving school (78-88) on x-axis, with lines for classes I, II; unclassified; IIInm; IIIm; and IV, V]

From: L. Paterson, 'Social origins of under-achievement amongst school leavers' in H. Maguiness (ed.), *Educational Opportunity: The Challenge of Under-achievement and Social Deprivation*, Local Government Centre, Paisley College, 1992.

Widest 95% confidence interval: ± 8%

as the appropriate work for 'real' men. However, in a more recent ethnographic study of working class pupils, Brown suggested that Willis' account was over-simplified[12]. The resistance depicted by Willis was only one, and certainly not the most common, response to schooling. Most working class pupils, both boys as well as girls, conform to the demands of school because they see it as a means of gaining access to a job with some security and a reasonable standard of living. Brown argued that :

> "... the ordinary kids' willingness to make an effort in school, albeit limited, was part of an attempt to maintain a sense of personal dignity and respect where they were not academically successful; and, in their own terms, to enhance their chances of making a working class career after they left school"[13].

According to Brown, the growth of unemployment and the collapse of the youth labour market were likely to have a marked effect on working class pupils' response to education, with conformity becoming a far less common strategy as the prospects of attaining a 'tidy' job diminished.

EDUCATION

Figure 6.4 Proportion entering any higher education by Registrar General's class of father's occupation.

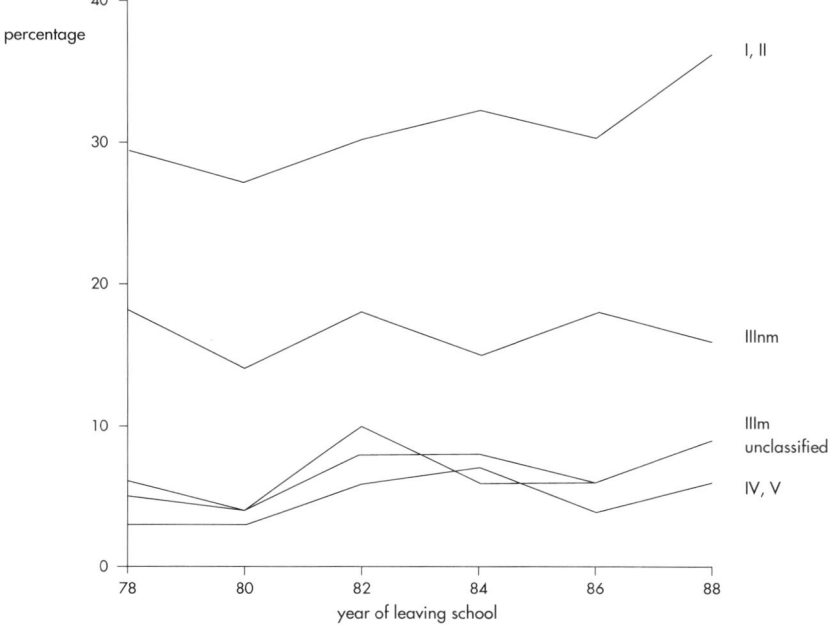

From: L. Paterson, 'Social origins of under-achievement amongst school leavers' in H. Maguiness (ed.), *Educational Opportunity: The Challenge of Under-achievement and Social Deprivation*, Local Government Centre, Paisley College, 1992.

Widest 95% confidence interval: ± 2%

In Scotland, few ethnographic studies of working class pupils' experience of education have been reported. Hughes, however, writing about social class from a teacher's perspective, provided some insights into the way in which Scottish comprehensive schools, often unintentionally, perpetuate inequality[14]. He noted the way in which the reputation of schools, based on their former status as junior or senior secondaries, tended to persist, and was reflected in their atmosphere and values. For example, former senior secondary schools on the whole had higher academic expectations of pupils, insisted on the wearing of uniform and attracted pupils from outwith the area. Although teachers were generally supportive of the principles of comprehensive schooling, they made conscious and unconscious judgements about pupils on the basis of their accent, dress, general demeanour and home neighbourhood. Potentially progressive curriculum developments, such as the increased element of coursework in Standard Grade examinations, also tended to favour middle class pupils with easy access to home computers, homework space and parental assistance, whilst school trips were often accessible only to those from more affluent backgrounds.

Practitioner accounts such as this provide important clues about the mechanisms by which social disadvantage is reproduced in schools. There is an urgent need for research which seeks to validate these anecdotal accounts and explores social processes in Scottish schools in greater depth. The mainstream Scottish tradition of educational research, then, has sought to quantify the relationship between social class and educational outcomes. However, among those categorised as working class and living on low incomes there are a number of groups for whom another part of their social identity may be particularly salient. The following sections consider two such groups, children of ethnic minority and single parent families.

(b) Ethnicity and educational disadvantage

Scottish studies of the relationship between ethnicity and educational outcomes are extremely scarce. Undoubtedly one reason for the neglect of this area is that there are relatively fewer people from ethnic minorities in Scotland than in the rest of the UK (according to the Scottish Office Central Research Unit the figure for Scotland is less than 1% of the total population, compared with a Labour Force Survey figure for Britain as a whole of over 4%). Smith reported the first large scale, general purpose survey of ethnic minorities in Scotland commissioned by the Scottish Office[15]. The survey revealed that 50% of ethnic minority householders were of Pakistani origin, 30% were originally from India and 20% were Chinese, mainly from Hong Kong; very few were of Afro-Caribbean origin.

The extent of poverty among ethnic minorities was indicated by their high rates of unemployment—a third higher than for the general population, with ethnic minority women having even higher rates. In addition to general levels of poverty, Smith's survey provided evidence of a general climate of racial intimidation in Scotland; Pakistani and Chinese people were more likely than whites to receive verbal abuse at work (15% of Chinese people reported such abuse).

There was also considerable evidence of educational disadvantage. Although only a small proportion (10% of males and 16% of females, particularly those of Pakistani origin) had never been in full time education, almost three-quarters of ethnic minority householders had no educational qualifications, compared with 50% of white householders. Relatively recent immigrants are particularly likely to experience problems in school as a result of lack of familiarity with the language and inadequate instruction and it was evident from the survey that only 10% of householders were born in Britain. However, Smith also noted that younger people were much better qualified than their parents. A range of factors such as size of family and density of house occupation have been shown to be associated with educational disadvantage and on both these measures ethnic minority groups in Scotland fared worse than the indigenous population.

To summarise, Smith's survey revealed that ethnic minority groups in Scotland experience particularly marked material and social deprivation. Detailed studies have not as yet been conducted to document the effect of this deprivation on educational experiences, but it is very likely to be translated into negative experiences of schooling and depressed levels of educational achievement.

Sharp and Fitzpatrick analyzed the examination results of ethnic minority candidates in Scotland whose first language was not English[16]. Their aim was not to compare the achievements of different groups, but to identify areas of the curriculum where ethnic minority candidates performed better or worse than expected. The general pattern was for ethnic minority groups to perform less well in English than in other subjects, suggesting that more attention needs to be paid to instruction in English as a second language.

Because of the absence of Scottish data on the relative performance of ethnic groups, it is interesting to look at data from south of the border, although the different composition of such groups underlines the need for caution in generalising from one context of such groups to the other. In their survey of educational achievement by ethnic groups in England and Wales, Drew and Gray found that social class was associated with educational achievement within each ethnic group[17]. When social class was taken into account, Asian pupils performed as well as white pupils, but Afro-Caribbean pupils did substantially worse than the other two groups. Mac an Ghaill and Gillborn both noted the way in which teachers held particularly negative views of Afro-Caribbean pupils, regarding Asian pupils as relatively studious[18][19]. With so few Afro-Caribbean students in Scottish schools, it would be very interesting to compare the relative performance and teachers' perceptions of Asian and white pupils.

In Scotland, there is clear evidence that ethnic minority groups experience material and social disadvantage generally associated with lower educational attainment. We currently lack studies which compare the examination performance of ethnic minority and white pupils in Scotland and we need more qualitative research which would provide a clearer picture of how such outcomes are produced in schools on a daily basis.

(c) Single parent families and educational disadvantage

Paterson has demonstrated that children of single parents perform considerably less well in school[20] and there is ongoing debate on the underlying reasons for this, with some commentators suggesting that the conventional two parent family is essential for the successful socialisation of children. It is easy to use such arguments to blame single parents for a status which they may well not have chosen and to ignore the fact that many single parents, most of whom are women, live in poverty. The proportion of families with dependent children headed by a single parent has increased from 8% in 1971, to 13% in 1981 and to 19% in 1991[21]. Scott has argued that throughout the world there is a trend towards the feminisation of poverty[22]. In the west, single mothers often become caught in the poverty trap, unable to take up paid work without losing social security benefit and unable to command a sufficiently high wage to pay for child care. Given the lower educational achievement of children from single parent families, it is essential to develop social policies which offer effective support, including adequate social security provision. In addition, we need to know more about the ways in which the economic disadvantage experienced by single parent families is translated into the educational failure of their children.

So far, then, research findings show that, in general, pupils from working class backgrounds perform less well than their more privileged peers in terms of examination results. Within the working class, there are other groups experiencing particular economic and educational disadvantages and some examples of these groups have been considered. More research is necessary to highlight the nature of the school experiences of these groups.

6.3 The Extent to Which Schools are Responsible for Educational Disadvantage

One of the most hotly contested debates of recent years concerns the extent to which schools are responsible for the educational outcomes of their pupils. In the 1950s and

1960s, researchers connected with the 'political arithmetic' tradition of social research—for example, Floud, Halsey and Martin—compared the chances of working class and middle class pupils of attaining professional employment status and found that the odds were heavily stacked against working class pupils[23]. Some educationists felt that the way to tackle this inequality was not by targeting resources on pupils in schools, but rather to reform the social structures which produce inequality in the first place. In a 1970 article, Bernstein suggested: 'We should stop thinking in terms of "compensatory education" but consider, instead, most seriously and systematically the conditions and contexts of the educational environment'[24]. In the collection of papers on consumer detriment published by the National Consumer Council in 1977, Eric Midwinter adopted a similar position, identifying an equalisation of social conditions as the means of straightening out the "flaws and kinks in the uneven tangle of English education"[25]. Others, like Halsey, have continued to champion compensatory education, particularly at the pre-school stage. Commenting on the long term effects of such programmes, he argued:

> "What Headstart and the EPA (Educational Priority Area) experience do show is that a pre-school programme, properly devised, can be a most economical investment for a government wishing to save money on schools. And for a government determined to relieve the handicaps of those who come from poor families, a pre-school programme discriminating in their favour seems to be one of the crucial weapons in the armoury. In that way education *can* compensate for society"[26].

The debate over whether schools make a difference to the educational outcomes of poor children was contested particularly strongly in the United States in the late 1970s. The work of Coleman et al. and Jencks et al. had been interpreted as indicating that the influence of the pupil's social background was so strong that schools made little difference to educational outcomes[27][28]. The inference which conservative politicians might draw from this work was that there was no point in investing in compensatory education programmes since the poor appeared to be ineducable. Black researchers like Ronald Edmonds made it their mission to prove that money spent on schools for the urban poor was not wasted, since high quality education was able to compensate for some of the effects of social deprivation[29]. Edmonds insisted that there was no lack of knowledge as to how to educate socially disadvantaged children; all that was lacking was the political will to put this into practice. Comparing a number of inner-city elementary schools with similar intakes, Edmonds found a very wide range of outcomes and concluded that a key factor was teachers' expectations of their pupils. He noted:

> "Many professional personnel in the less effective school attributed children's reading problems to nonschool factors and were pessimistic about their ability to have an impact, creating an environment in which children failed because they were not expected to succeed"[30].

Based on the observation that pupils with similar levels of social deprivation achieved success in some schools but not in others, Edmonds concluded:

> "The similarity in the characteristics of the two pupil populations permits us to infer the importance of school behaviour in making pupil performance independent of family background. The over-riding point here is that, in and of itself, pupil family background neither causes nor precludes elementary school instructional effectiveness"[31].

Since the early 1980s in the UK, the school effectiveness movement has gathered pace. Key studies of secondary schools by Rutter et al. and of primary schools by Mortimore et al. demonstrated that even though social class was the most important variable associated with educational outcome, if pupil progress became the focus of attention rather than unadjusted examination or test results, then very significant differences emerged between schools[32][33]. The development of multi-level statistical techniques in the 1980s has enabled researchers to separate out the effects of the school, the neighbourhood and the family. In Scotland, the Centre for Educational Sociology at Edinburgh University has undertaken a considerable amount of work on school effects[34][35][36]. Willms and Cuttance, for instance, reported a study of differences in educational outcomes between 15 secondary schools in a particular division of a Scottish education authority[37]. After controlling for family background and pupil attainment on entry to secondary school, they found that in the most effective schools the average pupil left with five or more 'O' Grade passes (A-C), whilst in the least effective schools, a similar pupil left with only one or two 'O' Grade passes.

Although studies have varied in their estimation of the size and nature of school effects, the findings are generally optimistic, offering hope that, at least to some extent, schools can compensate for social deprivation given appropriate forms of leadership, organisation and instruction. In theory, schools serving areas of low socio-economic status should be able to do at least as well as schools serving more advantaged areas if they are judged in terms of pupil progress rather than absolute measures of educational outcome. However, it is very difficult to separate out school factors from social background factors. Rutter et al., for instance, noted that a balanced social intake was strongly associated with effective schooling[38]. Pupils from less advantaged backgrounds may benefit from being educated alongside more privileged children because the expectations of the teachers are higher and the ethos of the school is orientated towards academic achievement. By the same token, where the majority of pupils in a school are from disadvantaged backgrounds, teachers' expectations are likely to be lower, and the performance of all pupils may be depressed.

Scheerens, after reviewing a large number of American, British and Dutch studies of school effectiveness, suggested that there may be a tendency for researchers to overestimate the size of the school effect and underestimate the influence of social background[39]. Despite the fact that arguments persist concerning the nature and extent of school effects, such studies have been helpful in publicising the up-beat message that schools play a significant part in enhancing or reducing progress, counteracting the view that schools were no more than 'marginal institutions' and as such had a very small part to play in remedying social inequality. However, it is important to remember that the level of attainment of children in a highly effective school of low socio-economic status is likely to be lower than that of children in a less effective, high socio-economic status school.

6.4 Factors Within Schools Which Tend to Help or Hinder Pupil Progress

If we accept that pupils, including those of lower socio-economic status, do considerably better in some schools than others, then it is clear that we need to look for explanations of depressed educational achievement not just in the material and social circumstances of pupils' families, but also within the dynamics of school and classroom processes. If it is possible to identify factors associated with effective (and ineffective) schooling, then this should be of assistance to schools in the process of change. A number of studies have sought to identify the characteristics of highly effective schools in terms of both academic and social outcomes[40][41][42]. In general terms, a number of key factors can be identified such as teachers' high expectations, clear school goals, a strong leadership role adopted by the headteacher and lessons which are clearly focused and give pupils maximum time on task. In their comparative study of grammar, secondary modern and comprehensive schools in South Wales, Reynolds and Sullivan found marked differences particularly with regard to their social outcomes. They identified two distinct strategies adopted by groups of schools, which they termed 'coercion' and 'incorporation':

> "Incorporation aims to achieve control through relationships, which are to be attained by blurring status hierarchies, involving pupils in the life of the school and ensuring therapeutic rather than punitive responses to pupil deviance if it occurs. Coercion, by contrast, aims to use external reinforcers of behaviour such as physical punishment, shaming or verbal sanctions in order to motivate pupils to be pro-social in their allegiance to school norms. In the two comprehensives, the strategy of incorporation was simply much more difficult to employ. Size made the development of primary relationships more difficult. The lack of consistency among teachers in their rule enforcement and expectations generated a more cynical pupil group"[43].

Although some progress has been made in identifying factors contributing to school effectiveness, translation of these into the area of school improvement has been rather slow. It is to be hoped that over the next decade there will be closer liaison between those working in the areas of school effectiveness and improvement.

An obvious question which arises in the context of consumer detriment is whether pupils of lower socio-economic status are performing less well in the education system simply because they are deprived of resources. It is certainly the case that middle class pupils continue to dominate higher education, thus commanding the lion's share of resources at this level. However, there is certainly not a straightforward link between level of resourcing and children's performance at primary and secondary levels. One reason for this is that most education authorities have used indices of social deprivation, such as entitlement to free school meals, to provide additional funding to schools serving disadvantaged areas on the grounds that these are likely to contain a high proportion of pupils with learning difficulties. In addition, even if they do not receive top-up funding, schools serving poorer areas are likely to cost more per pupil than those in more privileged neighbourhoods because they may have falling roles, a trend which is likely to continue as parents use the provisions of the Education (Scotland) Act 1981 to send their child to a school in a more affluent area. Popular schools in socially advantaged areas, by the same token, are likely to be cheaper per capita to run because of economies of scale. It is interesting to note that school effectiveness researchers have not found a clear-cut link between size of class and pupil progress. Intuitively, one might have expected children in smaller classes to do better, but the findings of Mortimore et al.[44] and others do not bear this out. As explained above, this is because the negative effect of low socio-economic status far outweighs the positive effect of small class size. To summarise, higher levels of spending per pupil and smaller class sizes, although likely to be beneficial, do not automatically produce better results. Pupils' progress and overall levels of achievement are influenced by the cumulative and interactive effects of the material and social situation of the family, reflected in parents' expectations of the child and the school, which in turn influence teachers' expectations and morale. Some people might use this evidence to maintain that preferential funding of lower socio-economic status schools does not represent an efficient use of resources. It could be argued, on the contrary, that additional resourcing is essential to support the work of schools in disadvantaged areas, but it can only mitigate, not eradicate, the detrimental effects of social deprivation.

The final section explores the present and future policy context and considers whether educational disadvantages are likely to diminish or intensify over the next decade.

6.5 Equalisation of Educational Opportunities—the Present and Future Policy Context

There is considerable disagreement over the effects of the reorganisation of secondary schools along comprehensive lines during the 1960s and 1970s. One of the central aims of comprehensive reorganisation, according to its supporters in the Labour Party, was to reduce social inequality by abandoning selection, thus opening up greater educational opportunities to all and reducing social inequalities between schools. Reviewing work on the effectiveness of comprehensive schooling in England and Wales, Reynolds and Sullivan commented on "the relative paucity of the overall effort that has gone into research on this question"[45]. Despite the inadequacy of the available data, which often compared comprehensives with grammar schools, commentators south of the border, such as Cox and Boyson, argued that comprehensive schools were failing and a return to selective education would benefit children at all levels of attainment[46]. Those of a more radical complexion such as Reynolds and Sullivan[47] and Hargreaves[48] maintained that comprehensives had failed because of their tendency to value a narrow range of mainly academic achievement, so that lower achieving children became alienated.

In Scotland, a much more positive view of the introduction of comprehensive schools has been offered. Using data from the 1977, 1981 and 1985 Scottish School Leavers' Surveys, McPherson and Willms argued that comprehensive education in Scotland has produced both equalisation and improvement. They commented:

> 'By "equalisation" we mean, not that equality of attainment between the social classes was achieved, but that inequality was reduced. By "improvement" we mean a rise in average levels of certified school attainment'[49].

They noted that the equalisation of school attainment was greatest in areas where pupils in comprehensive schools were not creamed off by the private sector and where there was a greater social mix; such schools tended to be in New Towns, small burghs and rural areas. In the cities, where the private sector survived and residential segregation led to schools which were predominantly working or middle class, the equalisation effect was less marked. As noted earlier, they also found that in the later stages of secondary schooling, equalisation was less evident, so that a far higher proportion of middle class than working class pupils continued to gain places in higher education.

In Scotland, it would appear that comprehensive education, whilst not removing social inequality, began to narrow the gap in attainment between working class and middle class pupils by giving all pupils access to public examinations, closing many junior secondary schools where teachers tended to have lower expectations of pupils and rearranging catchment areas to reduce social segregation. One might expect the process of equalisation to continue and gain momentum, as working class pupils who stayed on at school to gain qualifications in the 1970s become parents and pass on their higher aspirations to their own children. However, the encouragement of market forces in the educational arena, an important element of government policy, may hinder this process. Key aspects of this policy are summarised below.

Government policy documents make clear that parental choice is envisaged as the mechanism by which the marketisation of education is to be driven. For instance, as mentioned in section 6.4, the Education (Scotland) Act 1981 allowed parents the right to choose their child's school, rather than being allocated a place by the education authority. The underlying assumption of this measure is that parents, acting as critical consumers, will select a place for their child in a 'good' school and reject schools which they think are under-performing. In some urban areas, at the time of writing, 25% of parents were using schools outwith the neighbourhood and for Scotland as a whole the figure was 10%. Although there may be benefits for working class children attending schools in a more affluent neighbourhood, the detrimental effect for pupils who are left behind in a school with falling rolls, reduced resources and an increasingly demoralised staff is likely to be considerable. It is evident that middle class parents are more likely to use the parental choice legislation than are working class parents[50] and that the greatest movement of pupils is from schools in deprived areas with few middle class residents to schools in more affluent areas with a higher proportion of middle class pupils[51]. The emergence of these patterns confirms Ranson's warning that: "Under the guise of neutrality, the institution of the market actively confirms and reinforces the pre-existing social order of wealth and privilege"[52].

The obligation on schools to publish examination results, attendance and truancy rates and costs per pupil, as recommended in the Scottish Office Education Department consultation paper of November 1992[53], is likely to undermine further parents' confidence in schools in predominantly working class areas, since no information on school effectiveness measured by pupil progress is to be provided. The lack of value-added data was described by the Scottish Consumer Council as 'seriously misleading'[54]. It will be some time before the ultimate effect of this policy becomes clear, but there is a strong possibility that it will act as a brake on the process of equalisation associated with comprehensive reorganisation in Scotland.

Another example of government policy which may have a detrimental effect on the attainment of working class pupils is Devolved School Management, due to be introduced into all Scottish schools by April 1996[55]. Traditionally, education authorities have managed budgets centrally and have funded schools on the basis of the number of children and the particular circumstances of the school such as the level of social deprivation in the neighbourhood. Schools in disadvantaged areas with low school rolls have received more funding per capita than schools in advantaged areas with high enrolment. The principle of financial delegation is that education authorities retain a proportion of funds for central services, but devolve the majority of the budget to schools (80% according to the Scottish Office Education Department consultation paper published in November 1992)[56]. Explaining how education authorities should allocate funds, the Scottish Office Education Department emphasised the following point:

> "A further essential element is that schools should rapidly move towards the position where they (patterns of funding) are based on an assessment of the needs of the school by reference predominantly to pupil numbers (but also

taking account of other significant factors), rather than on historical patterns of expenditure"[57].

The extent to which preferential funding will continue to be allocated on the basis of social deprivation is unclear. However, a possible implication is that schools in disadvantaged areas with falling rolls will have their current levels of funding reduced, thus depressing the attainment of pupils even further. There is also anxiety that the 20% of the budget retained centrally will be inadequate to fund all the services on which schools now depend, particularly those for children with special educational needs. South of the border, experience of local management of schools (LMS), introduced by the Education Reform Act (1988), suggests that a rigid application of formula funding makes schools reluctant to accept children who are expensive and difficult to educate, such as those with cognitive and social, emotional and behavioural difficulties. A rise in exclusions and in requests for psychological assessments has been noted by researchers in England and Wales[58].

It is impossible at the time of writing to know what effect the recent spate of educational reforms will have on the experiences of children of lower socio-economic status in Scottish schools. A number of commentators south of the border are extremely pessimistic about the effects of the implementation of 'parentocracy', a term coined by Brown[59]. Within such a regime, educational outcomes are determined by the wealth and cultural capital of the parents rather than the ability of the child; the former system of meritocracy was in principle, if not in practice, based on the notion that success should be awarded on the basis of effort and ability. In Scotland, there is generally more optimism that the present emphasis on individualism will not replace the traditional commitment to social welfare. Munn argued that, with regard to issues such as national testing, parents have used their increased powers to support schools and teachers rather than the Government[60]. Paterson also maintained that the concern for social welfare in Scotland will continue to act as a bulwark against the marketisation of education[61]. He suggested that despite more than a decade of Conservative government, social class differences in educational outcomes are likely to continue narrowing because of the success of comprehensive reorganisation in Scotland. In addition, since take-up of higher education is already so high among middle class pupils, those of working class origin are particularly likely to benefit from the expansion of this sector. Ultimately, it is clear that only time will tell whether the process of equalisation in Scottish education, begun in the 1960s and 1970s, will continue throughout the 1990s or shift into reverse.

In the light of the possibility that parental choice as it is presently conceived may have the effect of increasing social inequality, the question arises as to whether it should be rejected as a guiding principle of education policy. Although this might have a superficial appeal, it is likely that the removal of choice would be very difficult for any government to justify and would have the negative consequence of reducing parents' stake in their children's education, with an associated loss of interest and commitment. Adler has suggested that a way forward might be to encourage diversity in schools but at the same time to provide parents with more information to enable them to match their child to a suitable school[62]. A problem with this suggestion is that diversity may easily produce inequality of status between different institutions, even if attempts are made to equalise resources. Ranson proposed that the principle of accountability should be maintained, but that parents should be encouraged to exercise choice not just to pursue the interests of their family, but to promote the well-being of others and the health of society, recognising the effect of their choices on others[63]. This might appear to be a somewhat utopian expectation in the current climate of competitive individualism, but it does offer a way of combining parental choice with a concern for collective welfare.

6.6 Conclusions

This paper began by drawing attention to the gulf in educational attainment between those of higher and lower socio-economic status and indicated some other factors associated with low income and educational disadvantage, including membership of single parent and ethnic minority families. The debate concerning the relative responsibility of school and society for educational failure has been outlined and suggests that, although some schools are undoubtedly more effective than others in helping working class pupils to make progress, they are not able to make much headway in compensating for the negative effects of social disadvantage. This implies that we should continue to monitor school effectiveness and identify key factors in those schools which are performing either better or worse than expected, with a view to emulating the former and remedying the latter. However, if other social policies are geared towards maximising individual and group differences, we should not expect education to be able to reverse this process.

Over the coming decade, it is evident that the educational arena will continue to be influenced by the prevailing political philosophy and at the time of writing this is characterised by an emphasis on the rights and power of the individual consumer, coupled with a tightening of centralised control. If we continue on a path which stresses the rights of those who are able to fulfil the role of critical consumer, then those who are unable to do so and who may have no one to act as their advocate are likely to be cast adrift. Children in families such as these will experience education of an increasingly impoverished quality. Even for working class children whose parents do succeed in gaining a place for them in a more privileged school, there is a strong possibility that they will be gradually lost from the system. However, rather than rejecting the principles of parental involvement and institutional accountability, it could be argued that the debate should focus on how parents may be involved in education in such a way that democratic choices do not diminish, but rather enhance, social welfare. This, clearly, is a major challenge for the future.

References to Chapter 6

1. Scottish Office, *The Parents' Charter in Scotland*, 1991.
2. L. Paterson, 'Social class in Scottish Education' in S. Brown and S. Riddell (eds), *Class, Race and Gender in Schools*, Scottish Council for Research in Education, 1992.
3. L. Bondi, 'Attainment at primary schools: an analysis of variations between schools', *British Educational Research Journal*, Vol. 17, No. 3, 1991, pp. 203-219.
4. Scottish Office Education Department, *Statistical Bulletin: School Leavers' Destinations*, The Scottish Office, 1992.
5. L. Paterson, 'Social origins of under-achievement amongst school leavers' in H. Maguiness (ed.), *Educational Opportunity : The Challenge of Under-achievement and Social Deprivation*, Local Government Centre, Paisley College, 1992.

6. Scottish Office Education Department, *Statistical Bulletin 12: Scottish Higher Education Statistics*, The Scottish Office, 1990.
7. L. Paterson, see reference 5.
8. L. Paterson, 'Socio-economic status and educational attainment : a multi-dimensional and multi-level study', *Evaluation and Research in Education*, 1992, pp. 97-121.
9. L. Paterson, see reference 8.
10. R. Sharp and A. Green, *Education and Social Control : A Case Study in Progressive Primary Education*, Penguin, 1975.
11. P. Willis, *Learning to Labour*, Saxon House, 1977.
12. P. Brown, *Schooling Ordinary Kids: inequality, unemployment and the new vocationalism*, Tavistock, 1987.
13. P. Brown, see reference 12.
14. D. Hughes, 'Social class and educational disadvantage: are the schools to blame? in S. Brown and S. Riddell (eds), *Class, Race and Gender in Schools*, Scottish Council for Research in Education, 1992.
15. P. Smith, *Ethnic Minorities in Scotland*, The Scottish Office, 1991.
16. S. Sharp and J. Fitzpatrick, 'The attainment in examinations of ethnic minority candidates in Scotland', *New Community*, Vol. 17, No. 2, 1991.
17. D. Drew and J. Gray, 'The black-white gap in examination results : a statistical critique of a decade's research', *New Community*, Vol. 17, No. 2, 1991, pp. 159 - 172.
18. M. Mac an Ghaill, *Young, Gifted and Black: student-teacher relations in the schooling of black youth*, Open University Press, 1988.
19. D. Gillborn, 'Racism and education : issues for research and practice' in S. Brown and S. Riddell (eds), *Class, Race and Gender in Schools*, Scottish Council for Research in Education, 1992.
20. L. Paterson, see reference 5.
21. Government Statistical Service, *General Household Survey 1991*, No. 22, HMSO, 1993.
22. H. Scott, *Working Your Way to the Bottom: The Feminization of Poverty*, Pandora Press, 1984.
23. J. E. Floud, A. H. Halsey and F. M. Martin, *Social Class and Educational Opportunity*, Heinemann, 1956.
24. B. Bernstein, 'Education cannot compensate for society', *New Society*, 26th February, 1970.
25. E. Midwinter, 'Education' in F. Williams (ed.), *Why the Poor Pay More*, MacMillan for the National Consumer Council, 1977.
26. A. H. Halsey, 'Education can compensate' in W. Swann (ed.), *The Practice of Special Education*, Blackwell, 1981.
27. J. S. Coleman, E. Q. Campbell, C. J. Hobson, J. McPartland, A. M. F. D. Mood and R. L. York, *Equality of Educational Opportunity*, US Office of Education, Centre for Educational Statistics, 1966.
28. C. Jencks et al., *Inequality : A Reassessment of the Effect of Family and School*, Basic Books, 1972.
29. R. R. Edmonds, 'Effective schools for the urban poor', *Educational Leadership*, Vol. 37, 1979, pp. 20-24.

30. R. Edmonds, see reference 29.
31. R. Edmonds, see reference 29.
32. M. Rutter, B. Maughan, P. Mortimore and J. Ouston, *Fifteen Thousand Hours : Secondary Schools and their Effects on Children*, Open Books, 1979.
33. P. Mortimore, P. Sammons, L. Stoll, D. Lewis and R. Ecob, *School Matters: The Junior Years*, Open Books, 1988.
34. J. Gray, A. McPherson and D. Raffe, *Reconstructions of Secondary Education: Theory, Myth and Practice Since the War*, Routledge and Kegan Paul, 1983.
35. D. Willms and P. Cuttance, 'School effects in Scottish secondary schools', *British Journal of Sociology of Education*, Vol. 6, No. 3, 1985, pp. 289 - 306.
36. P. Cuttance, *The Effectiveness of Catholic Schooling in Scotland*, University of Edinburgh, Centre for Educational Sociology, 1988.
37. D. Willms and P. Cuttance, see reference 35.
38. M. Rutter, B. Maughan, P. Mortimore and J. Ouston, see reference 32.
39. J. Scheerens, *Effective Schooling*, Cassell, 1989.
40. M. Rutter, B. Maughan, P. Mortimore and J. Ouston, see reference 32.
41. D. Reynolds and M. Sullivan, *The Comprehensive Experiment*, Falmer Press, 1987.
42. P Mortimore, P. Sammons, L. Stoll, D. Lewis and R. Ecob, see reference 33.
43. D. Reynolds and M Sullivan, see reference 41.
44. P Mortimore, P. Sammons, L. Stoll, D Lewis and R Ecob, see reference 33.
45. D. Reynolds and M. Sullivan, see reference 41.
46. C. B. Cox and R. Boyson, *Black Paper 1977*, Critical Quarterly, 1977.
47. D. Reynolds and M. Sullivan, see reference 41.
48. D. H. Hargreaves, *The Challenge for the Comprehensive School*, Routledge and Kegan Paul, 1982.
49. A. McPherson and J. D. Willms, 'Equalisation and improvement : some effects of comprehensive reorganisation in Scotland', *Sociology*, Vol. 21, No. 4, 1987, pp. 509-541.
50. F. Echols, A. McPherson and D. Willms, 'Parental choice in Scotland', *Journal of Education Policy*, Vol. 5, No.3, 1990, pp. 207-222.
51. M. Adler, A. Petch and J. Tweedie, *Parental Choice and Educational Policy*, Edinburgh University Press, 1989.
52. S. Ranson, 'From 1944 to 1988: education, citizenship and democracy' in M. Flude and M. Hammer (eds), *The Education Reform Act 1988: its origins and implications*, Falmer Press, 1990.
53. Scottish Office Education Department, *Better Information for Parents in Scotland. The Government's Proposals*, The Scottish Office Education Department, 1992.
54. Scottish Consumer Council, *The Parents' Charter: Better Information for Parents. Response of the Scottish Consumer Council to the Government's Proposals*, SCC, 1993.
55. Scottish Office Education Department, *Devolved School Management : Guidelines for Progress*, The Scottish Office Education Department, 1992.
56. Scottish Office Education Department, see reference 55.
57. Scottish Office Education Department, see reference 55.
58. D. Armstrong and D. Galloway, 'Special educational needs and problem behaviour: making policy in the classroom' in S. Riddell and S. Brown (eds), *Special Educational Needs Policy in the '90s*, Routledge, 1994.
59. P. Brown, "The 'third wave' : education and the ideology of parentocracy" *British Journal of Sociology of Education*, Vol. 11, No. 1, 1990, pp. 65-85.

60. P. Munn, 'Devolved management of schools and FE colleges: a victory of the producer over the consumer?' in L. Paterson and D. McCrone (eds), *The Scottish Government Yearbook 1992*, pp. 142-156, Edinburgh, Unit for the Study of Government in Scotland, 1992.
61. L. Paterson, see reference 5.
62. M. Adler, 'Parental choice and the enhancement of children's interests' in P. Munn (ed.), *Parents and Schools: Customers, Managers or Partners?*, Routledge, 1993.
63. S. Ranson, see reference 52.

Transport

by John Farrington

For many people transport is essential for getting to work, going shopping, visiting friends and pursuing leisure activities. In this chapter John Farrington shows that those on low incomes have very low levels of mobility and are consequently restricted in their daily lives. Few people on low incomes own or have access to a car and often rely on local bus services. At this end of the travel market some passengers face confusing and frequent changes to bus services and have no representative body to turn to when things go wrong. Although concessionary fares are available for some people on low incomes many others have to pay the full fare. Likely increases in bus and rail fares in the future will affect those on low incomes most acutely.

7.1 Introduction

Virtually everyone has a fundamental need to travel in order to access a range of activities and facilities. Our ability to access these activities and facilities governs, to a large extent, the standard of living and the quality of life we experience. The degree of access experienced by different consumers is determined largely by the type and quantity of travel physically and financially available to them. Most travel, by most consumers, is undertaken by using cars, buses, taxis and trains, since walking and cycling are sharply constrained by distance, and for some consumers by their personal physical mobility. In turn, the ability to pay for vehicular travel depends on personal or household income.

High income consumers can overcome the disadvantages of living in locations relatively remote from service and employment centres by paying for public transport (if it is available) or private transport. Low income consumers, on the other hand, are more likely to have their activity horizons constrained by their more limited spending power, even when public transport is available.

This chapter considers the implications for those on low incomes of the different types of transport which they can obtain. A variety of data is used to demonstrate the constraints acting on low income consumers and their ability to purchase transport. The main sources of information for the analysis of car ownership and public transport expenditure are tabulations of 1990 Scottish data from the Family Expenditure Survey (FES)[1] and the General Household Survey (GHS)[2]. These were commissioned specifically for this study from the ESRC Data Archive, and provide an important basis, not normally available, for analysis of the situation in Scotland[3][4].

It is rarely possible (without detailed field work which is beyond the scope of the present study) to analyse the situation in more detail than at the Scottish level, but where more detailed information is available, it is included in the analysis. Some comparisons with the situation in Britain as a whole are also provided.

The chapter is divided into the following sections:

- a consideration of the transport needs of low income consumers;

- an overview of the main transport policy developments of the last decade which have implications for consumers, particularly those on low incomes;
- an analysis of car ownership and public transport use among low income consumers;
- conclusions.

7.2 Transport and the Needs of Low Income Consumers

In relation to transport, low income consumers are a broad group in which it is possible to identify several sub-groups. These include those who are unemployed, pensioners, single parent families, those who are disabled, students, and those on low pay. These groups generally have a greater dependence on public transport than higher income groups.

Those depending on public transport need services which are affordable, reliable, accessible, appropriate for their needs, and of reasonable quality. They also need accurate and up-to-date information about public transport services, and a means of redress and representation when things go wrong.

The affordability of public transport is by definition a key issue for low income consumers. There are two main types of scheme which aim to address this issue—concessionary fares and discounted fares. Concessionary fare schemes are operated by the Regional and Islands Councils throughout Scotland, at a cost of £43.05 million in 1990/91, and are available for pensioners and disabled people, but they are not intended to address the financial constraints experienced by low income consumers in other groups. Other fare reductions on public transport are often available for all consumers, but these normally require advance purchase of cards or season tickets, and low income groups may not be able to make the necessary initial outlay. The benefits of concessionary fares to eligible consumers may be gauged from Strathclyde Passenger Transport Executive's (PTE) estimate that in 1991/92, 412,000 holders of concessionary travel cards made 73 million journeys, representing an average benefit of £60 per card holder[5]. Details of concessionary and discount fare schemes are given in Section 7.4c below.

Problems of accessibility to public transport may arise even where there may appear to be adequate public transport provision. For example, peripheral housing estates on the edge of the larger Scottish cities usually have frequent bus services to city centres, but these may involve: long walks to bus stops and difficulties for the elderly, disabled, and those with children and shopping; high costs in relation to incomes; and awkward cross-city journeys to work or job interviews, involving higher costs. Indeed, it can be cheaper and more convenient for a group of shoppers, for example, to share the cost of a taxi for this type of journey.

Many schemes are operated by the Regional Councils and by voluntary groups to provide transport for groups whose characteristics make access to public transport a particularly important issue, such as the disabled and elderly, involving features such as dial-a-ride and vehicles specifically designed for those with mobility difficulties. For example, Strathclyde Passenger Transport Executive's Dial-a-Bus service for mobility-handicapped people is available in those areas which contain nearly 95% of Strathclyde's population, and 241,000 people used it in 1991/92, about 60% of them making shopping trips[6].

All users of public transport require good quality information about the services they use, and about changes in those services, with sufficient advance notice to make adjustments to new schedules if necessary. They also expect reliable services which perform as scheduled in timetables. Bus deregulation and urban traffic congestion are two factors which have brought increasing pressure on information systems and on the reliability of bus services. Operators and local authorities are well aware of these difficulties and make significant efforts to improve them, but they remain key issues in consumers' perceptions of public transport. The provision of better information and more reliable bus services is inevitably related to the availability of resources, and to wider issues of planning for the alleviation of traffic congestion.

For some low income consumers, particularly those living in rural areas, public transport is inconvenient or unavailable, and car ownership is a necessity. In these cases, the proportion of income spent on the car will be high in comparison with higher income groups, and any changes in car ownership costs may have a significant effect on these consumers. Even when a household has a car, it will typically be used for the journey to work, leaving other household members dependent on public transport or lifts during the day; and this often results in young people in rural areas hitching lifts for journeys to and from towns, raising problems of safety.

The transport needs of low income consumers vary widely, but are fundamentally the same as those with higher incomes in similar locations and at similar life cycle stages. Public transport dependence is typically high, and car ownership low and marginal, for many consumers on low incomes. They are, therefore, particularly at risk of disadvantage because of restricted choice.

The systems for providing redress and pursuance of grievance by transport users in Scotland vary with the mode of transport. The Transport Users Consultative Committee for Scotland, based in Glasgow, deals with issues arising in relation to British Rail and Caledonian MacBrayne, the state-owned ferry operators. Air passengers can raise issues with the Air Transport Users Council, based in London. There is, however, no corresponding independent body which deals with issues relating to bus services.

Most transport operators take their responsibilities to their customers very seriously, and usually have their own administrative sections and procedures for dealing with complaints and other issues. The British Rail Passenger's Charter, introduced in 1992,[7] is an attractive idea but anecdotal evidence suggests that passengers would generally prefer to see money being spent on investment in the system to improve quality and reliability, rather than on compensation payments for late arrivals.

Increasing awareness of quality issues in the transport industry, as shown for example by the adoption of standards leading to BS 5750 by transport operators, is a positive sign that the interests of consumers are being given a high priority. This should indeed be the case in an industry where privatisation, competition, and responsiveness to markets are being so actively promoted by government policy.

Despite this emphasis on quality, it appears to be anomalous that the users of bus services, who make the majority of journeys by public transport, should not have an independent body such as a Users' Consultative Committee to deal with issues of grievance and possible redress. This would help to overcome the confusion that commonly arises in bus users' minds about the lines of responsibility (and complaint) for specific services. Local authorities are involved in the provision of subsidised services but do not have this role in relation to commercial services, and this distinction is not readily made by bus users. As is shown in Section 7.4, low income consumers tend to use bus services more than other groups do, and an independent users' body would help to represent their interests more directly, in the context of both specific and general issues, than the present rather diffuse pattern of responsibilities.

7.3 Transport Policy

Two main effects of transport policy since 1979 are relevant to the present context, and will be discussed in turn:

- The principal aim of transport policy since 1979, with important implications for public transport, has been to increase the significance of market forces in transport.

- A secondary aim, with some cost implications for car owners, has been to incorporate environmental considerations into vehicle legislation and transport policy.

(a) Market forces

Privatisation and deregulation of the bus industry have been the main tools used to inject market forces into the provision of public transport, together with financial controls on Strathclyde Passenger Transport Executive, the Regional and Islands Councils, and British Rail. Of these measures, bus deregulation has had the most significant direct effects on consumers.

Under the system which evolved in the late 1960s and through the 1970s, local authorities and PTEs were empowered to subsidise local bus services and rail services, and to co-ordinate these services in order to meet perceived public need. Bus services were regulated within a framework deriving from the 1930 Road Traffic Act. British Rail was also subsidised at the national level by means of the annual Public Service Obligation grant which made up the costs of loss-making passenger services, a category which includes all Scottish internal services.

The effect of this system was to develop co-ordination and to maintain largely intact the bus and rail networks in Scotland, but at the cost of increasing subsidy requirements. These were applied on a 'blanket' basis, and relatively little was known about the cost/revenue ratios of specific services, or the value for money being obtained. The trends in bus services and subsidy are shown by Bell and Cloke[8]: local government subsidies for public transport in Britain increased by 13 times in real terms between 1972 and 1982, while fares rose by 30% above the rate of inflation. The share of the travel market captured by buses and coaches fell from 42% to 8% between 1953 and 1982—a halving in absolute terms. British Rail did better in retaining approximately level numbers of passenger journeys, but their support from the state was approaching £1 billion by the early 1980s.

In 1980 the first moves towards the introduction of market forces in the supply of bus services came with the deregulation of long distance services. Competition quickly developed between independent operators and the Scottish Bus Group, the nationalised operator. There were benefits, many of which have endured, for low income consumers, such as students and pensioners, who make up a significant portion of the long distance bus market. Fares decreased, while the number and quality of some services increased. Consumer gains also resulted because British Rail responded with lower fares in order to maintain market share, though this strategy lost them revenue overall, and the long term consumer benefit is questionable because of the extra pressure placed on BR's finances.

The deregulation of local bus services under the Transport Act of 1985 took full effect in January 1987. Quality licensing, covering aspects of safety and operator fitness, was retained, but any operator meeting this requirement is free to run a commercial service, or to vary or withdraw the service, subject to 42 days' notice. The co-ordinating role of local authorities is replaced by a 'buying back' role in which services not run as commercial services, but judged by the local authority to be socially desirable, are subsidised via the tendering system. Local authorities appear to be satisfied that on the whole the basic structure of socially required services, such as rural routes and off-peak and Sunday services, has been retained. This has been possible due to a number of factors which include increasingly keen bidding for tenders by operators, and careful evaluation of the effects of service withdrawals by the local authorities[9]. This does not, however, preclude the possibility that the removal of a short link in a route, or a particular service—such as evening services used for educational, recreational or social purposes—may disrupt the established travel patterns of passengers dependent on bus services. Low income consumers without access to a car are particularly vulnerable to such changes, and their ability to make hospital visits, for example, can often depend on voluntary drivers and community services, while their participation in activities such as evening classes can be significantly curtailed.

Bus fare increases have generally been held below the level of inflation, and in this respect differ markedly from the overall experience in Britain. In 1990/91, local bus fares in Scotland had increased by 26.4% since 1985, whereas in Britain as a whole the increase was 48.1%. In the same period, the Retail Price Index had risen by 36.1%[10]. For many bus users, therefore, travel has become cheaper in real terms over the last few years though, for those whose incomes have risen by less than 26.4%, it has become more expensive, and for those on low incomes it may have remained expensive in relation to their resources. Furthermore, the average situation as reported in the Scottish Transport Statistics can, of course, mask variations. For example, fares on bus services supported by Strathclyde PTE as part of the 'social network' rose by about 5% between December 1991 and November 1992, while the Retail Price Index rose by about 3%. The future trend for bus fares in general may well be upwards in relation to inflation, since the market continues to decline (due mainly to transfer of journeys to cars, and to a reduction in travel due to unemployment) and the scope for further cost-saving within the industry as a whole is probably limited.

Difficulties continue to arise for all consumers from the very frequent changes in bus services which continue to occur, particularly in areas where operators' commercial services are in competition 'on the road' with other operators' commercial services, as for example in parts of Glasgow. Operators tend to tune their networks frequently in order to meet or to anticipate rivals' competition. This makes it difficult to ensure that the consumer has up-to-date, accurate information about services, and this has been identified as a significant problem arising from bus deregulation in Scotland, as far as the passenger is concerned[11][12][13]. It also leads to delay in identifying the need for subsidised services, and obtaining these replacement services where required. In Strathclyde, where the most active competition takes place, there was a total of 1,259 changes to registered bus services during the 1990/91 fiscal year[14]. Strathclyde Passenger Transport Executive has estimated that maintaining an up-to-date and accurate data base on bus services in Strathclyde, together with effective information supply systems for the public, would cost up to an additional £2 million on the PTE budget[15].

One consequence of bus deregulation appears to have been increasing under-investment in the bus industry[16]. As vehicles age, replacement will be necessary. The funding of this investment may well have implications for fare levels in the future, with a tendency for the rate of increase to speed up in order to finance vehicle replacement.

Rail fares have generally risen faster than the Retail Price Index due to financial pressures on British Rail and, possibly, to the preparations for privatisation. In contrast to the general trend in bus fares, therefore, many consumers, including those on low incomes, have found rail travel to be increasingly expensive in real terms. This has only been partly offset by the discounting available to certain groups. In the area served by Strathclyde PTE Section 20 rail services (which are operated by BR and funded by the PTE), however, fare increases have been at or around inflation rate as a result of PTE policy.

Rail privatisation, in the form presently proposed, has possible implications for low income rail users in Scotland. ScotRail is to be franchised as a single operation, though Anglo-Scottish services will be split between the InterCity East Coast Main Line to Edinburgh, Glasgow, Aberdeen and Inverness, to be franchised as a package, and the InterCity West Coast Main Line south of Glasgow. The Government has apparently undertaken to require franchisees to continue to offer discounts to disabled passengers but, with regard to elderly and young persons' railcards, has said only that it believes it would be "in the interests of franchisees to offer facilities of that sort"[17]. There also appears to be no requirement for franchisees to offer generally available discounted fares such as Savers. Section 7.4c includes a review of currently available discounted rail fares.

The systems of subsidy and support applied by the Scottish Office to Caledonian MacBrayne and P & O Ferries, the two main ferry operators on the west and north/east coast services respectively, are at present under review, following an earlier review in the late 1980s. The options in the review range widely, covering the structure of the operating companies themselves as well as the subsidy and support systems, and include the possible privatisation of Caledonian MacBrayne. It is difficult to gauge the possible effects of such changes on the consumer without detailed study. However, if it is supposed that one of the aims of privatisation in general is to reduce central support, then possible outcomes include pressure on wage levels and investment in the privatised industry, and on revenue raised from consumers, because increased efficiency—if it is there to be had—can often achieve only a limited reduction in costs. Unless there is a challengeable market in which real long term competition can be sustained, which is rarely the case in Scottish ferry services, privatisation may not offer consumer benefits, but may alter the pattern and cost of services which are literally 'lifelines' for many communities.

Air services are also of vital concern to many communities, particularly in the Highlands and Islands. While the costs of air travel are, of course, often higher than those of surface transport, the costs to consumers are offset in particular cases by the application of subsidy to specific services by the Government or Regional/Islands Councils, or by the provision of concessionary fares for the residents of particular islands or other concessionary groups. Examples are given in Section 7.4c.

(b) Environmental considerations

The main impacts on consumers in this area of policy stem from the Government and EC efforts to reduce the harmful effects of motor vehicle emissions. From the beginning of 1993, all new cars sold in the EC must be equipped with catalytic converters. The cost of this measure will to some extent feed down the chain of buyers, increasing the second-hand price of cars. Low income car owners tend to buy and sell at the lower (and older) end of the used-car market, and when they come to transfer up to cars equipped with catalytic converters they could incur some additional cost. On the other hand, they could then benefit from the price advantage of lead-free petrol which these cars (as well as many cars not equipped with converters) use; this at present stands at approximately 4.5p per litre. The net effect of these factors in the longer term should be fairly neutral, depending mainly on the amount of mileage travelled and fuel used.

The cost of fuel in rural areas is higher than in urban areas, and the differential tends to be even greater in the Highlands and Islands. Data for the winter period 1992/93 are available in the Rural Scotland Price Survey, and selected values are given in Table 7.1[18].

Table 7.1 Selected petrol prices, Winter 1992/93

	Leaded	Unleaded
	pence per litre	
Highlands & Islands average	55.94	51.25
Rural average	55.54	50.98
Aberdeen	51.90	47.90
Edinburgh	49.40	44.70
Dunfermline	51.90	47.20

Source: Mackay Consultants *Rural Scotland Price Survey*, Winter 1992/93, Mackay Consultants, Inverness, 1993, pp.7-8.

In other words, the average petrol costs in rural Scotland are 12.4% higher (leaded) and 14.1% higher (unleaded) than in Edinburgh and, though occasionally rural car users may have the opportunity to buy cheaper fuel in urban areas, they tend to have to pay more for their car use than urban dwellers, as well as covering greater distances.

A carbon tax is one option being considered by the Government as a means of achieving Britain's commitment to keep carbon dioxide emissions at 1990 levels by the year 2000. The budget of March 1993 did bring increases in fuel prices (12p per gallon, unleaded, and 15p per gallon, leaded) which will affect the cost of car use, and further increases in the future are likely, possibly involving increasing fuel prices by around 10% through taxation. Such steps, though ostensibly well motivated, have the effect of a regressive tax, and particularly affect low income car owners, especially those in rural areas dependent on cars for access to employment and services. The same could be said regarding exhaust emission standards in the MOT test; although this should not create problems for engines that are properly maintained, older and more worn engines, which are more likely to be owned by those on lower incomes, may have more difficulty in passing the test.

Road pricing and similar methods of charging for car use in urban centres is being actively considered as a means of reducing congestion and environmental impact, as well as raising revenue. Unfortunately this, like fuel taxation, has the effect of a regressive tax on mobility unless revenue is directly reinvested in the provision of better public transport at prices the low income consumer can afford.

(c) Summary—transport policy effects

As a generalisation, Scottish bus users appear to have benefited from fare increases below the rate of inflation, while rail users have experienced an opposite trend. Future trends in both transport modes appear likely to be upwards in real terms.

The rapidity of change in bus services causes difficulties for operators and local authorities in providing accurate and up-to-date information, and for consumers in planning their use of bus services. It may also delay the effective provision of subsidised services.

The costs of car ownership and use will probably be increased due to legislation designed to reduce environmental impact and to increase tax revenue, and these increases could be of significance to car owners on low incomes.

7.4 Car Ownership and Public Transport Use

(a) Car ownership and its effects

Car ownership confers significant advantages for the mobility of the household in general, and for those members with access to the car in particular. There is a wide variation in average household car ownership rates in Scotland, though the overall rate is low compared with other UK regions. The UK average rate in 1990 was 66.5%, while the Scottish average was 56.8%—the lowest of all the UK regions[19]. In Aberdeen in 1991, the rate was 60%, while Dundee's 48.3% and Glasgow's 34.5% reflect less prosperous economies with higher unemployment rates. These low car ownership rates in urban areas contrast with rural areas; for example, in Sutherland (Highland Region) in 1991, 69.7% of households owned a car, and in Gordon District (Grampian Region) 83.4% of households owned a car—one of the highest rates in Great Britain[20].

Household income exerts a strong influence on car ownership. Of the 50% of all households in Scotland which had a gross weekly income of £200 or less in 1990, 79% had no car. Of the 30% of households with a gross weekly income of £100 or less, 88% had no car. In contrast, of the 34% of households which had a gross weekly income of £300 or more, only 15% did not own a car. The strong association of car ownership with higher incomes can be expressed in another way: 75% of all the households which have no car have a gross weekly income of £200 or less[21].

Low car ownership rates have a direct bearing on overall mobility. Research in various parts of Britain has shown that in households without cars fewer journeys are made to a narrower range of places[22]. This means that the choice of shopping, employment, recreation and other activities is restricted. In Britain as a whole, in the mid-1980s, members of households with no vehicle made about half the number of weekly journeys (26.2) compared with households with one car (57.3). In terms of distance travelled the difference is more marked; members of households with no vehicle travelled about 115 km per week, and members of households with one car travelled 464 km per week.

Evidence of the same effect at a local scale in rural Scotland is available from household surveys carried out by the author for Grampian Regional Council which collected data from 550 households containing 1,140 adults in three rural areas in Speyside, Buchan and The Mearns (Laurencekirk area)[23][24][25]. The average weekly number of trips (all purposes, all modes) made by car drivers was 10.3, while adults in households without a car made only 1.9 trips, mainly by bus. This is a very low level of mobility, reflecting the rural nature of the survey area, the self-sufficiency (partly enforced) of the rural dweller and, to some extent, the personal immobility of the elderly members of the population.

This sharp contrast in mobility is only partly accounted for by the tendency for car-owning households to be located in less accessible places. There is also a real gain from car ownership in terms of obtaining access to a wider range of people, facilities and opportunities[26] (although car ownership involves some cost). In this way, car ownership conveys advantages in shopping, allowing access to lower prices at more distant supermarkets, and the possibility of bulk-buying (see section 4.8 in the chapter on food and nutrition and section 8.2 in the chapter on high street goods and services). Job-seeking is facilitated by car ownership, both for attending interviews and in terms of the job opportunities that can be considered, due to constraints on the journey to work. In addition to the economic advantages of car ownership, there are factors of comfort, convenience and flexibility involved in car ownership from which non-car households do not benefit.

(b) Public transport use

Use of public transport, particularly buses, is also clearly related to car ownership and income. People in households without cars in Britain make about twice as many bus journeys per week (3.1) as even non-drivers in car-owning households (1.6)[27]. People in households headed by semi-skilled or non-skilled manual workers make about twice as many bus trips per week (2.2) as those in households headed by managers and professional workers (1.0 bus trip per week)[28].

Rail travel in Britain tends not to be used by lower income groups as their alternative to car use; it is bus use rather than train use which increases with decreasing income, as shown in Table 7.2. This is probably due to the interaction between several factors, including the lower cost of bus travel, the longer journey to work often undertaken by higher income groups, and the greater car availability among higher income groups, which improves their access to rail services.

Walking also increases in importance for low income households. About half of all trips made by members of households with annual incomes of under £6,000 were on foot.

The other important point to note from Table 7.2 is the much lower overall mobility of low income households. The trip rate in the richest households (83 per week) is over four times greater than in the poorest households (18 per week). This is partly accounted for by the tendency for households in the lower income bands to include unemployed and retired people with no daily journey to work, but the difference in trip rates is much greater than this factor can explain.

It is clear that the low mobility levels of low income households result not only from low car ownership rates, but also because such households do not make up their mobility levels by using other means of travel such as public transport. In part this

Table 7.2 Percentage of journeys by different modes according to annual household income

Income (£000)	Under 3	3-6	6-10	10-12	12-15	15-20	20-25	Over 25	Total %
Walk	58	48	39	34	30	27	24	21	35
Bicycle	2	2	3	3	3	2	2	2	2
M/cycle	-	-	1	1	1	1	1	1	1
Car driver	8	18	26	30	33	37	40	44	29
Car passenger	11	15	17	20	21	22	21	21	19
Local bus	17	13	8	7	5	5	5	3	8
Train	1	1	1	1	2	2	3	4	2
Other	3	4	5	4	5	4	4	4	4
Note: percentages are rounded up									
Journeys per household per week	18	36	54	63	67	71	77	83	(av. 59)

Note: Income bands are at 1985/86 price levels.
Source: *National Travel Survey, 1985/86 Report Part 1; an analysis of personal travel*, HMSO, 1988 and S. Potter and P. Hughes, *Vital Travel Statistics*, Transport 2000, 1990.

may be because public transport is less convenient than the car, and in some areas and times of the day may not be available at all. But low income households also have less to spend on public transport. This is clear from Family Expenditure Survey data for Scotland in 1990.

Sixty per cent of households with a gross weekly income of less than £200 spend less than £1 per week on bus fares; yet, as already noted, 75% of households in this income group have no car. In other words, most of these households are not substituting public transport for the cars they do not have. In contrast, 34% of households with a gross weekly income of £300 or more spend more than £1 per week on bus fares, and 12% spend more than £5 per week on bus fares. This appears to confirm that the 15% of these households which do not own a car are able to increase their mobility by the use of public transport, unlike the households in the lower income groups.

A spending level of £1 or less per week on bus fares, as found in the lower income groups, represents a very low level of mobility, probably amounting to no more than one adult return trip per week at standard fares. For those living on peripheral estates or in rural areas, with few facilities within walking distance, mobility which is constrained to this extent strongly suggests a restricted quality of life. In view of this, the significance of discounted and concessionary fares in improving the mobility of low income consumers can be seen.

(c) Discounted and concessionary fares

A wide variety of discounted and concessionary fares for travel by consumers in Scotland is available. These are of particular significance to low income consumers, and are considered below.

Discounted rail and long distance bus fares are available to specific groups, which include many low income consumers. British Rail offer Railcards as follows:

Young Persons: age 16-23 plus students. Cost £16. One-third off most tickets.
Family: 1 to 4 adults aged 18 or over, plus 1 to 4 children under 16. Cost £20. For adults, one-quarter off Savers and Supersavers; one-third off most other tickets; children pay £1.
Senior: age 60 or over. Cost £16. One-third off most tickets.

As an example of the effect of these discounts, a Supersaver Aberdeen-Glasgow return ticket (excluding Friday travel) costs £32. With a Young Persons or Senior Railcard the fare would be £21.34. With a Family Railcard two adults and two children could travel for £50.

Long-distance bus operators such as Caledonian Express and Scottish Citylink offer discount cards for similar sections of the market. The cards cost £5 and give discounts of around one-third. A return journey Aberdeen-Glasgow (excluding Friday travel) normally costs £13.70 (Citylink) or £13.75 (Caledonian). With discounts, these fares are reduced to £9.13 and £9.75 respectively, while two adults and two children could travel by Citylink for under £23, or around half the cost of the equivalent rail journey.

The main problem with discounted fares requiring card purchase is that low income consumers are less likely to be able to take advantage of them because of the initial outlay involved and, for some groups such as the elderly, the possible difficulties of obtaining information. In contrast, concessionary fares do not have this drawback.

Concessionary fares for bus and rail travel are available for pensioners and disabled people through schemes designed and funded by the Regional and Islands Councils. Details are given in Table 7.3. (Note that concessions also apply to inter-Regional travel.)

There are variations in the concessions available, ranging from free travel to half fare, though the severely disabled are entitled to free travel in almost all Regions. Clearly these concessions are of great benefit to significant groups of low income consumers. Even greater benefit could be obtained by extension of the schemes to other groups such as the unemployed, where ability to travel in search of work is important. However, there would be a considerable cost attached to this type of extension.

Selective concessions are also available on some of the air and ferry services which are of particular significance in parts of western and northern Scotland. For example, on Aberdeen-Orkney/Shetland services, P & O Ferries give 10% discount off the full return fare to pensioners not resident on the islands and a further reduction for

TRANSPORT

Table 7.3 Concessionary travel

Cost of travel to concession holders:

	OAPs (non-disabled)		Disabled		Severely disabled		
	Bus	Rail	Bus	Rail	Bus	Rail	
Borders	Half	$	Half	$	–	–	$
Central	Quarter	Quarter	Quarter	Quarter	Free	Quarter	½ RC
D & G	Free	½ RC	Free	½ RC	–	–	Free off
Fife	Free off	Free 20	Free off	Free 20	–	–	Free 20
Grampian	Fifth	Fifth	Fifth	Fifth	Free	Free	#
Highland	Half	Half	Half	Half	Free	Free	
Lothian	30p max	30p	30p max	30p	Free	Free	
Strathclyde#	25p	25p/½	25p	25p/½	Free	Free	~
Tayside~	15p/¼	15p/¼	Free~	Free~	Free	Free	
W Isles@	Half	–	Half	–	Half	–	@
Shetland@	Free	–	Free	–	Free	–	
Orkney**	–	–	–	–	–	–	**

Notes * Those Regions which give severely disabled people a different benefit define them as follows:

Central Registered blind, deaf without speech, mentally handicapped or severely and permanently mentally ill (moderate or temporary get quarter fare) - all to be aged 16 or over. Main reason for free bus travel is to assist ease and speed of boarding.
Grampian Registered blind people.
Highland Registered blind people.
Lothian Registered blind or partially sighted people. No free travel on night buses.
Strathclyde Registered blind people.
Tayside Registered blind people.

$ Borders has no railway stations, hence no scheme.

½ RC Dumfries & Galloway offer BR Senior Citizens and Disabled Persons Railcards for sale at stations at half price.

Free off Fife give free off peak travel, half fare in peak. Includes companions. Peak is before 0900 and between 1530 and 1800 Monday to Friday.

Free 20 Fife give vouchers for 20 single journeys each year, half fare thereafter. Free travel includes companions.

Strathclyde give OAPs and (non severely) disabled people 25p flat fare travel until beyond about 10 miles, or to particular shopping centres; balance of fare thereafter on buses, half fare on trains (between two stations in Strathclyde); except in a.m. peak.

~ Tayside give OAPs 15p flat fare travel for fares up to and including 75p, quarter fare thereafter. Disabled people receive free travel except for those who can undertake full time employment who are restricted to the same benefit as OAPs (except that blind people can work and have free travel).

@ Concession also applies to inter-island ferries and air services. (Western Isles also provide one half-fare ferry trip to mainland per year).

** Assistance is applied through subsidy of bus and ferry services. In addition, residents of outer islands receive concessionary inter-island air travel.

Source: Draft Report, June 1992, courtesy of Association of Transport Coordinating Officers (Scotland), and personal communications. Note that the information given above is a summary and does not specify all conditions, exemptions, etc.

students. Orkney and Shetland residents also receive a discount, paying £66.50 and £93.70 respectively for the return journey. Pensioners and disabled people resident in Orkney or Shetland pay 30% of the full fare.

On their Ullapool-Stornoway route, Caledonian MacBrayne offer bulk-purchase discounts; whereas a full-price return costs £47.70, three return tickets purchased at once cost £38.65 each. This benefits Lewis residents, though it does require the expenditure of £115.95, which may well be difficult for people on low incomes.

Loganair have a 50% discount for pensioners, a condition being that the booking can only be made on the day before travel. The same airline offers students various discounts, depending on the route and the availability of seats.

British Airways offer Apex fares, the conditions for which are that the ticket must be booked at least 14 days in advance, and the passenger must stay over a Saturday night. Examples of the large discounts available are as follows:-

Glasgow-Inverness	Full return -	£134
	Apex return -	£79
Glasgow-Stornoway	Full return -	£192
	Apex return -	£114
Aberdeen-Shetland	Full return -	£208
	Apex return -	£124

(d) Summary—car ownership and public transport use

Car ownership in Scotland is strongly related to income, and ownership rates in low income households are very low. Moreover, the members of low income households do not fully substitute public transport for car use. As a result, their mobility levels are severely constrained, even when account is taken of the presence in low income households of retired and unemployed people who are not making a daily journey to work. Discounted fares requiring advance card purchase are not well-suited to low income consumers because of the initial outlay involved. The concessionary fares schemes operated by Regional Councils are of great significance in offering increased mobility for low income consumers, provided they fall into the eligible categories.

7.5 Conclusions

Low incomes constrain mobility to a very significant degree. This is a consequence of disposable income structures but it can be emphasised by geographical location, as, for example, in peripheral housing schemes or in rural areas. The main ways in which low income constrains mobility are through low rates of car ownership among low income consumers, and their inability to make up completely their mobility levels by substituting public transport use for car use, due to cost, inconvenience and, in some cases, unavailability.

Car ownership, where it exists among low income consumers, confers benefits which include the ability to reach a wider range of retail opportunities and cheaper prices. Taxation policy on fuel prices is likely to have significant impacts on low income car owners, particularly in rural areas.

Bus travel is an important means of mobility for low income consumers. The frequent changes in services which have resulted in some areas since deregulation make it difficult for bus users to be able to plan their mobility around these services. The availability of up-to-date and accurate information is of key importance to bus users and, although local authorities and bus operators try to provide this, there still appear to be difficulties.

It seems likely that future trends in bus fares will be upwards in relation to inflation, and this would affect low income consumers in particular. Also, proposals for rail privatisation appear likely to lead to upward pressure on fares, while concessionary fares are not guaranteed to continue. Such trends would affect low income consumers especially.

Concessionary fares schemes operated by local authorities are of great significance in assisting groups of low income consumers, and particularly pensioners and disabled people, to maintain their mobility levels. Since they are targeted at specific groups they are an effective way of structuring support for these groups.

Unless there are significant policy changes, the upward trend in car ownership in the UK is generally expected to continue over the next two decades, and to level out at about 30 million cars, 50% more than the present figure. While there will be a gradual increase in car ownership in the lower income groups, most of the growth is expected to occur through multiple car ownership in more affluent households. Moreover, the downward trend in the bus passenger market seems likely to continue, partly as a result of increased car ownership. Low income consumers, whose mobility is heavily dependent on bus use, may therefore experience increasing difficulty as bus services contract in the face of a declining market.

However, there are signs that policy shifts may occur as a result of the current debate about urban congestion, environmental impact and car use. If this happens, and the supply of public transport in urban areas, at least, is improved, this offers a more positive future for low income consumers in the medium to long term. It should not be forgotten, however, that the main constraint on the use of public transport by low income consumers is disposable income rather than the availability of services: public transport has to be affordable, as well as available.

References to Chapter 7

1. Central Statistical Office, *Family Spending: A Report on the 1990 Family Expenditure Survey,* HMSO, 1991.
2. Central Statistical Office, *General Household Survey,* 1990, HMSO, 1991.
3. Central Statistical Office, *Family Expenditure Survey 1990 - Scottish Data,* ESRC Data Archive, Essex, 1993.
4. Central Statistical Office, *General Household Survey 1990 - Scottish Data,* ESRC Data Archive, Essex 1993.
5. Strathclyde Passenger Transport Executive, *Annual Report and Accounts 1991-92,* 1992.
6. Strathclyde Passenger Transport Executive, see reference 5.
7. British Rail, *Passenger's Charter,* British Rail, 1992.
8. P. Bell and P. Cloke, *Deregulation and Transport,* Fulton, 1990, p.36.
9. Strathclyde Passenger Transport Executive, *Bus Service Provision in Strathclyde Four Years after Deregulation,* SPTE 1991, p.12.
10. Scottish Transport Statistics 1990/91, The Scottish Office, 1992, Table 2.7.
11. G.A. Mackay and J.H. Farrington, *Bus Deregulation Monitoring Study,* Report No. 1, Scottish Consumer Council, 1986.
12. G.A. Mackay and J.H. Farrington, *Bus Deregulation Monitoring Study,* Report No. 2, Scottish Consumer Council, 1987.
13. Strathclyde Passenger Transport Executive, see reference 9.

14. Strathclyde Passenger Transport Executive, see reference 9, p.6.
15. Strathclyde Passenger Transport Executive, see reference 9, p.7.
16. Strathclyde Passenger Transport Executive, see reference 9, p.1.
17. *The Independent,* 3 February, 1993, 'Tory MPs fear higher fares and poor services'.
18. Mackay Consultants, *Rural Scotland Price Survey,* Winter 1992/93 Mackay Consultants, Inverness, 1993.
19. Central Statistical Office, see reference 1.
20. General Register Office for Scotland - 1991 *Census Reports for:* Grampian, Highland, Tayside and Strathclyde Regions, Part 1, Table 21, HMSO, 1993.
21. Central Statistical Office, see reference 2.
22. M.J. Moseley, *Accessibility - The Rural Challenge,* Methuen, 1979.
23. J.H. Farrington, J.B. Sewel and D.W. Summers, *Public Transport and Travel in Speyside,* Grampian Regional Council, 1986.
24. J.H. Farrington, J.B. Sewel and D.W. Summers, *Public Transport and Travel in Mid- Buchan,* Grampian Regional Council, 1986.
25. J.H. Farrington, J.B. Sewel and D.W. Summers, *Public Transport and Travel in The Mearns,* Grampian Regional Council, 1986.
26. S. Potter and P. Hughes, *Vital Travel Statistics,* Transport 2000, 1990, pp. 17-19.
27. *National Travel Survey: 1985/86 Report Part 1; an analysis of personal travel,* HMSO, 1988, Table 7.4.
28. *National Travel Survey,* see reference 27, Table 7.9.

8 High Street Goods and Services

by Keri Davies and Mark Gabbott

Using high street services such as hairdressers or launderettes and buying high street goods such as clothes and furniture are part of everyday life. In many cases the prices paid by those on low incomes for these goods and services are not disproportionately high. But those with little money to spend may not be able to benefit from bulk-buying, forward-buying or special offers. Keri Davies and Mark Gabbott show that those on low incomes experience disadvantage as a result of poor access to high street goods and services chiefly because these shops and services are not located where they live. City centre and out-of-town sites are only convenient for those with cars or access to a good public transport system. Problems of access are not easily overcome and improving public transport services may be more effective in addressing disadvantage than relocation of shopping centres.

8.1 Introduction

Original research conducted in New York by Caplowitz in 1963 identified a number of factors which suggested that consumers on low incomes were 'paying' more for the goods and services they received[1]. (Paying in this work included both monetary and non-monetary considerations.) Caplowitz argued that low income consumers were forced to the margin of the economy through such mechanisms as high risk/high price credit, local brokers and the use of retail outlets where bartering and other forms of deferred credit were acceptable.

An effort to address consumer detriment across a wide range of consumer services in the United Kingdom by the National Consumer Council in 1977 argued that similar mechanisms were likely to operate here[2]. In the last 16 years, however, apparent changes to the modern UK economy and in particular the distribution of goods and services within it have made the issues facing low income consumers more complex. The argument is no longer simply one of access to the market in the sense that low income groups do participate in the mainstream economy, but the debate has moved on to consider the characteristics of that participation. The purpose of this chapter is first to define the problem and to assess the basis of the argument that consumers of high street goods and services face detriment. It then go on to consider problems of access to the market, price-quality and price-volume relationships, and the constraints upon consumers' access to market information. At present there is little published material which examines the situation of low income consumers and little empirical evidence on the issue. As a consequence, this review will draw on published secondary data as well as more mainstream material from the retail and marketing disciplines.

High street goods and services include all goods and services available for sale to individual private consumers which are not food or food derived—such as hairdressing, clothing, furniture and electrical goods. This is a wide definition and clearly there are particular problems associated with certain product and service categories. As a first stage, it is necessary to review briefly the characteristics of low income consumers of goods and services and of the sources of supply of these products. Following this, the main arguments which have been used to support the contention of consumer detriment for low income consumers are considered.

8.2 The Low Income Consumer of Goods and Services

It is difficult to define the exact size of the low income group and the characteristics of the consumers of whom it is composed (see sections 1.3 and 1.4 in the introductory chapter). Relative to the rest of the UK, Scotland has, however, a higher proportion of low income households (see Table 1.2 in the introductory chapter).

Low income households have specific social characteristics. Most consist of a single adult and the largest group is made up of single retired pensioners. In 1990, for example, one-quarter of all the recipients of regular weekly grants of income support in Scotland were over 70 years of age[3]. However, there is also a sizeable number of non-retired households in the under-£100 income group, including single parent families with one or more children. Between 1980 and 1990 the number of single parent families in Scotland receiving benefit almost doubled from 44,000 to 82,000, even though the overall population of the country declined[4]. It is a combination of income, family structure, employment and age rather than income alone, therefore, which leads to the low income consumer being characterised as having a low level of mobility and restricted purchasing patterns.

One of the major problems is how to define 'disadvantage'. There are two general classifications of disadvantaged consumers which can be identified. First, there are disadvantages which stem from the economic circumstances of certain groups, which include low income, residential area and a lack of access to private transport. These would be associated generally with the term 'low income consumers'. However, there are other disadvantages which are also strongly, if not uniquely, associated with the low income group. These are disadvantages associated with age, physical or mental disability and special responsibilities, such as for young children, and elderly or dependent relatives. It is not possible to separate these two general classes of disadvantaged consumers in a consideration of the effects of low income since many of the latter group are also members of the former group.

The definition of household goods and services described above in section 8.1 includes a number of the expenditure categories used in the Family Expenditure Survey[5]. Using a combination of classifications we can estimate that households which represent the lowest 20% of gross weekly income (an average gross weekly income of under £100) spent approximately £22 per week on household goods and services compared to an average figure for all households of £71 (on an average weekly income of £300). It could be anticipated that actual weekly expenditure across the range would be less for low income groups but there is some evidence that the low income groups spend a greater proportion of their income on household and personal goods and services, as well as leisure services, than upper income groups.

We can elaborate on these figures in a number of ways. First, income levels and expenditure also tend to vary from area to area. Estimates of consumer expenditure on comparison goods by Lothian Regional Council for the mid-1980s show this trend even at a local authority level (Table 8.1). Within this pattern there are likely to be smaller areas, such as local authority housing estates and run-down privately rented housing, which will have higher concentrations of low income households and constrained spending on non-food items.

Table 8.1 Consumer expenditure per head on comparison goods* (£ per annum)

	1985	1986
Edinburgh	720	784
East Lothian	633	689
Midlothian	593	645
West Lothian	580	632

* Comparison goods are primarily non-food items such as clothing, shoes, furniture, etc for which consumers are prepared to shop around, comparing prices and quality in the process.

Source: Lothian Regional Council, *Shopping Needs in Lothian Region*, Department of Planning, Lothian Regional Council, 1988, p.34.

Second, if we take housing tenure to have some relationship to income, then government statistics for Scotland show that households with forms of tenure associated with low income, such as housing rented from local authorities, have lower levels of ownership of the major consumer durable goods (Table 8.2). (A similar relationship is found if we compare households with economically active and inactive heads of household[6]). Even in those categories where ownership levels are relatively high, it can be argued that low income households will be the slowest adopters of many products. In a variation on Townsend's argument for the existence of 'relative poverty', the pressures experienced by all consumers from such sources as children, peer groups or advertising may weigh particularly on low income consumers[7]. For example, the pressure from children to possess goods such as a television, video recorder or games console may push a single parent family even further into debt or into using poor quality goods.

Finally, there is one other major consumer durable whose ownership both reflects income levels and affects the purchase of other goods and services: the motor car (see section 7.4a in the chapter on transport). Car ownership levels in Scotland, and particularly parts of Strathclyde, have long been among the lowest in the UK. While the number of households in Scotland without a motor car dropped between 1981 and 1991, the differences between Scotland and the rest of the UK have stayed constant[8]. (In 1991 half of households in Strathclyde were without a car and in Glasgow City that figure rose to two-thirds)[9]. Yet again, however, the picture is quite complex. For example, the 1991 Census of Population shows that whilst the number of single pensioner households has risen in all parts of Scotland since 1981 (standing between 14% and 18% of all households in most regions), the percentage of pensioner households without a car has fallen over the same period[10]. So, not only is it dangerous to see more pensioner households as automatically leading to lower mobility levels overall, but the figures also show that pensioner households in rural areas tend to have higher car ownership levels than those in urban areas, which are presumed to have better public transport networks.

Table 8.2 Scottish households with consumer durables by tenure, 1983 and 1990

Percentage with:	Owner occupied		Rented privately or from a housing association		Rented from local authority, new town or Scottish Homes	
	1983	1990	1983	1990	1983	1990
TV	89	97	68	91	77	91
Telephone	87	97	69	78	65	70
Washing machine	90	96	71	75	84	85
Deep freezer	66	86	50	60	38	62
Video	20	73	14	51	16	51
Tumble Drier	36	59	26	36	23	36
Microwave oven	–	57	–	43	–	28
Home computer	–	23	–	13	–	11
Dish washer	7	17	4	8	0	1

– not collected

Source: Scottish Office, *Scottish Abstract of Statistics 1991*, The Scottish Office, 1992, p.131; and The Scottish Office, *Scottish Abstract of Statistics 1992*, The Scottish Office, 1993, p.141.

Nonetheless, one recent study has gone so far as to suggest that "the carless shopper appears largely by-passed by the retail revolution"[11]. It is worth quoting at length from its conclusions of a study of disadvantage in Swansea.

"Car ownership emerged as by far the most important differentiator of shopping behaviour patterns in the study area. However, behavioural variations independent of mobility considerations were demonstrated to be related to area of residence and to age, but not to socio-economic status differentials. A distance decay effect associated with area of residence was reflected in terms of the particular convenience shopping destination rather than in the type of outlet patronized for both mobility groups. Similarly, elderly respondents tended to display significantly more constrained patterns of shopping behaviour than their younger counterparts. *For differences in socio-economic status, however, the behavioural variations noted appear simply to reflect mobility considerations.*

"Clearly, limited disposable income is the critical contextual determinant of the shopping behaviour patterns of the majority of disadvantaged consumers. The Swansea survey shows that the lack of a car is disproportionately associated with characteristics of social disadvantage, such as unemployment, old age,

lower levels of home-ownership and single parent families. However, it does not necessarily follow that the carless shopper is a disadvantaged consumer...Because they are making such limited use of the new shopping facilities, carless households seem to have failed to benefit from the retail revolution. However, although the less mobile shopper makes greater use of the more traditional and localized facilities, it is unclear whether this always constitutes disadvantage in terms of travel, finance, available shopping opportunities, or perceived life circumstances. The evidence, both from the research reported here and from that in other studies, is inconclusive"[12].
(sentence in italics: our emphasis)

So, low income consumers are less likely to own a car and this will affect their shopping behaviour, but it is difficult to say whether they are truly disadvantaged as a result. The simple examination of income and expenditure on high street goods and services tells us something about low income consumers and the choices which they face, but it does not characterise the detriment faced by these groups in terms of their shopping behaviour. In order to begin our discussion of this specific issue, we need first to outline the nature of the retail system which consumers face in the early 1990s.

8.3 The Provision of High Street Goods and Services in Scotland

In the quarter of a century since Caplowitz first raised his concerns about the consumption opportunities accorded to the poor, the retail scene in the UK has changed markedly. Dawson and Broadbridge have pointed to a number of major areas of change in Scotland, including:

- a decline in the number of retail businesses and in the number of retail establishments;
- an increase in the market share of the larger firms;
- operational changes;
- consumer changes;
- locational trends[13].

We shall consider each of these in turn.

(a) A decline in the number of retail businesses and in the number of retail establishments

Table 8.3 shows that the number of shops selling non-food products has declined quite sharply since 1961, although the rate of decline slowed during the 1980s. This has come about, in part, because of the redevelopment of many town and city centres, but mainly because of a decline in the number and status of small, independent shops and a lower level of growth in the number of shops run by large, multiple chains, including mixed retail businesses.

(b) An increase in the market share of the larger firms

As the multiple chains get bigger, so they are coming to dominate the markets in which they operate. There are no comparable figures for Scotland but statistics for the whole of Britain show that in 1988 the largest ten enterprises accounted for 49.5% of clothing and footwear sales, 29% of household goods sales and 32% of the sales of

Table 8.3 Retailing in Scotland—estimates of shop numbers

	1961	1971	1980	1986	1991
Food retailers	24,000	18,400	11,300	8,300	7,300
Drink, confectionery and tobacco	8,500	5,500	4,800	4,600	4,400
Clothing, footwear	8,200	7,400	4,700	3,900	4,000
Household goods	4,600	5,300	4,500	3,400	3,200
Other non-food	5,100	5,200	3,000	3,600	3,800
Mixed retail businesses	400	600	1,200	1,500	1,400
TOTAL	50,800	42,400	29,500	25,300	24,100

Source: J.A. Dawson and A. Broadbridge, *Retailing in Scotland 2005*, Institute for Retail Studies, Stirling, 1988.

other non-food goods[14]. The growth of such a concentration of market power has been a controversial issue. Some commentators have argued that as they get bigger, so the large firms have been instrumental in distributing new and innovative products and in keeping down prices through their economies of scale and their improved ability to put pressure on manufacturers. Others have claimed that they have reached near monopoly positions in some market sectors, such as DIY products, and that lacking clear reference points to provide a basis for comparison consumers are being duped into paying more than they need to for products.

There is some evidence provided by the Retail Price Index that large, multiple retailers may have kept prices down in recent years. (The Retail Price Index allows comparison between sectors by restating the actual price in each sector in the first year of any comparison—*the base year*—as 100 and then showing the relative increases or decreases in later years.) The Index shows that between 1987 and 1991 prices rose from a base of 100 (1987) to 117.7 for leisure goods, 118.5 for clothing and footwear, 122.5 for household goods and services, 129.5 for household services and 133.4 for personal goods and services. At a time of inflationary pressures, these price performances were markedly lower than those for housing (160.8), catering (139), alcohol (139) and leisure services (138.8)[15]. For example, Mintel report that:

> "It is clear that price cutting by multiple retailers has kept the retail value of the [toy] market down, even when consumer spending in general was advancing rapidly. This squeezing of margins must have damaged smaller retailers which depend on all year round sales, and, in fact, may have forced some of the larger chains to go into liquidation over the last couple of years"[16].

(c) Operational changes

Retailing during the 1980s saw a polarisation in many sectors into chains of large stores and chains of small stores, each targeted at specific consumer groups and needs. Large stores, often located either on out-of-town or edge-of-town sites—for example,

Asda, B&Q and MFI—offered consumers one-stop shopping and the benefits of economies of scale; chains of small stores—such as Next, Dixons and Radio Rentals—were used to target very precisely small customer groups or market niches. Both formats had the benefits of being part of large chains with their purchasing power and professional management. During the 1980s there was a tendency for many of these chains—for example, MFI and Radio Rentals —to trade up or go 'up-market' in terms of the products and services that they were offering. So, there was a greater focus on 'value for money' and product quality relative to competitors rather than an over-emphasis on price. Nonetheless, discount stores such as What Everyone Wants and Poundstretcher have also been built up during the same period and charities such as Oxfam run some of the largest chains of shops in the country.

(d) Consumer changes

It is argued that many of the changes in retailing in Scotland have reflected changes in the way in which Scottish consumers approach retailing. Shopping activities can be divided on the basis of how much time they take up, so that essential or convenience shopping will be undertaken so as to minimise the amount of time involved, whereas there has also been an increase in leisure (or fun) shopping, which takes longer and where the surroundings are as important as the task at hand. Commentators have pointed to the paradox that those consumers who are 'time rich', such as the elderly and the unemployed, are not in a position to make full use of such facilities due to their low incomes; whereas those consumers at whom such facilities are directed may be 'time poor' and able to use them only at weekends.

Non-store or forms of home shopping such as mail order catalogues have declined slightly in importance during the 1980s, from 3.4% of total retail sales in 1983 to 2.6% in 1992[17]. They are likely to remain important, however, for those in rural areas or those with low mobility who cannot get to a choice of shops[18]. Catalogues can also offer the advantages to low income consumers of being able to try out and return goods without any obligation and of being able to pay in instalments, giving an easily available, if expensive, form of credit. The cost of this convenience is higher prices than those generally available on the high street.

(e) Locational trends

As a result of both the trends within the structure of retailing itself and the consumer changes, the location of many forms of retailing has shifted too. Leisure shopping has been provided for in town centres and in new, purpose built shopping centres, sometimes within existing centres, as with the St Enoch Centre or Princes Square in Glasgow city centre, or out-of-town, as at South Gyle in Edinburgh. Similarly, non-food superstores have provided comparable convenience but only for those who can reach them.

To summarise, then, recent changes to retailing in Scotland have brought significant benefits to consumers. These have been identified as increased choice, better retail environments and improved quality of merchandise. However, most of these benefits have been concentrated upon consumers who have two main attributes: they are affluent, in the sense that they have a significant disposable income, and they are mobile, usually owning a car. As a consequence, the pattern of retail development in Scotland has tended to be steered towards these sections of the community. For instance, site location has been driven by good access from major trunk road networks and proximity to affluent residential areas.

This has meant that residential areas which are local authority owned, and hence likely to be less affluent in general than owner occupied areas, have been neglected in terms of modern retail development. The result is that the more prosperous areas or those with particularly good road access, such as Corstorphine in Edinburgh or Newton Mearns in Glasgow, benefit fully from better shopping facilities and increased competition, whereas other areas, such as Craigmillar in Edinburgh, may be starved of development through a decline in new investment as well as experiencing loss of shopping provision due to the impact of alternative shopping facilities arising elsewhere. This situation can lead to a cycle of decline where consumers in the areas with lower mobility either through poor road access, the lack of access to public transport or the lack of access to private cars, become 'trapped' consumers. The shops they have access to are characterised by declining investment, monopoly pricing, a limited range of merchandise and poor quality goods. The provision of shopping facilities and the location of development and investment can, to an extent, be tackled using planning controls to prevent the cycle of decline but this only affects the location of shopping provision; it does not change the lack of real choice or access to information.

8.4 Problems of Access to the Market

Agencies involved with the control of retailing, land-use planning authorities in particular, have been most concerned to ensure that all sections of the community have access to competitive retail facilities. Consider the following statement from the Planning Department of Glasgow District Council which is very clear in its view that retail change has disadvantaged certain groups in society.

> "Although recent changes in retailing have brought many benefits, less fortunate shoppers, especially those without access to private transport, have faced increasing disadvantage. In their case, the 'retail revolution' has largely passed by, and the loss of traditional outlets has been particularly felt. An important function of retail planning is to seek to redress this type of imbalance and to ensure that all shoppers have access to an adequate range of modern retail facilities"[19].

It has already been noted that the types of location favoured by retailers operating in Scotland have changed. Planning policies have attempted to strengthen town and city centres, whilst certain types of non-food retailers have been concerned to develop large stores (sometimes called retail warehouses) in out-of-town or off-centre locations. It has also been noted that many of these companies aim to provide a package or retail environment which includes not just price but also product quality and availability, location, store design and staff development. The public perception of retail warehouses is that they offer very low prices but because of the costs of providing this environment the prices may not be as low as companies claim. On the other hand, it can be argued that the 'good old days' were not quite as they have been portrayed. The presence of many small shops did not necessarily lead to competition but perhaps to inefficient retailing with higher overall price levels, low product quality and expensive credit.

It is surprising that given the emphasis among planning departments and other agencies towards alleviating the disadvantages suffered by those on low pay, the elderly and people with disabilities, so little work should have been done to study the problem. Too often, documents and plans carry platitudes which, whilst they may be justifiable in terms of food shopping and some services, are translated into broadly based statements which are not necessarily related to other forms of retailing.

Studies which have been conducted, including those on shopping for food and non-food items, show that lower income consumers tend to choose stores that are closer to their homes, and that higher income consumers tend to select stores that are close to other stores which they wish to use, either in town centres or shopping centres[20]. Closeness to home may be related here to the mobility of the low income consumer and much will depend upon where such consumers live. In parts of rural Scotland, where choice is less and population density insufficient to attract large retailers, consumers from all income groups are still paying 2½% more on average for high street goods and services than in a large city and their choices are reduced too[21]. Only some highly mobile consumers will be able and willing to travel to the larger towns and cities on a regular basis for their shopping, although it is possible to substitute mail order and other non-store forms of shopping for local sources of supply of many non-food items[22]. On the other hand, residents in the Gorbals area of Glasgow have access to a wide range of shops in Glasgow city centre. For example, almost three-quarters of the clothing needs of Gorbals residents is met by shops in the city centre, with a further 14% taken by mail order where the choice of products may be different and where credit availability is also important[23].

However, studies such as those by Lloyd and Jennings also imply that low income consumers may differ from higher income groups in that they have fewer proposed outcomes (usually purchases) from each shopping trip and a smaller or restricted network of places to shop[24]. This would accord very well with the theoretical discussion on the relationship between poverty and consumption advanced by Douglas and Isherwood, according to which the poor lose out because of their restricted access to information (considered in detail below) and because they have a narrower set of objectives[25]. They are more likely to make a shopping trip for just one specified item and less likely to enter shops unless they have a specific purchase in mind. This latter point is borne out by recent research for the National Consumer Council which shows that in Scotland respondents were far less likely to visit non-food shops without actually making a purchase if they belonged to households with low incomes, were pensioners, were lower social class or were from households with children[26].

8.5 Price-Quality and Price-Volume Relationships

The theoretical arguments concerning general consumer disadvantage associated with low incomes are based upon observation of shopping behaviour and assumptions about the relationships between the price of a product and other product characteristics, in particular:

- the existence of a relationship between the price and the quality of a product i.e. that as price increases, so does quality;
- the existence of a relationship between the price and volume of a product which is bought i.e. that the larger the volume bought, the cheaper the price per unit bought.

(a) The price-quality relationship

Consumers categorise brands and products in many different ways, one of which is the quality of the product. In itself, quality is difficult to define but we can consider quality to be an assessment of the intrinsic value of the product. In some circumstances the consumer may not be in a position to assess the quality of the product, especially if it is packaged, technically complex, or is a product with which they have little previous experience. This is frequently the case in the purchase of large household products such as furniture, carpets or electronic goods and is especially true of services where the intangibility of the product makes pre-purchase inspection impossible. In these circumstances consumers have to use other product attributes in order to assess quality, such as the brand name or country of origin or, more commonly, the price of the product, where a high price is assumed to indicate high quality.

The presumption underlying the relationship is that if product X costs more than product Y, then product X must be of a better quality, all other things being equal. The argument assumes that the relationship is linear—that is, that increments in price are reflected in increments in real product quality. This is represented by the line marked *a* in Figure 8.1. If this relationship exists then low income consumers have access only at the lower quality end of a particular market offering. This situation simply describes a market with a range of quality offerings; for higher quality you need to pay a higher price. In this sense lower income consumers are indeed at a disadvantage but only because they do not have more money.

Figure 8.1 The price-quality relationship

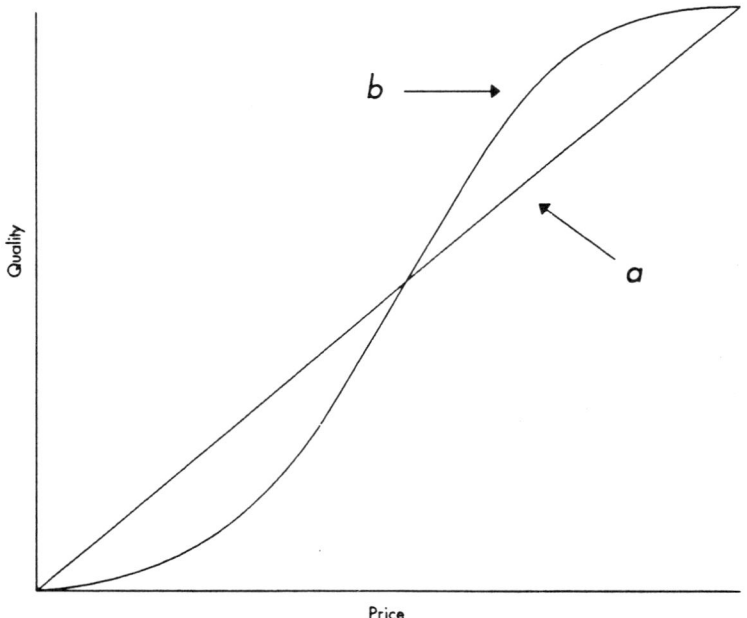

However, it is also possible for quality to degrade much more quickly at lower prices. That is, the relationship may be curvilinear, where quality increases disproportionately or in the opposite direction to price, as in shown by the line marked *b* in Figure 8.1. This would describe a situation where low income consumers are paying higher prices for goods and services expecting higher quality but where there is little actual increase in the quality of the product. The same could also be true of higher income consumers where the attachment of brand labels associated in some instances with higher prices do not, in fact, reflect higher quality. Measurement of this phenomenon is particularly difficult.

The views of retailers in markets such as health and personal care products are that, despite the increasing emphasis on price which has come with the current recession, the long term consumer trend is for value for money. This comes instead of the acceptance of low prices alone. Multiple retailers have used their size to dictate prices to their suppliers and have, in general, passed such savings on to consumers[27].

(b) The price-volume relationship

In most purchases it is possible to gain discount for buying greater volume; for example, the difference between buying two 250 ml bottles of shampoo and one 500 ml bottle of shampoo can be quite large. This relationship is most appropriate to food purchases but it is also found in terms of many high street goods and services. We can see numerous examples of short term promotional offers of the 'three for the price of two' kind in clothing, electrical accessories and household products. Low income groups may be unable to gain access to these offers since they cannot afford to forward-buy to take advantage of the offer. The price-volume relationship working against low income consumers can also be seen in many promotional offers based upon expenditure, such as 'buy £100 worth of goods and we will give you a £10 voucher towards a future purchase'. Any promotional campaign encouraging and rewarding increased expenditure is bound to discriminate against low income groups.

Part of the problem with relying upon the price-quality and price-volume relationships can be seen by looking at the issue of 'discounts'. Low income consumers can take some comfort from the fact that price is becoming a dominant issue once again in high street retailing. The economic recession of the late 1980s and early 1990s has encouraged retailers to seek higher volumes of sales by lowering prices, either through special offers or through sales, etc. However, the trend to use shop sales, discount stores and other sources of cheaper products such as charity shops and second-hand shops is not necessarily characteristic of low income groups; indeed, the tendency is most marked for the higher income groups rather than the lower income groups[28]. One could argue that an increase in the number of off-price and discount retail outlets would be of benefit to the low income consumer as much as any other consumer group. However, price reductions through discount retailers, car boot sales and public markets may still be inaccessible without access to a car. Charity shops and second-hand shops tend to be concentrated in town centres, and away from suburban and peripheral areas, again raising the issue of access. The polarisation of formal low price retail outlets into out-of-town discount centres and town centres can be viewed as a wider distribution of the retail offering but, for consumers who are restricted in travel, this process has served to emphasise their locational disadvantages. Based upon price alone, there appears to be no significant difference in shopping patterns among low income consumers; indeed, most of the recent change appears to be among middle to high income groups who are moving to off-price and discount outlets.

8.6 Access to Market Information

The final argument about consumer disadvantage concerns access to information upon which to make an informed choice. Of all the arguments this is perhaps the most contentious since 'informed choice' is a highly subjective term. In today's economy the consumer is assailed with an extremely wide number of choices in all product categories. In addition, in choosing non-food items, and especially services, consumers need information, with the emphasis on the quality of that information rather than its quantity[29]. Most consumers still use point of sale information from a combination of retail outlets, which they add to their own experience[30][31]. However, it could be argued that low income consumers are less likely to use impartial sources of pre-purchase information. This is on the basis that information from such sources is not usually free of charge (as in the case of Consumers' Association membership) or they do not know of or have access to free sources of such information, including libraries and resource centres[32]. The crux of the argument is that low income consumers are more reliant upon information provided by general media and particularly media which have no travel cost associated with them but which are marketer controlled rather than independent, such as advertising on TV and radio and the national newspapers[33]. They are also disadvantaged through being unable to 'shop around', primarily through restrictions on mobility, but also due to the constraints offered by price.

These disadvantages are also apparent in the post-purchase phase. Evidence concerning the propensity to complain about goods and services based upon income variations is misleading. On the one hand, low income groups have more investment in seeking a satisfactory solution to a complaint; yet, on the other, they have less knowledge of their legal rights. The elderly particularly are less likely to pursue complaints. However, this group through income constraint is likely to have access to poorer quality goods in most product classes and is, therefore, likely to have the highest incidence of complaint. There is some debate concerning the response of sellers to complaints at the low price/low quality end of the market. Based upon restricted shopping patterns and the importance of market stalls, second-hand shops and deep discount outlets, it has been argued that the chance of getting full redress is significantly weakened. This is due to the itinerant nature of many of the sellers, the marginal nature of many low price businesses and the absence of choice for a low income group.

8.7 Conclusions

It is clear that in some respects low income groups have been disadvantaged in recent years but that the pattern is not uniform for all groups or all areas. Retail innovation in the UK has been successful because it has responded to changing shopping needs among consumers. However, most of this change has been concerned with offering new retail formats and locations to groups of consumers who have become more affluent and more mobile. In this respect, low income groups have in the majority of cases been bypassed and are increasingly isolated through factors which are associated with their low income status, principally their lack of mobility. Equally, some groups of consumers fall into the low income group because of their age, disabilities or because they have young children. There is evidence that the needs of these groups are different from those of the mobile consumer. For instance, older people prefer traditional ways of shopping and often require to buy products in smaller quantities. All of these groups tend to seek retail provision closer to home and find travelling both difficult and expensive. These needs may not be met by current retail innovation and the result is a doubly disadvantaged group.

Lack of a car, which is not confined to poor consumers alone, is a major determinant of shopping behaviour. There is also some evidence that low income groups pay more for a number of reasons, including not being able to buy in bulk, not being able to take advantage of special offers and having to pay public transport costs if they do not possess a car.

However, this is not the whole story. First, there are problems in defining the unique needs of an amorphous and fragmented group of consumers. Second, there are problems in providing measurable dimensions of disadvantage. Third, the arguments are demonstrably weak in characterising only low income experiences. For instance, in the case of the price-quality relationship, a curvilinear relationship could be interpreted equally as evidence that high income consumers pay more as a result of excessive branding or innovative retail formats as it can be applied to low income consumers.

A number of questions must be considered in conjunction with this evidence. Accepting that the evidence is inconclusive, we can say that Scotland has a high proportion of consumers who display low income characteristics. However, the case for real disadvantage appears to be more closely associated with access rather than any structural imperfection in the market which is price and income driven. The issue here is a distinction between relative disadvantage (a position in which one group is worse off than another) and absolute disadvantage (an ideal versus reality). It is suggested here that characterising the low income group as relatively disadvantaged is more persuasive than any argument for absolute disadvantage and that questions of access, mobility and geography provide a basis for understanding the experiences of low income consumers in Scotland. The land-use planning system in Scotland has been the prime proponent of the access approach but it is not clear that it has actually been successful, even in its own terms. Dawson and Broadbridge, for example, have argued that other forms of intervention may be preferable.

"Even if, however, there is a need for public policy support for these groups, the mechanisms for such support are not necessarily clear. For instance, specific supports, through the social service system, directly to these groups of consumers may be preferable to the use of planning controls on new developments which, while they help to protect these groups, disadvantage the mass market of consumers"[34].

However, it should also be clear that even this approach is likely to founder on the difficulties of defining the group of low income consumers who are likely to be disadvantaged when shopping for high street goods and services. The diversity of the target group and the diversity of the industry with which they are faced is likely to make any attempt at a blanket approach unworkable and unwise.

References to Chapter 8

1. D. Caplowitz, *The Poor Pay More*, The Free Press of Glencoe, 1963.
2. National Consumer Council, *Why The Poor Pay More*, MacMillan, 1977.
3. Scottish Office, *Scottish Abstract of Statistics 1991*, The Scottish Office, 1992, p.19.
4. Scottish Office, see reference 3, p.17.
5. Central Statistical Office, *Family Spending: A Report on the 1991 Family Expenditure Survey*, HMSO, 1992.
6. Central Statistical Office, *Social Trends* No. 23, HMSO, 1991, p.83.
7. P. Townsend, *Poverty in the United Kingdom*, Allen Lane, 1979.
8. Central Statistical Office, *Regional Trends* No. 27, HMSO, 1992 and *Regional Trends* No.28, HMSO, 1993.

9. General Register Office Scotland *1991 Census. Report for Scotland Part 1,* Vol. 1, General Register Office Scotland, 1993.
10. General Register Office Scotland, see reference 9.
11. R.D.F. Bromley and C.J. Thomas, 'The retail revolution, the carless shopper and disadvantage', *Transactions of the Institute of British Geographers*, N.S. Vol. 18, No. 2, 1993, pp. 222-236.
12. R.D.F. Bromley and C.J. Thomas, see reference 11.
13. J.A. Dawson and A. Broadbridge, *Retailing in Scotland 2005*, Institute for Retail Studies, Stirling, 1988.
14. A. Broadbridge, *Distributive Trades Profile 1991. A Statistical Digest*, Institute for Retail Studies, Stirling, 1992.
15. A. Broadbridge, see reference 14, p.60.
16. Mintel, 'Specialist Toy Retailers', *Retail Intelligence*, Vol. 1, 1993.
17. A. Broadbridge, see reference 14, p.71.
18. G.A. Mackay and G. Laing, *Consumer Problems in Rural Areas*, Scottish Consumer Council, 1982.
19. Glasgow District Council *Shopping Policy Review 1992*, Planning Department, September, 1992.
20. R. Lloyd and D. Jennings, 'Shopping behaviour and income: comparisons in an urban environment', *Economic Geography*, Vol. 54, 1987, pp.157-167.
21. G. A. Mackay and Y. Macleod, *Rural Scotland Price Survey. Summer 1992*, Mackay Consultants, 1992.
22. G. A. Mackay and G. Laing, see reference 18.
23. Strathclyde Regional Council, *Strathclyde Regional Council Shopping Survey 1987*, Department of Physical Planning, 1987.
24. R. Lloyd and D. Jennings, see reference 20.
25. M. Douglas and B. Isherwood, *The World of Goods*, Allen Lane, 1979.
26. National Consumer Council, *Consumer Concerns 1992: A consumer view of high street goods and services*, NCC, 1992.
27. Mintel, 'Personal care and healthcare goods retailers', *Retail Intelligence*, Vol. 6, 1992.
28. Mintel, 'Discount and off-price retailers', *Retail Intelligence*, Vol. 2, 1991.
29. K. Keller and R. Staelin, 'Effects of quality and quantity of information on decision effectiveness', *Journal of Consumer Research*, Vol. 14, September, 1987, pp.200-213.
30. J.W. Newman and R. Staelin, 'Pre-purchase information seeking for new cars and major household appliances', *Journal of Marketing Research*, Vol.9, August, 1972, pp.249-257.
31. J.D. Claxton, J. N. Fury and B. Portis, 'A taxonomy of prepurchase information gathering patterns', *Journal of Consumer Research*, Vol.1, December, 1974, pp.35-42.
32. A. Westbrook and C. Fornell, 'Patterns of information source usage among durable goods buyers', *Journal of Marketing Research*, Vol. 16, August, 1979, pp.303-312.
33. D. Furse, G. Punj and D. Stewart, 'A typology of individual search strategies among purchasers of new automobiles', *Journal of Consumer Research*, Vol. 10, March, 1984, pp.417-431.
34. J. A. Dawson and A. Broadbridge, see reference 13.

Social Security
by Angus Erskine

In this chapter Angus Erskine examines the extent to which the social security system meets the needs of those it was designed to help. Many of the poorest people in Britain today, including a high proportion of Scots, are dependent on social security. This dependence on benefits traps many below, or close to, the poverty line. Although this chapter indicates many ways in which those on low incomes experience detriment, the Government is currently assessing plans to reduce overall spending on social security. The failure of the present system to meet needs has prompted calls from many quarters for it to be reviewed and redesigned.

9.1 Introduction

Social security ill serves the interests of its consumers. Those who are most in need rely upon the worst elements of the system. The structure of means tested benefits, for example, traps many pensioners and those on low pay in poverty. The standard of living of those who are unemployed is rapidly falling below that of the rest of the community. Single parents are under attack in the media and are trapped on benefit because of current benefit regulations.

At the same time social security expenditure is under scrutiny and the costs of the welfare state are being questioned. The Conservative Party, committed to reducing direct taxation and controlling public expenditure, is examining this—the largest element of public expenditure. The Labour Party, through the Commission on Social Justice, is developing plans to modernise social security provision to ensure that it meets the economic and social objectives of the party.

This cross-party interest in social security is not surprising. The social security budget is an increasing share of government expenditure and whether the current benefits system is perceived from the left or the right it acts against their social and economic objectives.

For the right, the social security system produces 'perverse incentives' by encouraging people to act in ways in which they would not otherwise do. According to this critique, young women in their early teens become pregnant to live a life of security on the largesse of the tax payer; those who are unemployed remain unemployed not because of the lack of employment opportunities, but because they prefer the security of benefits. Meanwhile, the cost of social security reflected in high taxation reduces the incentive to entrepreneurs to generate wealth that will trickle down through the economy in the form of jobs. Social security consumed 30% of general government expenditure in 1992/93 and, because it is partly based on universal benefits which go to people independent of income, is not sufficiently targeted on those who are most in need. The right suggests that low levels of social protection will result in a strong economy.

For the left, the social security system traps people in poverty. For those who are able to work, there are insufficient exits from dependence upon social security benefits. For those who cannot work benefits are too low to allow them to share in the prosperity of the country. The left points out that those European countries that are economically strong have good social provision.

Our current social security system was designed for very different times from those in which we live now. In that sense politicians are right in identifying the need to re-examine it.

There are four main areas of expenditure on social security—on pensions, on sickness and disability, on child benefit and on unemployment. (See Table 9.1 for a list of the major benefits.) The British social security system is nominally based upon the principle of social insurance through the National Insurance Fund. This is the system as envisaged by Beveridge and with roots that go back to the 1911 National Insurance Act. Predictable events during a person's life such as old age, unemployment

Table 9.1 Cost of the main benefits and numbers of recipients in 1991/92

Benefit	No of recipients (1,000s)	Expenditure (£m)
Retirement Pension	9920	25588
Widows Benefit	345	1012
Unemployment Benefit	675	1604
Sickness Benefit	120	273
Statutory Sick Pay	330	700
Invalidity Benefit	1365	5347
Maternity Allowance	15	31
Statutory Maternity Pay	85	345
Non-contributory Retirement Pension	30	36
War Pension	280	842
Attendance Allowance	975	1706
Invalid Care Allowance	170	285
Severe Disablement Allowance	305	596
Mobility Allowance*	665	1062
Industrial Disablement Benefit	295	587
Industrial Death Benefit	25	64
Income Support*	4660	11612
Child Benefit (families)	6760	5199
One Parent Benefit	835	249
Family Credit*	355	626
Housing Benefit*	4110	2226
Community Charge Benefit*	6335	1074

* indicates means tested benefits
Source: Cm 2213 Social Security Departmental Report, *The Government's Expenditure Plans 1993-94 to 1995-96*, HMSO, London, 1993 Tables 6 & 8.

and sickness or disability were to be covered by National Insurance. The reality is that most expenditure and most people dependent upon benefit rely upon means tested social security benefits. More and more people are reliant upon means tested benefits and it is the poorest who suffer.

National Insurance was designed by Beveridge on the basis of four key assumptions:

- That there would be full male employment. Unemployment while not being abolished would be a temporary phenomenon. While in work, contributions would be paid to provide insurance payments when out of work and for old age, sickness or disability.

- That the insurance scheme would spread the risks amongst the population. A National Insurance system would allow for the build up of a surplus which would provide an income to allow for the payment of benefits during recession without an increased call on the taxpayer.

- That National Insurance benefits would be established at a level which would ensure that means tested benefits would become a residual element in the social security system.

- That most women would be married and their main role would be outside the labour market, caring for children.

Political and social change have meant that we live in a very different world from that which Beveridge envisaged and all four assumptions no longer hold true. What the political debates leave aside is the position of those who are poorest. What does the social security system do for those who are on the lowest incomes?

As dependence upon the social security system has increased, its inadequacies have become more prominent. From the perspective of the claimant, the benefit system is complex and inflexible.

9.2 The Extent of Dependence

Social security payments make up a larger proportion of personal incomes in Scotland than in Great Britain as a whole. In 1992 social security payments made up 17.0% of gross household income in Scotland compared with 13.1% in the UK.[1] This reflects the greater poverty in Scotland, and the lower wages and the changes experienced in the labour market during the 1980s.

This dependence upon the social security system comes through one of two routes. There are those who cannot do paid work and, having no other source of income, rely upon state benefits. Among these are many pensioners, carers and those unable to work through disability, sickness or unemployment. There are others who may have a small income either from paid work, savings or occupational pensions and are entitled to social security benefits as a supplement. Among these are those who are low paid and receive Family Credit, and those whose income is near to the income support level and are entitled to housing benefit to assist them with their housing costs.

Since 1979 and particularly since the series of social security reforms of the mid- to late-1980s, eligibility for social security benefits has been curtailed[2]. There have been a number of significant changes which has meant the exclusion of groups of people from the social security system. The removal of entitlement to benefit from 16 and 17 year olds has resulted in extreme hardship being suffered by young people who do not have recourse to other income[3]. The changes to housing benefit have meant that, particularly among pensioners, those with an income which raises them just above income support level have a restricted entitlement to benefit[4]. Changes in conditions for benefit for those who are unemployed have hit many who are without paid work[5].

Despite these restrictions, expenditure on benefits has continued to rise. The overall impact of piecemeal changes has yet to be fully documented, but it is clear that attempts to reduce expenditure on social security have not succeeded in reducing the overall proportion of public expenditure devoted to it[6]. Yet, these restrictions in eligibility have had a very significant impact on the lives of those who depend upon social security to bring their income up to a minimal level[7].

How minimal social security benefits are is apparent to those who have to live on them, but is often forgotten by the rest of the population. In 1992, a pensioner couple who have worked throughout their lives, contributing taxes and National Insurance payments, but who do not have an occupational or earnings related pension, would have received £86.70 a week, 27% of the average wage[8]. An unemployed couple would receive £69.70 a week, 22% of the average wage.

Concentrating only upon those who receive social security benefits disregards the plight of those who are entitled to them but do not claim:

- 4.35 million people in the UK in 1989 were living in families whose relative net resources were below 100% of the income support level, but did not receive income support due either to disqualification from benefit or to non-take-up of benefit. This represents nearly 8% of the population.

- 1.28 million people over pension age are not receiving income support but are living below the income support level (13% of all pensioner households)[9].

There is clearly a problem within our system of social security benefits if people are going without their entitlement, as citizens of Britain, to even a basic minimum.

Of those who were claiming and were dependent upon means tested benefits, in 1991:

- Nearly 8 million people in the UK, of whom nearly 2.5 million were children, were dependent on income support.

- Approximately 0.5 million people in Scotland received income support.[10] Including dependants, 850,000 people in Scotland were reliant upon means tested income support for all or part of their income.

- Another 250,000 in Scotland were receiving housing benefit but were not on income support[11].

- At least 364,000 people in Scotland over the age of 60 are living in households for whom the benefits' level will be their maximum income for the remainder of their lives.

The population dependent on income support in Scotland differs from that of Great Britain as a whole. People who are unemployed or have disabilities are over-represented and those over 60 are under-represented (Table 9.2).

Over the past decade and a half there have been two consistent trends in Great Britain. First, among the unemployed population of working age, there has been an increasing reliance on means tested income support and decreasing eligibility for National Insurance benefits (Table 9.3).

Table 9.2 Numbers and proportions of recipients of income support at 31st May 1991 (thousands)

	Over 60		Unemployed		Disabled		Single Parents		Other		All	
	N	%	N	%	N	%	N	%	N	%	N	%
Scotland	156	32.0	148	30.3	46	9.4	98	20.1	40	8.2	488	100
England	1330	35.5	1115	29.8	300	8.0	725	19.4	273	7.3	3743	100
GB	1575	35.1	1335	29.8	375	8.4	871	19.4	331	7.4	4487	100

Source: Department of Social Security, *Social Security Statistics 1992*, HMSO, London, 1992 Table A2.03.

Table 9.3 Numbers and proportions of unemployed people in receipt of National Insurance or means tested support at November (thousands)

	1977		1982		1991	
	N	%	N	%	N	%
NI Unemployment Benefit only	440	40.0	714	29.7	507	25.2
NI Benefit & Income Support (SB)	121	11.0	262	10.9	119	5.9
Income Support (SB) only	539	49.0	1428	59.4	1385	68.9
Total	1100	100.0	2404	100.0	2011	100.0

Derived from: Department of Social Security, *Social Security Statistics* 1992, HMSO, London 1992 Table C1.01. Because of inaccuracies and inconsistencies in Table C1.01, the figures for 1982 and 1977 have been derived from Table 1.36 from 1983 & 1977 editions.

- In 1976, 7% of payments from the National Insurance Fund went on National Insurance benefit to those who were unemployed but, by 1991, this had decreased to 3% of payments[12][13].
- In 1976, 48% of men who were claiming benefit as unemployed received National Insurance unemployment benefit but, by 1991, this had decreased to only 25%;
- In 1976 only 36% of men claiming benefit as unemployed had to rely solely on supplementary benefit but, by 1991, 69% relied solely on its replacement, income support[14].

Second, there has been a substantial increase (by 153%) in the numbers of single parents dependent upon income support (Table 9.4).

Table 9.4 Recipients of regular weekly payments of supplementary benefit/income support 1978-1991 Great Britain (thousands)

	1978		1982		1986		1991		Variation
	N	%	N	%	N	%	N	%	1978-1991
60+	1738	59.3	1781	41.7	1717	34.8	1575	35.1	-9%
Unemployed	598	20.4	1722	40.3	2121	43.0	1335	29.8	+123%
Disabled or sick	223	7.6	240	5.6	301	6.1	375	8.4	+68%
Single parents	344	11.7	435	10.2	595	12.0	871	19.4	+153%
Others	30	1.0	90	2.1	204	4.1	331	7.4	+1003%
Total	2933	100.0	4268	100.0	4938	100.0	4487	100.0	+53%

Derived from: Department of Social Security, *Social Security Statistics*, HMSO, London (Annual): Tables 34.34 for 1978; 1982; 1986 & Table A2.03 for 1991.

- In 1978 there were 344,000 single parents in Great Britain in receipt of supplementary benefit, 12% of the claimant population. By 1991, there were 871,000, 19% of the claimant population.

9.3 Claimant Need

The relationship between the level of social security payment and the needs of claimants has always been weak. This involves two issues. First, claimants of social security—pensioners, people with disabilities, families, students, the homeless, young people and those in low paid work—have a wide variety of differing needs, which the social security system has to address within a uniform structure. Second, adequacy has not been central to the determination of social security payments. Beveridge proposed that the level of benefits should be related to a determination of basic needs derived from the work of Rowntree[15][16]. However, the level at which Beveridge wished to establish family allowances was considered by the Treasury to have been too high and was set at a much lower level than that proposed[17].

At the heart of the social security system there has always been a concern with ensuring minimum standards of living for those who have no alternative income and this minimum has been maintained, albeit at a very low level. An alternative perspective would be to suggest that benefits, as in some other European countries such as the Netherlands, should ensure that the living standards of those who are unemployed or retired should not diverge dramatically from the standards enjoyed by the rest of the population.

There are two ways that the adequacy of benefits can be judged, either against an absolute standard—a minimum level to meet needs—or relative to the standard of living of the rest of the population.

In real terms, the value of National Insurance retirement pension and unemployment benefit has nearly doubled since 1948[18]. This absolute measure of the value of benefits is misleading, however, since it is based upon the General Index of Retail Prices (RPI). The evidence suggests that the spending patterns of those on low incomes is such that the RPI may conceal the impact of price rises on living standards. In particular poorer households spend a much larger proportion of their income on food than the average household[19]. (For more detail on the cost of food see sections 4.5 and 4.6 in the chapter on food and nutrition). Changes in government taxation policy, in particular the shift from direct taxation on incomes to indirect taxation on consumption, further increases, disproportionately, the burden on the poorest.

Research by the Family Budget Unit at the University of York[20] shows that income support levels are insufficient for claimants to meet a low cost budget and that the cost of children is not covered by any child related benefits. They calculated a low cost budget which includes only items which two-thirds of people described as necessities in the 1991 Breadline Britain Survey[21], and found that more than half of all single pensioners and single mothers failed to reach this standard. The low cost budgets for households with children were about one-third greater than the 1992/93 income support rates.

In another study, Townsend and Gordon found that "according to the subjective opinions of Londoners, the minimum incomes required for different types of household to surmount poverty averaged 61 per cent above the minimum rates of means-tested benefits payable at the time"[22]. Also, Huby and Dix in their study of the Social Fund found that their respondents who were on benefit "clearly experienced some difficulty in meeting regular expenses associated with living costs"[23].

The evidence that benefits are not set at a sufficiently high level to allow for participation in society is fairly unambiguous. What that level would be in practice is more open to debate.

The level of benefit is not set on the basis of the needs of those who receive it, but according to the overall public expenditure impact. During the last major review of social security in 1985, the Government established three main objectives:

- that the social security system must be capable of meeting genuine need;
- that the system must be consistent with the Government's overall objectives for the economy;
- that the system must be simpler to understand and easier to administer [24].

During the review, the issue of whether benefit levels were adequate to meet needs was not addressed, and the outcome of the review suggested that the Government was mostly concerned with the overall objectives for the economy and in increasing means testing to ensure needs were 'genuine'.

However, at times, an element has been added to benefits to allow for a particular cost. An example of this is the compensation element built into benefit rates to cover the 20% of the Community Charge which all claimants became responsible for in 1988. A once and for all compensation was added to the income support rate. In 1990/91, nationally, benefits were uprated by 5% to allow for retail price inflation whereas, for example, the Community Charge in the Districts of Strathclyde Region rose by 11%[25].

While benefits have been increasing in real terms, they have not been increasing in line with the general rise in living standards. National Insurance unemployment benefit for an unemployed couple represented 31% of the average earnings of male manual workers in 1948, but by 1991 that had decreased to 26% of average male manual workers' earnings[26].

At the least, the most effective way of ensuring that those who have to live on benefits are not further deprived is to raise benefits in line with earnings, not with prices. During the 1970s and early 1980s when the Retirement Pension was linked to increases in earnings, its comparative value rose to 38% of average male manual workers' earnings in 1982, before dropping back to 32% in 1991[27].

9.4 The Workings of the Benefit System

The British social security system is increasingly characterised by its use of means testing. Safety net benefits are set at a low level and are payable upon a test of means. This was not the intention of the National Insurance system proposed by Beveridge, who foresaw means tested benefits as becoming limited in scope to only a number of special cases[28]. It is not the pattern in other countries where means tested benefits play a more residual role than they do in Britain.

This reliance upon income related benefits produces distortions within the system and leads to high marginal tax rates experienced by those on benefit and to the accompanying poverty and unemployment traps.[29] The marginal tax rate is the proportion of increased gross income which is lost through reduced social security benefits and increased income tax and National Insurance payments. For those on the margins of social security and income tax this proportion can be very high.

High marginal tax rates are a product of the rapid rate of withdrawal of means tested benefits above a certain level of income.

- Family Credit is withdrawn at a rate of 70p per extra pound of income.
- Housing benefit is withdrawn at the rate of 65p on income above the income support level.
- Council tax benefit is withdrawn at a rate of 15p in the pound.

In 1992/93, in the UK, half a million claimants experienced marginal tax rates of 70% or more[30].

These marginal tax rates affect those whose income is growing and who should be climbing out of poverty. Equally, there is an impact on those whose incomes are decreasing. Small drops in income result in disproportionate increases in benefit entitlement. It is these high marginal tax rates which create the poverty trap[31]. To deal with the poverty trap, where income related benefits exist, it is necessary to take a number of measures:

- to increase the threshold at which benefits begin to be withdrawn;
- to reduce the rate at which benefits are withdrawn so that the proportion of benefit removed is smaller for each pound increase in income;
- to introduce a lower income tax rate for low paid workers, thus reducing the combined impact of benefit withdrawal and eligibility for income tax and National Insurance contributions;
- to ensure that housing costs are more effectively met than through the current housing benefit system.

The unemployment trap is also a feature of means tested benefits. As more people are encouraged to take work at low levels of wages and wages protection is abolished, the impact of the unemployment trap will increase.

For some who are on benefit, particularly where they have a large family, wages from work are not likely to result in an increase in income compared with income from benefit. Work involves additional costs related to child care, clothing, travel and food which means that a direct comparison between incomes in and out of work is not possible.

The unemployment trap is best overcome by two measures: first, an adequate minimum wage and, second, child benefits at a higher level than at present to ensure that those who have large families and are in work receive an income which meets their needs.

There are two other significant ways in which the benefit system works against some claimants. Single parents, who in the absence of adequate child care and access to employment are likely to remain on very low incomes for a considerable period of time, are subject to 100% marginal tax rates because of the treatment of the three possible elements of their income—maintenance, wages and social security. Maintenance payments are taken into account fully in calculating social security payments, thus creating a 100% tax rate. If single parents work, they experience the same interaction between wages and benefits which others experience, but they also have additional expenses associated with working such as child care costs, for which there is inadequate allowance.

Pensioners who either have small occupational pensions or small capital sums are a second group who are disadvantaged. A new pensions trap is being created alongside the poverty and unemployment traps. A small occupational pension reduces pensioners' entitlement to means tested housing benefit or income support. The value of their occupational pension is not to them, but to the Exchequer in savings in benefit payments. They remain on a low income.

Many pensioners may have saved small capital sums to protect them in their retirement. However, capital is very harshly treated in relation to means tested benefits. For housing benefit purposes, capital over £3,000 is treated as having an income of £1 per week for each £250 of capital. This represents a return on investment of nearly 21% per annum. Clearly, those with small capital sums do have access to more resources than those without and, within an income related system, it has to be taken into account. However, increasing the level at which it restricts benefit reduces the numbers affected rather than making the system itself more equitable.

9.5 The Social Fund

Meeting special needs is a particular challenge to a universal, regulated social security system. There will always be some people who, unless the basic level of benefit was set very high, have special one-off needs which the basic benefit cannot be expected to meet. The British social security system has dealt with these special needs by shifting from a discretionary system of payments up until 1980, to a regulated system of single payments, and now grants and loans through the discretionary Social Fund. The objectives of the Social Fund are to provide flexibility in dealing with special one-off needs which arise for income support claimants while, at the same time, ensuring control over the levels of expenditure. The Social Fund relies upon loans for most payments, which are then repaid by direct deduction from benefit.

In practice what this means is that people can be considered too poor to receive a loan. Officers may recognise a need which they judge is legitimate, and there may be resources in the Fund to make a loan but, because of the financial circumstances of claimants, they are too poor to repay the loan and, therefore, do not receive one. The effect of this is that for the poorest of claimants, faced with financial crises, their only resort to credit is in its most expensive forms. (See section 10.8 in the chapter on credit and debt.)

The Social Fund is discretionary and it is cash limited at the level of local offices. Under an open ended discretionary system, where officers are satisfied that the need is genuine, then payment may be made. With a cash limited system, the need may be recognised, but the cash is not available.

The Social Fund was introduced to near universal criticism in 1988. Since then the evidence which supports the criticisms which were made has been accumulating[32]. The Fund is allocated on the basis of directions and guidance laid down by the Secretary of State; the state of the local office's budget; the nature of the local office priorities; and the discretionary judgements of Social Fund officers.

A study of the operation of the Social Fund at the level of local offices found that there was considerable diversity in how the fund was operated between local offices:

> "... identical social fund applications may have a different outcome depending on the office to which they are made"[33].

Walker, Dix and Huby found that some offices could only make awards where the circumstances were extreme while other offices met virtually all applications[34] and a major evaluation of the Social Fund funded by the DSS found that:

> "After careful examination of the available evidence, we cannot say that people who receive social fund awards are in greater general need than those who are refused ..."[35].

The report points out that the needs of those who are eligible but do not apply and those not eligible are similar to those who have received help from the fund.

Huby and Dix report that in their sample of people receiving Social Fund loans, the average repayment rate was over 13% of weekly income[36]. In addition two-thirds of the sample were making payments from their income to cover other forms of credit or borrowing. When these were included, on average, a total of 22% of income was being spent on borrowing.

Overall the evidence suggests that the Social Fund has succeeded in controlling expenditure but the flexibility and discretion upon which the fund is based has resulted in inconsistent treatment for claimants.

9.6 The Interaction Between National Insurance and Income Support

The National Insurance system continues to work well as a non means tested system which provides a small additional income for those who are unemployed, sick or elderly, as long as they have sufficient other resources to lift them out of poverty. It does not work for those who are in irregular or low paid work, because they will become dependent upon means tested benefits.

In particular, for women, the National Insurance system does not provide benefit. Many married women will have worked part time at wage levels which do not involve making National Insurance contributions and, therefore, are not entitled to National Insurance benefit[37]. Others will find that their National Insurance benefit, although calculated upon their own contributions, counts as family income when they and their partner are unemployed or elderly. This affects women in particular because they are often in part time or more precarious employment.

Means tested benefits are not only costly in global public expenditure terms but are also costly to administer. Since they involve an assessment of means, the time spent in calculating entitlement is longer. As dependence upon income related benefits has increased, so the administrative cost of the DSS has increased.

- In 1985/86 the DSS distributed £41 billion in benefits which cost £1.8 billion to administer (4.5%).
- In 1991/92 the DSS distributed £65 billion in benefits which cost £3.6 billion to administer (5.5%).

The administrative costs of income support and the Social Fund are 12% and 45% of the cost of the benefit respectively[38].

The substantial costs of means tested benefits are likely to increase. In recent years, there has been a greater emphasis upon family income supplement, now Family Credit, as a way out of poverty for families in low paid work. At the same time there has been decreasing protection for those on low wages, with for example the system of wages council protection being abolished and the Government arguing that wages should be allowed to be freely negotiated at whatever level. In Scotland a larger proportion of the workforce are low paid compared to Britain as a whole[39] (see section 1.7 in the introductory chapter).

There is a severe detriment for those on low pay who receive Family Credit in terms of the time they have to wait to receive it. The targets which the DSS set for the determination of claims in 1992/93 were 60% of claims in 13 working days and 95% in 45 working days. During this time, a person with a family will have to exist on inadequate wages. In addition, low paid work tends to be insecure and may lead to unemployment. The target clearance time for a new claim for income support as unemployed is four working days[40]. Reliance upon means tested income support and Family Credit rather than child benefit to support large families creates a severe disadvantage for poorer families.

Resolving these problems involves three measures:

- the extension of social insurance cover not just to narrowly defined contributors but also to citizens who have some connection with the labour market;
- the raising of insurance benefit levels to ensure that fewer people require both insurance and means tested benefits;
- the raising of child benefit to a level which reduces entitlement to Family Credit to all but very large families.

These measures would involve the Government in a greater redistribution of income than at present. Some of the additional expenditure to meet this could be met if higher rate tax payers were taxed on child benefit and from savings in Family Credit payments and administration.

A further element of detriment which is produced by the divide between National Insurance and means tested benefits is the treatment of claimants. Claiming means tested benefit involves greater intrusion into the claimant's life, not only in relation to testing income. It involves, in the case of households, the investigation of sexual relationships within the household. Also, people with disabilities are faced with a double test involving a test of extent of disability as well as a test of means[41].

A benefits' system which relies upon tests of income and household tests is expensive to administer, militates against the poorest and results in discriminatory practices which are not based upon need. This can be contrasted with a system which is based upon categorical entitlement. Claimants would have to be able to prove that they fall within the category for whom benefit is payable, for example having dependent children for child benefit or being over a certain age for a pension. The costs of such a universal categorical system can be met, in part, by reducing the administrative costs of means tested benefits and taxing categorical benefits where they are received by those who pay tax at the higher rate. However, to provide universal categorical benefits, independent of a test of means, requires a consideration of the costs to the public purse of benefits received by those who are well off through tax allowances and occupational benefits.

9.7 Occupational and State Welfare

Over the past ten years there has been increased emphasis upon occupational benefits, which have existed and been recognised for a long time[42]. More recently their distributional impact has been more thoroughly analysed[43] and their regulation and control have become a matter of public concern and debate through the affairs of a number of occupational pension schemes, most notably the Maxwell Fraud[44].

Occupational benefits provide advantage to those who are better off; the most generous occupational schemes go not to the part time cleaner in the office, or the part time catering worker, but to the best paid executive. They represent part of their remuneration and income package which adds to their already privileged position. In many cases these benefits are promoted by employers because they are 'tax efficient', reducing the tax liability of both employer and employee.

They are important also because they represent a shift in control. Occupational pension funds are significant financial assets—£482 billion in 1989[45]—which are controlled by private interests. These assets are, unlike other personal assets, not under the control of those who are the nominal beneficiaries.

A second element of the shift in control is the change from state financing and delivering of benefits to the state financing but employer delivery of benefits. This is the case with statutory sick pay and statutory maternity pay, where the benefit, paid for through the public purse, is delivered through the employer and the wage packet. The evidence suggests that the existence of statutory sick pay has led to a tightening up of labour discipline over manual workers and a net benefit to non-manual workers. A study which examined the effect of the introduction of statutory sick pay found that, between 1981 and 1984, there was no significant overall change in the rate of absenteeism through sickness. However, this concealed a reduction of absenteeism among unskilled manual workers and an increase in the incidence among more skilled and non-manual workers[46].

Recent government policy has been to reduce the controls and regulations under which businesses operate. Without effective controls, state financed, but employer delivered, benefits are open to abuse by employers. This is most likely to occur in marginal small enterprises whose workforce is poorly organised and poorly paid and may involve, at the least, employers depriving workers of their statutory rights and, at the worst, employers defrauding the National Insurance fund by making false deductions against their National Insurance contributions.

The long term effect of transferring the administration of benefits to employers is to reduce the ability of the most marginal workers to ensure their rights. At the same time, the increased emphasis on occupational and private pension schemes, which has accompanied the downgrading of the State Earnings Related Pension Scheme, has the effect of ensuring that those who are poor during their working life are also going to be poor when they are old.

Occupational benefits have been accurately characterised as upside down benefits which benefit the better off rather than the poorest. The way that occupational pensions are treated by the tax system makes this worse: tax relief on occupational pension contributions is estimated by the Treasury as being £8.1 billion in 1992/93[47], more than one-third of the total expenditure on retirement pensions. For those in the higher tax bracket, these contributions are an effective way of deferring income until they are older and in a lower tax bracket. In addition to this, tax relief is granted on investment income and on lump sum benefits. The largest proportion of these reliefs goes to the already well paid, but they are paid for by all tax payers, poor as well as rich.

9.8 Appeals, Adjudication and Policing

Any system of social security which relies upon regulation requires an effective system of appeal and adjudication. With the exception of the Social Fund, the social security system is based on fairly clearly defined rules of entitlement. Two parallel trends have been taking place over recent years. First, entitlement has become increasingly complex as rules are more narrowly defined. Eligibility for income support as unemployed is now determined by a form (B1) which is 18 pages long and involves almost a 100 different questions. Eligibility for Family Credit involves a form (FC1) which is 14 pages long. Despite efforts by local authorities to simplify housing benefit application procedures, housing benefit forms are notoriously complicated, involving decision making about eligible rent, eligible income and household composition. (See section 2.4 in the chapter on housing.)

Second, fraud has been a major preoccupation of the DSS over recent years. Cook points out the very different treatment of those suspected or guilty of fraud by the Inland Revenue compared with the DSS[48]. Those suspected of DSS fraud may have their benefit stopped, but the Inland Revenue cannot increase its collection on the basis of a suspicion of fraud.

The fraud targets which the Benefits Agency has set will result in an increase in claimants being pursued on the suspicion of fraud. In many cases this results in claims being voluntarily withdrawn in cases which would not stand up to examination in a court of law. This preoccupation with fraud was given added emphasis by the Secretary of State for Social Security in his speech to the 1992 Conservative Party Conference. The target for fraud detection has been increased from £460 million in 1992/93 to £557 million in 1993/94[49].

It is against this background that the system of appeals and adjudication should be viewed. In 1991, there were 36,782 appeals registered at Social Security Appeals Tribunals in Scotland. Of those which were eventually adjudicated upon, 36% were found in favour of the appellant.

There has been a dramatic increase in the length of time that it takes for appeals to be heard in Scotland.

- In 1991, 64% out of the 36,782 appeals were outstanding[50].
- In 1988, when there were nearly two and a half times the number of appeals registered (89,000), only 27% were outstanding[51].

Baldwin, Wikeley and Young in their study of social security adjudication found that adjudication officers who are responsible for the initial decision making about claims operate in an environment which is under-resourced and where hurried decisions are expected[52]. Their ability to perform their quasi-judicial role is undermined by the pressure of work which is placed on them as low grade civil servants. In addition, their formal independence within social security offices has become compromised by their other workloads.

> "The local offices are so severely under-resourced that poor quality work is now the norm. Corners are cut in routine fashion in local offices as adjudication officers struggle to keep abreast of the workload"[53].

Appeal tribunals are regarded by staff as being a 'safety net' which means that adjudication officers cut corners to process work quickly, leaving final decisions to appeal if the claimant decides to make use of a tribunal. There is, however, a low rate of attendance at appeal hearings, with just one in two appellants attending their hearing (see section 11.3a in the chapter on legal services for more detail about tribunals in general).

9.9 Advice, Information and Services for Claimants

Despite the attempt of the 1988 reforms to simplify it, the British social security system remains extraordinarily complex. The interaction of National Insurance benefits with means tested benefits, the number of means tested benefits geared to claimants in different categories and the increasing dependence of claimants on both forms of benefit mean that claimants, if they are to ensure that their entitlements are met, rely upon good advice.

One of the hidden administrative costs of the social security system is services paid for by local and central government rather than the DSS. Citizens Advice Bureaux, local authority welfare rights services and voluntary organisations provide either specialist advice to groups of claimants or offer advice about social security benefits as part of a generalist advice service.

There are three free sources of advice for claimants. The DSS provides publicity about benefits and leaflets as well as a freephone service. Local authorities and voluntary agencies mount take-up publicity campaigns, and provide advice to individuals and representation at tribunals. Under legal aid, solicitors may advise claimants, on a one off basis, on points of law, but cannot represent them at tribunals.

All three sources of advice are limited. From the claimants' perspective it is difficult to accept the impartiality of the DSS as advisors, since one of the objectives of the DSS is to ensure that benefits are not provided to those who are not entitled to them—not to ensure that those who claim receive all of their entitlement. None of the performance targets established for the Benefits Agency are concerned with ensuring that claimants are informed of their entitlements. The main ones are concerned with ensuring accuracy of payment, timescale and fraud detection.

Local authorities and voluntary agencies have been experiencing financial constraints which makes take-up campaigns and advice giving increasingly difficult to provide. Representation of claimants at tribunals is time consuming and costly. Few solicitors have knowledge of the detail of the social security system and, except in exceptional circumstances, they are unable to claim legal aid for the representation of claimants at tribunals.

In Scotland, the problem that claimants face in obtaining good quality, independent advice is particularly severe in rural areas and peripheral housing estates, as visiting or telephoning the local office of the DSS is an expensive business. In rural areas it will take a full day and an expensive bus or train fare to make a personal visit. Local authorities and voluntary agencies rarely provide an expert service over a wide area to a geographically scattered population.

As means tested benefits become more important for claimants' income, the problems become more severe. Means tested benefits are not only difficult for the DSS to administer and claimants to understand, but also many of those eligible do not claim them[54].

Claiming, particularly when there is a public campaign against 'scrounging', is stigmatising. Family Credit, as a benefit for low paid workers was designed to encourage take-up. Its predecessor, Family Income Support, had a low take-up rate of 51% in 1986/87[55]. Family Credit has not been a great success either in terms of take-up. In 1988/89, which is the latest date for which the Government has provided figures, the take-up rate of Family Credit was 57% of eligible recipients.

In 1989, income support had a take-up rate of 75% of eligible recipients and 87% by expenditure. It is clear that the individual entitlements are small but for claimants on such a low income they are of much greater significance[56].

The DSS has established targets for quality of service within the social security system, but take-up rates are not one of the indicators of performance. Indeed, the annual reporting of take-up rates was removed in 1992 from the annual Social Security Statistics.

The Benefits Agency's Customer Charter details their commitment to 'customers'[57]. It commits the Benefits Agency to providing a service which is courteous, fair, confidential, private and accessible. The payment of benefit is to be prompt and accurate and the Agency is committed to providing clear and accessible help and information. The key measure of how well the Benefits Agency is doing is to be the level of satisfaction reported by 'customers'. The service standards and targets set for the Agency are administrative and concerned with clearance times for claims.

The objectives laid out in the Charter are entirely rhetorical. It would be difficult to imagine any agency which would not wish to be courteous, fair or accessible. What is of importance for consumers is what is ignored. The take-up of benefits, appeal procedures and quality of information are not mentioned. The Customer Charter does not contain the other performance indicators for the Benefits Agency which are set out in the Social Security Department's Expenditure Plans. These are much more hostile towards the customer and include targets for the recovery of Social Fund loans, benefit savings through detection and fraud, the recovery of income support overpayments and the achieving of efficiency savings of £54 million[58].

The current concentration on managerial issues is reflected in the new structures being adopted as part of the Next Step programme. The DSS is being divided into five Agencies: the Benefits Agency, the Contributions Agency, the Information Technology Services Agency, the Resettlement Agency and the Child Support Agency. The largest Agency, the Benefits Agency, began operating in 1991 and the Child Support Agency started in April 1993.

9.10 Conclusions

As it operates at present the social security system serves the interests of its consumers badly, with those most in need relying upon the worst element of the system—

income support. Income support was designed to target those most in need but the evidence suggests that it misses a very large part of the target.

For some better off pensioners and prosperous families with children the system provides a useful, if not essential, supplement to their income. For others who live on very low incomes, the system fails to meet even their basic needs. There are three groups who are particularly ill served by the present structure. First, there are those whose incomes are just above the income support levels. The structure of means tested benefits traps pensioners with small occupational pensions and those on low pay in poverty.

Second, the long term unemployed experience detriment. As National Insurance benefits are increasingly replaced by means tested benefits and eligibility is restricted, the long term unemployed are subjected to increasing controls. Their standard of living falls rapidly behind that of the rest of society. The Social Fund is a haphazard and inadequate way of meeting the one off needs which inevitably occur in long periods dependent upon benefits.

Third, women experience detriment. The system of benefits through National Insurance was based upon a model of male breadwinners providing for the needs of their families. It ignores the reality that most women work, as well as care for children. When married women become unemployed, they may receive National Insurance benefits on the basis of their contributions. But many married women are employed in part time, low paid work and will not have paid contributions. Their entitlement to social security will depend upon their husbands. Single parents, more than 90% of whom are women, are particularly disadvantaged. If they are claiming they are subjected to the cohabitation rule which may mean that they cannot enter into a new relationship without loss of benefit. If they are alone, under the regulations of the Child Support Agency, they are penalised by deductions from income support: if they receive maintenance; if they do not receive maintenance; or if they work.

References and footnotes to Chapter 9

1. Central Statistical Office, *Family Spending: A Report on the 1992 Family Expenditure Survey*, HMSO, 1993, Table 40.
2. For a list of all social security benefits which have been abolished or have had availability restricted since 1979 see *Hansard*, Vol. 215, No. 89, c503-4w.
3. *Excluding Youth*, Bridges Project and Edinburgh Centre for Social Welfare Research, University of Edinburgh, 1991.
4. In 1983 there were 1,370,000 pensioner households in receipt of housing benefit but no means tested supplementary benefit. By 1991, this had dropped to 916,700, although the number of pensioner households will have increased. Source: Department of Social Security, *Social Security Statistics*, 1985, Table 35.05 & *Social Security Statistics*, 1992, Table A3.20.
5. A. Atkinson and J. Micklewright, 'Turning the screw: benefits for the unemployed, 1979-1988' in A. B. Atkinson, *Poverty and Social Security*, Harvester Wheatsheaf, 1989.
6. J. Hills (ed.), *The State of Welfare: The Welfare State in Britain since 1974*, Clarendon Paperbacks, 1991.
7. J. Hills, see reference 6.
8. Central Statistical Office, *Regional Trends*, No. 27, HMSO, 1992, Table 8.3.

9. House of Commons Social Security Committee, *Low Income Statistics: Low Income Families 1979-1989*, Second Report, 1992/93 HC359, HMSO, London, 1992, Table 3.
10. Department of Social Security *Social Security Statistics 1992*, HMSO, London, 1992, Table A2.03 & A2.08.
11. Department of Social Security, see reference 10, Table A3.02.
12. Department of Social Security, *Social Security Statistics 1991*, HMSO, 1991, Tables H 2.03 & HC33.
13. *National Insurance Fund Accounts 1990/91*, HMSO, 1992.
14. Department of Social Security, *Social Security Statistics 1992*, HMSO, 1992 Table A2.03 & *Social Security Statistics 1989*, Table 1.32.
15. J. Veit Wilson, `Muddle or mendacity? The Beveridge Committee and the poverty line', *Journal of Social Policy*, Vol. 21, Pt 3, 1992.
16. A. B. Atkinson, `A National Minimum? A History of Ambiguity in the Determination of Benefit Scales in Britain' in T. Wilson and D. Wilson (eds), *The State and Social Welfare*, Longman, 1991.
17. J. Harris, *William Beveridge*, Clarendon Press, 1977.
18. Department of Social Security, *Social Security Statistics 1991*, HMSO, 1991, Tables H3.04 & H3.06.
19. S. Leather, `Less Money, Less Choice' in National Consumer Council *Your Food: Whose Choice*, HMSO, 1992.
20. *Social Policy Research Findings No. 31*, Joseph Rowntree Foundation, 1992.
21. J. Mack and S. Lansley, *Breadline Britain in the 1990s*, Routledge, 1991.
22. P. Townsend and D. Gordon, 'What is enough? New evidence on poverty allowing the definition of a minimum benefit', in M. Adler, C. Bell, J. Clasen and A. Sinfield, (eds) *The Sociology of Social Security*, Edinburgh University Press, 1991.
23. M. Huby and G. Dix, *Evaluating the Social Fund*, HMSO, 1992.
24. Cmnd 9517 *Reform of Social Security*, HMSO, 1985, Vol. 1, para 1.12.
25. C. Mair, *The Community Charge Rebate Scheme*. Paper prepared for the Scottish Foundation for Economic Research, 1990.
26. Department of Social Security *Social Security Statistics 1991*, HMSO, 1991, Table H3.04. This figure is not calculated on the same basis as the earlier one referred to for 1992 (see reference 8). This is because in 1992 the DSS stopped reporting on this trend and the 1992 figure had to be calculated by the author from publicly available sources.
27. Department of Social Security, see reference 26, Table H3.06.
28. Cmd 640 *Social Insurance and Allied Services*, HMSO, 1942, para 371.
29. J. Bradshaw and A. Deacon, *Reserved for the Poor*, Blackwell and Martin Robertson, 1983.
30. Cm 2213 Social Security Departmental Report, *The Government's Expenditure Plans 1993-94 to 1995-96*, HMSO, 1993, Figure 19.
31. The term `poverty trap' refers to when people are in work and an increase in their gross earnings results in their being little or no better off. The term `unemployment trap' is when net income in work is little greater than, or even less than, net income out of work.
32. G. Craig (ed.), *Your Flexible Friend?*, Social Security Consortium, 1989.
33. R. Walker, G. Dix and M. Huby, *Working the Social Fund*, HMSO, 1992.

34. R. Walker, G. Dix and M. Huby, see reference 33.
35. M. Huby and G. Dix, see reference 23.
36. M. Huby and G. Dix, see reference 23.
37. C. Hakim, 'Workforce restructuring, social insurance coverage and the black economy', *Journal of Social Policy*, Vol. 18, 4, 1989.
38. Cm 2213 Social Security Departmental Report, see reference 30, Table 1 & Figure 27.
39. The Scottish Office *Scottish Abstract of Statistics 1992*, HMSO, Table 10.5.
40. Benefits Agency, *Customer Charter*, 1992.
41. C. Barnes, 'Discrimination, disability benefits and the 1980s', *Benefits* 3, January/February 1992.
42. R. Titmuss, 'The Social Division of Welfare' in *Essays on 'The Welfare State'*, Unwin University Books, 1958.
43. A. Sinfield, 'Why some are more secure than others', *Benefits* 2, September/October 1991.
44. House of Commons Social Security Committee, *The Operation of Pension Funds*, 2nd Report, 1991/2 HC 61-II, HMSO, 1992.
45. House of Commons Social Security Committee, see reference 44, Table 1.
46. H. Dean and P. Taylor Gooby, 'Sick pay and the control of sickness absence', *Journal of Social Policy*, Vol. 19, Part 1, January 1990.
47. Cm 2219 HM Treasury, *Public Expenditure Analyses to 1995-96 Statistical Supplement to the 1992 Autumn Statement*, HMSO, 1993.
48. D. Cook, *Rich Law, Poor Law*, Open University Press, 1989.
49. Cm 2213 Social Security Departmental Report, see reference 30, Figure 38.
50. Department of Social Security, see reference 10, Table H3.01.
51. Department of Social Security, *Social Security Statistics 1989*, HMSO, 1989, Table 49.04.
52. J. Baldwin, N. Wikeley and R. Young, *Judging Social Security*, Clarendon Press, 1992.
53. J. Baldwin, N. Wikeley and R. Young, see reference 52.
54. V. Fry and G. Stark, 'The take up of supplementary benefit: gaps in the safety net', *Fiscal Studies*, November 1987.
55. Department of Social Security, see reference 26, Table H5.01.
56. Department of Social Security, *Income Related Benefits Estimates of Take Up in 1989*, Government Statistical Service, 1993.
57. Benefits Agency, see reference 40.
58. Cm 2213 Social Security Departmental Report, see reference 30, Figure 38.

Credit and Debt

by Michael Adler and David McMillan

In this chapter Michael Adler and David McMillan explain what types of credit are used by those on low incomes and why they may fall into debt. The growth in consumer credit accompanied by improved credit referencing has meant that those on low incomes may be unfairly discriminated against or offered credit they cannot repay. People fall into debt for many different reasons, but chiefly as a result of a sudden change in circumstances or long periods of time living in poverty. There is a clear need for a co-ordinated debt advice service in Scotland to help address increasing debt problems.

10.1 Introduction

This chapter considers the position of low income households in relation to consumer credit and consumer indebtedness. Section 10.2 outlines the development of the consumer credit market. The considerable growth in consumer credit has been made possible by improved methods of credit referencing, and section 10.3 describes the use of credit scoring to assess the credit-worthiness of potential borrowers. Section 10.4 examines patterns of indebtedness and explains how people get into debt and why low income households tend to use the more expensive forms of credit; while section 10.5 reviews the availability of debt advice and debt counselling in Scotland. This is followed, in section 10.6, by an analysis of recent trends in the number of payment actions raised and disposed of in the courts. Section 10.7 examines developments that have been of advantage to consumers and assesses the extent to which they have benefited low income households. Section 10.8 considers forms of credit such as mail order firms, money lenders and credit unions which are of particular importance to households on low incomes. Section 10.9 analyses the functions of bodies which were set up to regulate the consumer credit market, examines recent consumer credit legislation and the voluntary codes of practice, and assesses whether or not they provide an effective regulatory framework. Finally section 10.10 pulls the evidence together and sets out an overall assessment of the impact of recent developments in consumer credit and consumer indebtedness on low income households.

10.2 The Extent of Consumer Credit and Consumer Indebtedness

There are no figures on the extent of arrears on consumer credit agreements—they are simply not collected. In the absence of such figures, data on credit extended by, and outstanding to, creditors are a useful indicator of the possible extent of the problem. It should be noted that these figures refer to the UK as a whole and that there are no separate data for Scotland.

As can be seen from Table 10.1 below, there has been a large and sustained increase in the amount of consumer credit extended since 1984 (the first year for which complete data are available). This only started to slow down at the end of the decade, probably due to the economic uncertainty caused by the recession and the concurrent tightening by creditors of their lending policies. Between 1984 and 1991, the amount of consumer credit extended increased almost three-fold. The data include bank credit cards, loans from finance houses and other specialist credit granters (for example retailers and insurance companies), and unsecured Building Society loans (known as Class 3 loans) but exclude bank loans and loans for house purchase.

Table 10.1 Total levels of new credit extended, 1984-1992 (UK)

Year	Amount extended (£m)	Index (1984=100)	% increase
1984	18,910	100.0	
1985	22,622	119.6	19.6
1986	28,057	148.6	24.9
1987	34,734	183.7	23.8
1988	41,171	217.7	18.5
1989	45,888	242.7	11.5
1990	50,780	268.5	10.7
1991	51,772	273.8	2.0
1992	53,631	283.6	3.6

Note: The data from *Financial Statistics* slightly overestimate the actual level of consumer credit as they include figures for individuals who are self-employed and borrow money for their businesses. The figures used from other sources do not have this problem. In addition, there are slight discrepancies between the CSO statistics and those used by the Monopolies and Mergers Commission. However, these are of little significance.

Sources : Central Statistical Office, *Credit Business Bulletin*, December 1992; Central Statistical Office, *Financial Statistics*, various years, Table 9.3; Monopolies and Mergers Commission, *Credit Card Services*, Cm.718, 1979, Table 3.2.

At the same time, the amount of credit outstanding more than doubled (see Table 10.2). It is clear, however, that, like the large annual increases in the amount of new credit extended, the large annual increases in the amount of credit outstanding which were common a few years ago have now slowed down.

Table 10.3 shows that different forms of consumer credit increased at different rates. The three-fold increase in Building Society Class 3 loans since 1988 is particularly striking. The very rapid increase in this figure is mainly due to the relaxation of restrictions on the granting of unsecured loans by building societies in 1986. Further increases are likely in the near future since the further relaxation of such restrictions was approved by the Government in 1992. However, the continued rise in the amount of credit advanced through bank credit cards is perhaps even more

Table 10.2 Total levels of credit outstanding, 1984-1991 (UK)

Year	Amount outstanding (£m)	Index (1984=100)	% increase
1984	22,307	100.0	
1985	26,112	117.0	17.0
1986	30,548	136.9	17.0
1987	36,174	162.2	18.4
1988	42,544	190.7	17.6
1989	48,404	217.0	13.8
1990	52,579	235.7	8.6
1991	53,617	240.3	2.0

Source : Central Statistical Office, *Financial Statistics*, various years, Table 9.3.

significant. Credit cards have now become the major form of consumer credit in the UK in terms of the amount of credit extended. This stark fact could be misleading, however, because people use different forms of credit in different ways. Credit cards are used by many people to purchase goods and services without having to carry around large sums of money or as a convenient form of interest-free, short term credit for paying bills before interest charges are incurred. In 1988 some 24.9 million credit cards were in circulation in the UK and about 38% of the adult population held an Access or a Visa card[1]. It has been estimated that 30% of credit card users regularly pay their bills before charges are levied[2]. This contrasts with other forms of consumer credit, in particular credit from finance houses, which tend to be used to buy larger items such as a car or household furniture and which can take several months or even years to pay off. Such forms of credit necessarily entail the payment of interest.

The growth in consumer credit has substantially exceeded the rate of inflation during the last ten years[3]. This is due to a number of factors including the deregulation of financial services which resulted in aggressive marketing by some lenders and the increased availability of credit made possible by improved methods of credit referencing (see section 10.3 below). Although it has been suggested that changing consumer attitudes are also a reason for increased consumer credit, a recent study[4] indicates that attitudes have not changed to any great extent since 1979[5].

It has proved very difficult to obtain data about Scotland from industry sources, but the Committee of Scottish Clearing Banks was able to provide information for the period 1990-92. A comparison of the figures shown in Table 10.4 with figures for the UK as a whole points to a lower level of banking credit in Scotland. Figures for personal loans three months or more in arrears and the average size of personal loans were not available from all the banks and the figures in Table 10.4 have,

Table 10.3 New credit extended 1988-1992 : finance houses and other specialist money lenders, building societies, bank credit cards and retailers (UK)

Year	Building Society Class 3 Loans		Bank Credit Cards		Finance Houses etc.		Retailers	
	New Credit (£m)	Index (1988 = 100)	New Credit (£m)	Index (1988 = 100)	New Credit (£m)	Index (1988 = 100)	New Credit (£m)	Index (1988 = 100)
1988	488	100.0	20,338	100.0	15,480	100.0	4,635	100.0
1989	963	197.3	23,708	116.6	16,835	108.8	4,659	100.5
1990	1,237	253.5	27,633	135.9	17,275	111.6	4,750	102.5
1991	1,436	294.3	29,299	144.1	16,377	105.5	4,975	107.3
1992	1,626	333.2	31,433	154.6	16,172	104.5	5,032	108.6

Source : Central Statistical Office, *Credit Business Bulletin*, December 1992.

Table 10.4 Credit from the four Scottish clearing banks: personal loans, 1990-1992

Year	No. of personal loans	Credit outstanding (£m)	Average personal loan (£)	No. of personal loans 3 months or more in arrears
1990	581,000	948	1,632	11,039
1991	592,000	1,035	1,784	14,800
1992	553,000	1,003	1,814	15,484

Source : Committee of Scottish Clearing Banks, personal communication, March 1993.

therefore, been estimated from those banks that were able to provide data. Data were also provided for the number of agreed overdrafts. A rough estimate would suggest that there were about 430,000 agreed overdrafts from Scottish banks in Scotland in 1992.

The increase in consumer credit which occurred during the 1980s does not necessarily mean that there has been a corresponding increase in the number of debt problems. All that can be said for certain is that the growth in consumer credit increased the potential for problem debts.

10.3 Credit Scoring

During the 1970s, and to a greater extent during the 1980s, the increase in the size of the market for credit meant that the traditional methods of requesting references to check on credit-worthiness became too cumbersome and time-consuming. Instead, lenders turned to credit referencing as a way of responding quickly to applications for credit and protecting themselves against large increases in the percentage of defaulters.

Credit referencing uses three basic types of check:
- The lender checks the identity and address of the applicant on lists kept by credit referencing agencies.
- The lender checks a list to see if there are any court judgments against the applicant.
- The lender makes a search of data on recent and current credit transactions which all lenders agree to share through credit reference agencies. These data are only available to licensed lenders[6].

Some lenders then take these raw data and put them through a credit scoring system to determine whether or not the applicant is a suitable recipient of credit. Credit scoring systems are used to assess both the likelihood of default by individual applicants and the corresponding level of risk to a lender. Only if the final credit score is above the level required by the company will the applicant be offered credit. Each company has its own customised credit scoring system which requires regular updating. These systems are expensive and are, therefore, only used by the larger lenders. In general, they have had a positive effect since they have allowed credit to be advanced in a relatively non-discriminatory way to a wider section of the public than would otherwise have been the case without the price of credit becoming prohibitive. However, there are a number of concerns about credit scoring systems which affect those on low incomes. These fall into two main categories: being unfairly discriminated against and being offered credit that they are unable to repay.

Being unfairly discriminated against can occur as a result of using third-party information. For example, when checking for court judgments, the lender looks for judgments during the previous six years at the applicant's address. This can result in persons who are economically independent of the applicant (e.g. previous occupants, or flat-sharers) being used to judge an applicant's credit-worthiness and as those on low incomes may be more mobile and more likely to share accommodation it is more likely to apply to them. It can have the effect either of denying credit to persons who are able to pay or of granting credit to persons who are unable to pay. However, the Data Protection Agency has recently[7] begun to serve enforcement orders on lenders limiting the use of third-party information to persons who are thought to be part of the family unit. This should restrict the use of third-party information though the problem will still remain.

Those on low incomes can also be discriminated against due to the practice known as 'red-lining'. This involves systematically denying people credit because of the area in which they live. The Office of Fair Trading (OFT) has found no evidence of outright 'red-lining'[8]; however, there is considerable evidence of it in a watered down form as a person's area of residence is frequently used as one of the variables in a credit scoring system. While there is little wrong with its inclusion as one of a number of variables, there is a need for further monitoring to ensure that the weighting given to area of residence is not so strong as to make it almost impossible for an applicant from a poor neighbourhood to gain credit.

The second area of concern referred to above is that people on low incomes may be offered credit that they cannot afford. This situation can arise in several ways. Certain types of information are not kept by credit referencing agencies. In particular, gas and electricity transactions and information on secured loans are not used despite indications that these are the types of credit that are the first not to be paid and act as a kind of early warning system of other debt problems[9]. There are also serious gaps in the information available to lenders from credit referencing agencies. This is because the five main credit referencing agencies in Britain do not pool their information on credit transactions. As most companies only subscribe to one agency (on grounds of cost) there may be serious deficiencies in their knowledge of applicants for credit. There is thus the possibility that people who are already overstretched or have serious debt problems will be offered more credit. If a way of sharing information between agencies could be found and if information on fuel debts and secured loans could be included, credit scoring systems would be improved and less bad debt would occur.

A further concern with credit scoring systems is that ability to pay is often not included by lenders. Among their reasons for not including it, creditors claim that it is a poor predictor of default and that, in any case, it is often difficult to confirm a person's income and outgoings. While this means that credit may be granted to those on low incomes, it also means that those on low incomes who are unable to repay the money in the time allowed may be offered credit. The OFT has recently called for all lenders to take into account people's ability to pay when considering them for credit[10].

Credit scoring enables lenders to assess the credit-worthiness of a large number of applicants for credit quickly and in a standardised manner, and has facilitated the expansion of consumer credit. However, its main purpose is to protect lenders rather than borrowers and, as such, it can be manipulated by lenders to reflect the risks they are willing to take. Although its advocates claim that it operates in a non-discriminatory way, there is evidence to suggest that low income households may lose out by being offered credit that they cannot afford (and then having to pay high interest charges) and by being refused credit when they are able to pay if they live in an area with a high default rate.

10.4 Patterns of Indebtedness

Credit is clearly not offered to everyone on an equal basis. Nor is the cost of borrowing the same for everyone. Moreover, credit is used in different ways and for different reasons by different groups of people. The reason why credit is sought, the social background and outlook of the potential borrower, and the policies of credit granters can all affect the types and amounts of credit that are available and the uses to which credit is put.

The costs of different forms of credit are affected by the amount of security that a lender can obtain on the loan and the borrower's likely ability to pay. So, for example, mortgages tend to have the lowest interest rates because a house can act as security, while loans from money lenders tend to attract the highest rates of interest, in part because they are unsecured. Large scale lenders can assess the borrower's ability to pay fairly accurately using credit scoring (see section 10.3 above). However, smaller lenders do not have access to such expensive checks and so have to use less accurate methods. This is confirmed by research which shows that 49% of people who had a loan from a money lender claimed that they had not been asked about their ability to pay, while the comparative figure for finance houses was 18%, for banks 10% and for building societies 2%[11]. Small companies which do not check ability to pay thoroughly tend to offer comparatively small loans to those on lower incomes and to charge higher interest rates. Lower income groups are more likely to be excluded from the cheaper forms of credit through 'red lining' or because they have fewer resources with which to pay. As a result, those on low incomes are often forced to use the more expensive forms of credit.

While those with higher incomes are more likely to use credit to acquire assets, those with lower incomes are more likely to use it to cope with adversity. However, using credit in this way can give rise to a vicious circle in which the present problem is solved at the expense of larger commitments in the future and the build-up of problem debts. It seems likely that many of those who use a particular form of credit do so through habit, convenience, and in ignorance of the existence and availability of other forms of credit for the purpose they have in mind[12].

Those on low incomes are often paid weekly and so are more likely to prefer forms of credit, such as mail order firms, tallymen, or trading checks, where payment is made weekly. Credit cards and bank loans, which are generally paid monthly, are not as attractive to those who receive their wages weekly. Also, many people on low incomes use small creditors with whom they have developed a personal relationship, such as those who collect at the door on a weekly basis.

Research on why people get into debt indicates that an important causal factor is a sudden, adverse change in circumstances—for example, unemployment, redundancy, sickness, childbirth or marital breakdown—which has the effect of either reducing income or increasing expenditure. Commitments taken on in good times may be difficult to meet in less favourable circumstances. Research also indicates that poverty leads to indebtedness since the poor simply do not have enough money to meet their everyday requirements[13]. The first of these explanations will be exacerbated if those affected by a change in circumstances are already heavily committed by borrowing up to the limit of their ability to repay; the second will be heightened by living in poverty for a long period of time. Fuel debts, rent arrears and loans taken out to cover these bills are very common among the long term poor.

The majority of debtors make regular payments for a considerable period before falling into debt. Research which has looked into the characteristics of consumer debtors suggests that few of them are either 'feckless' (unable to look after their financial affairs) or 'immoral' (deliberately trying to avoid payment); rather, most of them are ordinary citizens who fall into debt through 'misfortune' due to either a loss of income caused by an adverse change in their circumstances or long term poverty where they are simply unable to cover their outgoings[14].

Among the population as a whole, however, low income is not related to indebtedness because pensioners, despite having low incomes, do not often get into serious debt. This can be explained in terms of their attitudes to credit (they are the age group that is by far the most hostile to it and so use it least) and by the fact that the low income they receive in retirement is both regular and stable. If pensioners are excluded, then income becomes a much more significant factor in determining whether people have debt problems: according to the 1992 PSI survey, the proportion of non-pensioner households with problem debts, the average number of such debts and the number of debts per 100 commitments are all inversely related to household income[15]. The data on problem debts summarised in Table 10.5 refer to the UK as a whole, but it can be assumed that the patterns they reveal apply equally to Scotland.

Table 10.5 Problem debts by household income (UK)

	Up to £100	£100-£150	£150-£200	£200-£250	£250-£300	£300-£400	£400 plus
Proportion with:							
Any problem debts	33%	22%	13%	9%	10%	8%	2%
Three or more debts	10%	4%	4%	2%	1%	1%	0%
Average number of debts	0.69	0.40	0.29	0.19	0.18	0.13	0.04
Debts per 100 commitments	12.8	6.5	4.2	2.6	2.3	1.7	0.5
Number of respondents	255	176	255	201	177	284	206

Source : R. Berthoud and E. Kempson, *Credit and Debt : the PSI Survey*, Routledge, 1992, Table 8.5.

The introduction of student loans, combined with reductions in the value of student grants and changes in eligibility for benefits, has led to a substantial increase in debt among this group of consumers. A survey carried out by Edinburgh University Students' Association (EUSA) indicated that 52.2% of students had debts averaging £949.15 at the end of the academic year (July) and 39.8% still owed an average of £717.25 at the beginning of the following year (October)[16].

10.5 Debt Advice

Although debt advice in Scotland is provided by many agencies, Citizens Advice Scotland, through its 64 Bureaux and 11 full time money advice workers, deals with the majority of cases. Figures from these Bureaux (summarised in Table 10.6) suggest that money and debt advice are becoming an ever increasing part of their workload with the number of debt enquiries increasing more than three-fold between 1986 and 1993 (see also section 11.6b in the chapter on legal services).

While the greatest number of cases are dealt with by CABx, several other agencies also offer debt advice. A network of Independent Money Advice Centres (mainly financed by local authorities) is involved in debt work along with more general enquiries. These centres vary enormously in size and in the range of services they offer. Debt advice is also given out by local authority Social Work Departments, local authority Consumer Protection/Trading Standards Departments and by Social Fund Officers in the Benefits Agency.

While there clearly is a need for a co-ordinated, well organised and efficiently run system of debt advice in Scotland, and there have been some positive moves towards this goal with the setting up of Money Advice Scotland to help improve communication between the various organisations involved in money advice, for this to be successful the rivalry which appears to exist between the various debt advice agencies would have to end[17].

The possibility of additional funding urgently needs to be explored. One possibility is to raise money from agencies which grant credit. The level of private funding is currently very low, accounting for only 16% of funding for CABx in Scotland[18].

CREDIT AND DEBT

Table 10.6 Money advice and debt enquiries at Scottish CABx, 1986-1992

Year	Totals enquiries	Money Advice enquiries	Money Advice enquiries as % of total	Debt enquiries	Debt enquiries as % of total
1985-86	445,647	131,012	29.4	28,057	6.3
1986-87	495,796	n/a	n/a	42,114	8.5
1987-88	508,319	195,575	38.5	54,165	10.7
1988-89	511,824	219,327	42.9	55,517	10.7
1989-90	556,954	258,734	46.5	60,023	10.8
1990-91	562,705	255,301	45.4	69,395	12.3
1991-92	628,562	279,916	44.5	81,220	12.9
1992-93	629,570	293,955	46.7	93,818	14.9

Source : Citizens Advice Scotland, *Annual Review*, various years.

There is an element of self-interest in this for the private sector that should be stressed: debt counselling can be in the interests of the creditor as well as the debtor in that it can both lead to a negotiated settlement and persuade them to abandon expensive attempts at recovery when there is no chance of repayment.

10.6 Debt Enforcement Through the Courts

As indicated in earlier sections, the consumer credit market has grown dramatically in the last 15 years or so and it is clear that the number of debt problems has also risen steeply. This section looks at the extent to which debtors have been subject to diligence—that is, to court-sanctioned debt enforcement procedures.

The activity of the Scottish courts between 1980 and 1990 might have been expected to keep pace with the rise of consumer credit. However, this has not occurred. Although there was a modest increase in the number of debt actions raised, the amount of diligence actually fell[19]. Between 1985 and 1990, the number of court actions[20] rose by less than 10% from 163,124 to 184,217 while the number of poindings and warrant sales fell (the former from 16,468 to 9,225, the latter from 693 to 640)[21].

This being the case, there are two possible explanations for the relative decline during the 1980s in the use of the courts as a means of debt enforcement:

- The first is that court procedures have become more expensive or less effective and, as a result, less attractive to creditors as a means of recovering debts. It is clear that many creditors regard recovery through the courts as a cumbersome way of enforcing the debt. Indeed many companies see the main advantage of court action as increasing the pressure on the individual to come to an agreement about repaying the debt rather than as a direct means of recovering the money[22]. However, it is hard to see why there should have been a sufficiently marked increase in the level of disenchantment to explain the relative decline in the use of the courts. Indeed, the Debtors (Scotland) Act 1987 which reformed the law of diligence was designed, among other things, to make debt enforcement through the courts more efficient and to appeal to creditors[23]. The development of debt counselling services may have resulted in successful negotiations with creditors over debts which would otherwise have gone to court, and may have helped to make creditors aware that there is little point in taking debtors to court if they have no assets. Disenchantment with the courts by creditors may have contributed to the relative decline in the extent to which they are used, but it is clearly not the only relevant factor.

- This leaves what has been termed 'systemic rationalisation'[24][25]. This refers to developments in consumer credit that have increased the attractiveness of debt settlement without resort to the courts. These developments have been many and varied. They include:
    — changes in the range of available credit facilities to allow for more flexible payment of debts, such as the increased use of credit cards;
    — the increased domination in the credit market of larger companies which can afford to finance the rescheduling of repayments without suffering undue financial hardship;
    — the increased use of direct debit, standing order and overdraft facilities to ease the repayment of debts and the similar effect of direct deductions from social security payments;
    — the increased use of pre-payment arrangements, especially in the utilities industries.

These developments are very diverse but all have the effect of making resort to the courts less likely[26]. In fact systemic rationalisation is probably the major reason for the comparative drop in the number of court actions despite the rise in consumer credit. Whether this has been a positive or a negative development for the consumer is still unclear.

Overall, there appears to have been a move away from a public form of debt enforcement through the courts to private forms of debt enforcement through charging high rates of interest on outstanding loans and, in some cases, refusing further credit[27]. However, this shift has not affected the low income consumer to the same extent as those with higher incomes. Those with low incomes, who are less likely to have bank accounts, credit cards or access to 'modern' forms of credit, have benefited less from systemic rationalisation than those with higher incomes. One consequence of this is that court actions are more directed than ever at low income consumers.

Another important change in the legal system was the introduction of the Small Claims procedure (see also section 11.3b in the chapter on legal services). This was introduced in 1988 and aimed to simplify claims made for relatively small amounts (under £750). The intention was to encourage individuals to come forward to sort out disputes and small debt problems in the courts. The evidence from the first year of implementation, however, indicated that 90% of the litigants were larger businesses and public utilities[28]. This suggests that, rather than being a way for individual citizens to settle disputes, the new procedure may be providing an easier means for large firms to enforce their smaller debts. Whether or not this is beneficial depends on whether creditors use the new procedures to collect small debts from the poor (who would otherwise have had greater flexibility to repay) and whether creditors use the courts instead of private enforcement procedures (which may be even harsher on the poor because of, for example, high interest rates).

One final change in the legal system, which came into effect on 1 April 1993, concerns voluntary sequestration. Under the Bankruptcy (Scotland) Act 1985, a person may be declared bankrupt and have his estate sequestrated by the Sheriff Court or the Court of Session. The number of awards made by the courts is set out in Table 10.7. It can be seen that there was a particularly sharp increase in the number of awards made by the Sheriff Court which increased more than ten-fold from 508 in 1987 to 5,387 in 1991.

Table 10.7 Number of awards of sequestration, 1987-1991

	1987	1988	1989	1990	1991
Court of Session	52	31	52	39	64
Sheriff Court	508	920	1,560	2,579	5,387
Total	560	951	1,612	2,608	5,491

Source : *Annual Report of the Accountant in Bankruptcy 1992,* The Scottish Office, 1993.

Specialised insolvency practitioners have played a key role in providing expert advice about sequestration but their remuneration from public funds will cease when the Bankruptcy (Scotland) Act 1992 comes into effect. Although the Government has announced an extension of the legal aid scheme to allow solicitors to prepare debtors' petitions and present them in court, there are not enough legal aid solicitors for this work and those who are available have less time and less expertise than insolvency practitioners. As a result, the use of sequestration and the opportunity it provided for insolvent debtors to rehabilitate themselves are likely to decline.

10.7 Convenient Credit

Much of this chapter has concentrated on the negative aspects of credit. Yet it is undoubtedly the case that credit is, in general, beneficial since it allows people to get by in difficult times and to afford goods that would otherwise be beyond their reach. There have been a number of positive developments in credit in recent years that have made credit arrangements cheaper and more convenient. The rise in standing orders and the more recent, more dramatic, rise in direct debits have allowed people with bank accounts to ensure that their finances are simplified by having certain bills paid automatically by the banks[29]. However, the impact of these arrangements on those with low incomes is relatively small, as few of them possess a bank account or have a steady enough income to be able to make use of such facilities.

The monthly payment schemes which are now operated by the fuel companies enable people to pay their annual fuel bills in fixed monthly instalments throughout the year without the traditional seasonal fluctuations. These schemes make it easier for people to budget for their bills and enable them to predict what they will have to pay each month. Scottish Power had 280,000 households paying monthly in April 1992, though many did so using direct debit or standing orders, suggesting that many of those who used the scheme were not on low incomes[30]. However, those in receipt of income support who are in arrears may have money deducted from their benefit to pay off their arrears and towards their next bill. Although this does ensure that the fuel bill gets paid, it can mean that other debts build up due to the loss of income (see also section 3.5a in the chapter on energy and fuel consumption).

Another form of credit which can work to the consumers' advantage is a hire purchase agreement where this is offered interest-free (and the retailer has not made a price increase to cover the cost of the interest). Interest-free agreements are sometimes offered by retailers as a form of sales promotion in which the retailer pays the interest leaving the consumer to pay only the basic sale price of the goods. It is estimated that up to 20% of all hire purchase agreements are interest-free[31].

10.8 Alternative Forms of Credit

Some types of credit are particularly important for those on lower incomes. Mail order firms are used fairly evenly across all income groups and mail order is the most popular form of credit with 30% of all households using it according to a 1989 PSI survey[32]. It is, however, more important for low income households since they do not use as many of the other types of credit. Mail order is generally used to buy clothes and shoes, with some expenditure on household goods. It is most commonly used by parents with children and by women. Despite its importance for people on low incomes it has a comparatively low default rate although, when problems do occur, mail order companies are often among the most aggressive in trying to recoup their money, threatening court action at an early stage and not attempting to find out about the defaulter's financial situation or personal circumstances[33]. (See also section 8.3d in the chapter on high street goods and services.)

Other money lenders, such as check traders, tallymen and pawnbrokers, deal almost exclusively with lower income groups although the numbers involved are relatively small[34]. They have far higher rates of 'problem debts' than other groups of lenders, the risk being six times that of finance house loans and HP agreements. Their importance is both because they provide a readily available form of credit for those who are unable to obtain credit elsewhere and because they are seen to be less rigid than other lenders. This is in spite of the fact that they often charge extremely high rates of interest.

Another form of credit which is used frequently by those on low incomes, but is often ignored in discussions of credit, is money borrowed from family and friends. This form of credit is especially useful as it is generally interest-free, and 10% of families in the 1989 PSI survey reported that they had borrowed in this way in the previous 12 months[35]. These loans were also the least likely to become problem debts with less than 1% causing problems, probably because people give top priority to paying them off. While this form of credit is interest-free, people are generally very reluctant to borrow from family or friends as they often feel ashamed to have to ask them and worry a great deal about repaying these loans[36].

A further form of credit used by those with low incomes is the Social Fund. This provides two types of interest-free loans to people on a discretionary basis : budgeting loans which are made to enable recipients who have been on income support for at least 26 weeks to spread the cost of relatively expensive items (such as a bed, other items of furniture, or a washing machine) over a longer period; and crisis loans which are intended to prevent a serious risk to the health or safety of recipients (who do not need to be in receipt of income support) and their dependents in the event of an emergency or following a disaster. Budgeting loans and crisis loans are both repayable by direct deductions from social security payments: most loans are repaid within 78 weeks and the normal weekly rate of repayment is 15% of the applicant's personal income support allowance. Decisions about who should get such loans are made by Social Fund Officers who have to take into account the monthly budgetary allocation for loans and the level of repayments achieved. Thus, 'cash limits' play a vital role in deciding whether or not to provide someone with a loan (see section 9.5 in the chapter on social security for more about the Social Fund).

Although Social Fund loans are interest-free, people are frequently reluctant to apply for them unless their situation is desperate as they have a number of perceived drawbacks:

- Applicants often feel degraded by the experience of applying for loans.
- Applicants are uncertain about the outcome and many requests are refused.
- Repayment by means of direct deductions from social security payments is disliked as it does not give people the option of missing an occasional payment when they are having a difficult week[37].

As can be seen from Table 10.8, a substantial number of people are refused Social Fund loans, in particular budgeting loans. This is of concern because these loans are restricted to people on very low incomes and, as already mentioned, people tend only to apply as a last resort. The most frequent reasons for refusing a budgeting loan are that the request has 'insufficient priority', an elastic term which is adjusted to match the state of the local Social Fund budget (cited in 183,565 cases, i.e. 31.0% of refusals in 1991/2) and being on income support for less than 26 weeks (cited in 166,399 cases, i.e. 28.1% of cases). Of even greater concern is that, in 31,595 cases (i.e. 5.3% of refusals), the reason cited is that the applicant cannot afford to repay the loan. Many of those who are refused a Social Fund loan have no option but to turn to one of the more convenient but much more expensive forms of credit described in section 10.7 above.

A final form of credit which may be of help to those on low incomes is provided through a credit union. Credit unions are savings and loans co-operatives in which members have a common bond. Members agree to save money into a pool which can then be used to finance loans at fixed rates of interest. Credit unions have been very slow to take off in Scotland (and more generally in the UK), although recent evidence suggests that they have now begun to grow more quickly. This is illustrated by figures in Table 10.9 from Lothian Region which show that membership has increased eight-fold and assets by a factor of 40 over the last five years.

Credit unions can certainly be a useful way of enabling those on low incomes to gain access to comparatively cheap credit. At the same time, they can help those on low incomes to save, even if this only involves very small amounts each week. Nevertheless, they do not live up to all the claims made for them. Even among their

Table 10.8 Loans from the Social Fund, 1991-1992 (UK)*

	Budgeting Loans	Crisis Loans
Applications received	1,360,000	711,000
Awards	711,000	592,000
Awards as % of applications processed	53%	88%
Refusals	591,862	75,388
Average award (£)	£217	£62

* data refer to the period April 1991 - March 1992
Source : *Annual Report of the Social Fund 1991-1992*, Cm.1992, HMSO, 1993.

Table 10.9 Credit Unions in Lothian Region, 1988-1992

Year	Number of members	Index (1987-88=100)	Total Assets	Index (1987-88=100)
1987-88	382	100.0	27,485	100.0
1988-89	657	172.0	82,244	299.2
1989-90	2,254	590.1	441,815	1,607.5
1990-91	2,662	696.9	660,591	2,403.5
1991-92	3,281	858.9	1,099,320	3,999.7

Source : Lothian Region Credit Union Development Agency, *Annual Report*, 1991/92.

own members, credit unions are not the main form of credit. Thus, while they can be of assistance, they do not serve people's entire credit needs. Furthermore they are often centred around the workplace and, as a result, comprise a high proportion of middle income members and are not particularly significant for those on lower incomes. The largest community-based credit union in Scotland is Dalmuir Credit Union with 2,800 members. While credit union membership is increasing fairly rapidly, it is doing so from a very small base and, while the development of credit unions is to be encouraged, it is not going to make a great deal of difference to most people, particularly those on low incomes, in the short term.

10.9 The Regulation of Consumer Credit

The Office of Fair Trading (OFT) and Trading Standards Authorities are responsible for regulating the consumer credit market. The responsibility of the Director General of the OFT and his staff includes:

- the surveillance of trading practices;
- reporting bad trading practices to the Secretary of State for Trade and Industry and recommending action to remedy them;
- taking action against traders who are persistently unfair in their business;
- encouraging voluntary codes of practice;
- publishing information and advice for consumers.

The OFT does not deal with individual complaints but does collate information about them so that it is aware of any general problems in the consumer credit market and can recommend suitable action where this is necessary. The OFT allocates credit licences to traders and can refuse or withdraw them where this is considered appropriate. These licences are a useful indicator of the number of secondary credit institutions that have developed around the credit industry. These secondary institutions comprise credit reference agencies and debt collecting agencies.

Table 10.10 shows that there has been a very large increase in the number of licences granted to debt collection agencies between 1985 and 1992. Although there is no available information concerning the socio-economic characteristics of those from whom they attempt to recover outstanding debt, it is clear that this includes a high proportion of those on low incomes.

Table 10.10 Debt collection agency licences granted by OFT, 1985-1990 (UK)

Year	Number of New Licences Granted
1985	1,417
1986	1,441
1987	1,821
1988	1,921
1989	2,325
1990	2,256
1991	2,906
1992	3,038

Source : Office of Fair Trading, personal communication, April 1993.

Although the OFT formulates policy relating to the regulation of consumer credit, it is Trading Standards Authorities that actually enforce consumer credit law. Strathclyde Region Trading Standards Department has set up a special unit for dealing with illegal money lending and other forms of consumer fraud. It is currently investigating 200 cases of alleged money lending and claims to have a 90% success rate. The unit works closely with the police and the procurator fiscal, who decides whether or not to prosecute on the evidence uncovered by the unit's investigations. There are currently about ten prosecutions per year.

The 1974 Consumer Credit Act lays down the legal framework for consumer credit agreements. The use of the Annual Percentage Rate (APR) as a general measure of the cost of interest was introduced by the Act so that people could compare the terms offered by different traders. APR is a measure which takes into account the reduction of the debt as the loan is paid up and so gives a more accurate measure of the interest rate on the loan. Its main problem is its complexity; for example, when asked, most people do not know what APR stands for[38]. It would be far simpler for people to understand what it means if a whole figure rather than a percentage were used or even if a system of written statements was introduced in which credit costs were banded and the consumer told in written form which band the agreement falls into—for instance 'high cost', 'very low cost', similar to the system for describing the tar content in cigarettes[39].

Other measures in the Consumer Credit Act include: a five day 'cooling off' period for agreements signed outwith retail premises, mainly aimed at stopping purchases resulting from pressure selling on the doorstep; an insistence that traders must serve a 'default notice' which states what consumers have done wrong and gives them seven days to remedy the situation before any further action is taken (for instance to reclaim goods); and provisions which enable the OFT to demand a 'cease and desist' assurance from a trader who has been operating in an unfair way. If this order is ignored, the trader can be prosecuted and face the prospect of a fine or imprisonment.

The regulation of consumer credit has been frequently amended since 1974. One area in which the OFT is currently recommending further changes, which could be of particular advantage to those on low incomes, relates to the concept of 'extortionate' credit. This concept was intended to protect vulnerable low income consumers from being charged overly high interest rates on credit. However, between 1977 and 1991 only 20 cases against creditors on this ground made it to court in the UK[40]. Even when such cases do get to court, the legislation is weighted heavily in favour of the creditor with evidence needed from the pursuer to prove that the interest rate charges were 'grossly exorbitant', a very high standard of proof. The OFT is now recommending that 'extortionate' credit be replaced with the legal concept of an 'unjust credit transaction'. Credit would then have to be proved 'excessive' rather than 'grossly exorbitant' for the case to be found against the creditor[41]. While this is a move in the right direction, it will not help those who are unwilling to come forward to complain about 'unjust credit' because they are afraid of losing the only form of credit to which they have access.

One of the OFT's other functions is to encourage the setting up of voluntary codes of practice by trade associations. One area where this is currently going on is the banking sector where the 'Banking Code of Practice' has been in operation since March 1992 and is currently under review. A recent study by the Consumers' Association suggests that many Building Societies and banks are not adequately publicising the Code of Banking Practice or the existence of the Banking and the Building Society Ombudsmen[42]. This is of real concern as awareness of such schemes is low and they are of no use to people who do not know of their existence.

Although low income households are most in need of protection, they are least likely to benefit from these voluntary codes of practice. This is because they are least likely to have a bank account or an account with a Building Society[43] and because voluntary codes of practice do not (as yet) apply to the types of credit which are most important for them (see section 10.8 above). The recent introduction by the banks of 'maintenance charges' on personal accounts which fall below a given threshold[44] will have a disproportionate effect on those with low incomes and may discourage them from opening or maintaining bank accounts and thus benefiting from bank services such as direct debits, standing orders and agreed overdrafts (see section 10.7 above). One low income group who will almost certainly experience the first of these effects, although not necessarily the second, is students.

10.10 Conclusions

The evidence reviewed in this chapter makes it clear that there has been an enormous expansion in the amount of credit extended in recent years. For most people this has been a very welcome development since it has enabled them to purchase goods and services, which would otherwise have been beyond their reach, through paying by instalments over a period of time. However, for many people, in particular those with low incomes, these developments have resulted in serious financial problems. The amount of credit outstanding has increased in parallel with the amount extended and substantial numbers of people have found themselves unable to make the required repayments. There has been a massive increase in the number of requests for money advice and debt counselling from advice agencies, so much so that the available resources are stretched to breaking point. The casualties of the consumer credit boom have mainly been households with young children who have either experienced an unanticipated deterioration in their financial circumstances or spent long periods in or on the margins of poverty. For them, the increase in the availability of consumer credit has not expanded their horizons but, rather, has magnified their problems, as they are forced to borrow more on less favourable terms to avoid the consequences of failing to meet the repayments for goods and services that they had purchased on credit in the past.

Despite the enormous expansion in the amount of credit outstanding, with one notable exception, there has been no corresponding increase in the number of court actions initiated by creditors[45]. Lenders have increasingly preferred to use other methods of enforcing payment. These other means include, for example, charging high interest rates, withdrawing credit and selling debts to debt collecting agencies. Whether these changes, which reflect a privatisation of debt enforcement, have been beneficial for the borrower, especially the low income borrower, must be an open question because so little is known about these activities and their impact on those who cannot keep up with their repayments.

Although in recent years there have been a number of positive developments that have eased the financial position of consumers and reduced the risk of default (for instance, the greater availability of standing orders, direct debits and instalment payments), many of them have been of little advantage to the poor since they tend not to have bank accounts or a sufficiently regular income to qualify. The same is true of credit unions, which offer cheap loans and encourage people to save. These have not only been slow to develop but due to registration requirements are almost invariably associated with the workplace. Thus, they are of little or no help to the unemployed or to those whose employment fluctuates.

Of course, some developments have been specifically aimed at the poor, such as the use of direct deductions from social security benefits and pre-payment facilities for electricity consumers. However, closer inspection of both these schemes suggests that they may actually exacerbate the problems of low income households. The decline in the value of social security benefits (in particular for the unemployed) means that direct deductions may impose very severe financial problems on those affected, while the use of pre-payment facilities deprives users of credit (except short term emergency credit) and makes them liable to cut themselves off and end up, if only for short periods, without electricity.

There is a good deal of indirect evidence to support the conclusion that low income households are most likely to experience problems with consumer credit and that these difficulties are worse for them than for people who are better placed financially. Unfortunately there is little direct evidence, because the poor do not come forward to complain about their experiences. The OFT and local Trading Standards Departments are to some extent reactive in their approaches and, therefore, lack systematic information about the workings of the consumer credit market or the need for further regulation to address the particular problems faced by those on low incomes.

That notwithstanding, it should be stressed that the special problems experienced by low income households in relation to consumer credit are due as much to their poverty as to the operation of the consumer credit market. The need to address these problems, important though that is, should not divert attention away from the need to improve the financial circumstances of low income households.

References and footnotes to Chapter 10

1. Monopolies and Mergers Commission, *Credit Card Services: a report on the supply of credit services in the United Kingdom,* Cm.718, London, HMSO, 1989.
2. According to the Monopolies and Mergers Commission Report, about 30% of cardholders paid all their statements in full, 30% paid interest continuously over a 12 month period while the remaining 40% took extended credit for at least one month (but less than 12 months) in the year. These estimates refer to 1987.
3. Central Statistical Office, *Annual Abstract of Statistics,* various years.
4. R. Berthoud and E. Kempson, *Credit and Debt: the PSI Survey,* Routledge, 1992.
5. National Consumer Council, *Consumers and Credit,* NCC, 1980.
6. Office of Fair Trading, *Credit Scoring,* Office of Fair Trading, 1992.
7. These enforcement orders came into effect on 31 July 1993.
8. Office of Fair Trading, see reference 6.
9. J. Ford, *The Indebted Society : Credit and Default in the 1980s,* Routledge, 1988.
10. Office of Fair Trading, see reference 6.
11. R. Berthoud and E. Kempson, see reference 4.
12. G. Parker, *Credit,* Chapter 12 in R. Walker and G. Parker (eds) *Money Matters,* Sage, 1988.
13. M. Adler, *The Economic and Social Situation of Consumer Debtors in Great Britain* in G. Hörmann (ed.), *Consumer Credit and Consumer Indebtedness,* University of Bremen Press, 1986. For more up-to-date evidence, see R. Berthoud and E. Kempson, reference 4.
14. M. Adler and E. Wozniak, *More and Less Coercive Ways of Settling Debts* in H. M. and N. L. Drucker (eds), *The Scottish Government Yearbook 1980,* Paul Harris, 1979.

15. R. Berthoud and E. Kempson, see reference 4.
16. Based on a sample of 1,201 students representing approximately 10.1% of all undergraduates and 14.0% of returning undergraduates at Edinburgh University. See *EUSA Matriculation Poll Report (Student Finances and Employment)*, October 1992.
17. T. Hinton and R. Berthoud, *Money Advice Services*, Policy Studies Institute Research Report 660, London, PSI, 1988.
18. CEI Consultants, *Money Advice in Scotland : a New Opportunity*, Final Report of a Development Study for the Scottish Development Agency, 1990.
19. Diligence comprises the court-sanctioned remedies which may be applied to a debtor when the creditor has obtained decree. They include arrestment of wages as well as the poinding and sale of moveable property.
20. Court actions include ordinary causes (where the sum involved is over £1,500), summary causes (where the sum involved is less than this) and cases brought under the Small Claims procedure. Although they include a number of different types of action, debt actions are by far the largest category, comprising more than 50% of the total.
21. Figures from *Civil Judicial Statistics*, various years. There are no published figures for decrees obtained by the pursuer. Statistics relating to arrestments have only been published since 1989.
22. T. Hinton and R. Berthoud, see reference 17.
23. It was also intended to make the practice of diligence less oppressive. The main changes as regards debtors were extending the list of items which are exempt from warrant sale, introducing new Time-to-Pay Directions and Orders which replaced Instalment Decrees and reforms to the arrestment of wages. These measures are intended to benefit both parties; the reduction of the amount arrested imposes less financial pressure on the debtor while the debt is being paid off and continuous arrestments enable the creditor to recover the debt in full without having to raise actions repeatedly in court. For a fuller account, see D. I. Nichols, *The Debtors (Scotland) Act 1987*, W. Green and Son, 1987.
24. R. A. Kagan, `The routinisation of debt collection : an essay on social change and conflict in the courts', *Law and Society Review,* Vol.18 (3), 1984.
25. M. Adler and G. Hörmann, *Schuldbeitreibung und die Gerichte : Bundesrepublik und Gross Britannien im Vergleich (Debt Enforcement and the Courts : West Germany and Great Britain Compared)* in E. Blankenburg and R. Voigt (eds) *Implementation von Gerichtsentscheidungen*, Westdeutshcer Verlag, 1987.
26. Research on creditors' policies and practices is currently being undertaken by the Scottish Office Central Research Unit.
27. M. Adler and G. Hörmann, see reference 25.
28. H. Jones et al., *Small Claims in the Sheriff Court in Scotland,* Central Research Unit Papers, The Scottish Office, 1991.
29. According to figures provided by the Association for Payment and Clearing Services (APACS), the volume of direct debits has grown almost five-fold in the last ten years (from 871,000 per day in 1982 to 3,923,000 per day in 1992) while standing orders have now stabilised at around 900,000 per day. The figures refer to the UK as a whole.

30. Scottish Power, *Annual Report and Accounts*, Glasgow, 1992.
31. R. Berthoud and E. Kempson, see reference 4.
32. R. Berthoud and E. Kempson, see reference 4.
33. R. Berthoud and E. Kempson, see reference 4.
34. National Consumer Council, *Credit and Debt : the Consumer Interest*, HMSO, 1990.
35. R. Berthoud and E. Kempson, see reference 4.
36. J. Ford, Consuming Credit : *Debt and Poverty in the UK*, Child Poverty Action Group, 1991.
37. R. Cohen, *Debt and the Social Fund*, Family Service Unit, 1991.
38. R. Berthoud and E. Kempson, see reference 4.
39. Consumers' Association, *Handbook of Consumer Law* (3rd edition),1991.
40. J. Ford, see reference 36.
41. Office of Fair Trading, *Unjust Credit Transactions*, 1991.
42. Building societies were the worst culprits with fewer than a quarter displaying signs advertising the Ombudsman and fewer than a third able to hand out leaflets when asked. See *The Independent*, 8 April 1993.
43. The Social Security Advisory Committee has commissioned an independent report into why a fifth of all households do not have a bank account. The report is due to be published early in 1994.
44. The Royal Bank of Scotland charges £3.00 per month on accounts which fall below £50.00.
45. The one exception is the very sharp increase in possession actions raised by building societies and other mortgage lenders.

11 Legal Services

by Elizabeth Macdonald

In this chapter Elizabeth Macdonald describes the ways in which those on low incomes are disadvantaged in their use of legal services. Although legal services provided under the legal aid scheme may be free for those who are very poor, many others on low incomes are faced with expensive bills. Reduced eligibility for legal aid means that many in Scotland will no longer get free legal aid or will have to make a contribution they cannot afford. Procedures at tribunals and in Small Claims cases are too formal and lack of representation puts claimants at a disadvantage. Poor access to legal services, a lack of advisers with appropriate expertise, lack of knowledge about legal rights and attitudes to the legal system all create barriers for those on low incomes to overcome.

11.1 Introduction

Legal services may become important to people unexpectedly and in stressful circumstances. The existence of a legal remedy may become critical if your landlord wants to make you homeless, if you want to be protected from a violent spouse, if your employer wants to dismiss you or if you have had an accident at work. But the existence of legal rights or remedies is only of academic interest if individuals have no access to the legal services which enable them to enforce their rights.

Consumers on low incomes may be disadvantaged as a result of the nature of substantive law: for instance, in the area of housing, the replacement of regulated tenancies by assured tenancies in the Housing (Scotland) Act 1988 has strengthened the position of the landlord in relation to the tenant; similarly the abolition of the Wages Councils has removed a legal right to a minimum level of pay in certain areas of employment. Although this chapter focuses on legal services, if the goal of legal services' policy is defined in terms of equal access to justice, then attention cannot be restricted to the means by which legal services are provided, but must extend to accessible procedures and laws.

There is evidence that despite the attempts that have been made to ensure that legal services are available to those who may need them, individuals very often forego their rights[1]. The legal system is perceived as being intimidating and costly. The individual, who rarely comes into contact with its workings, is at a disadvantage compared with the 'repeat players' such as insurance companies who use the courts frequently. While most people will come into contact with the legal system at some point in their lives, they will only approach lawyers with some reluctance and possibly only after discussing their problem with more accessible advisors such as Citizens Advice Bureaux staff or volunteers.

In any consideration of legal services it is important that their definition should not be restricted to 'services provided by lawyers'. The Royal Commission for Legal Services in Scotland (the Hughes Commission) which reported in 1980 shared this starting-point, arguing that lawyers may give advice which is not of a legal nature and, equally, many people other than lawyers—for example trading standards officers, trade union officers, and Citizens Advice Bureaux volunteers—can provide legal advice. The courts and court staff are also involved in providing legal services, and important legal advice can also be conveyed by other means, for example through information provided in leaflets, advertisements and booklets. The Hughes Commission chose to define legal services as falling into two parts:

> "Firstly enabling the client to identify and, if he judges appropriate, to choose a legal solution; and secondly, enabling the client to pursue a given legal solution"[2].

This definition is echoed by the Legal Aid Board for England and Wales which in its 1990/91 Annual Report described access to legal services being achieved when,

> "individuals are aware of their need for legal services and can select and actually obtain legal services of an appropriate quality, at a price within reach."

These definitions highlight the essential points which any attempt to assess the adequacy of provision of legal services must address i.e. information, accessibility, choice, value for money, affordability and appropriateness of service.

This chapter is concerned with the extent to which the provision of legal services to consumers on low incomes is adequate, the ways in which those on low incomes are disadvantaged, and the extent to which changes could be made to the pattern of provision of legal services so as to increase the information about, the access to, the appropriateness of, and the affordability of legal services. The focus is on Scotland but, as the pattern of provision is broadly similar in England and Wales, reference will also be made to the system there.

The Scottish legal system is quite distinct from the system in England and Wales. It has its own body of substantive law with the principle-led approach of the Roman based civil law tradition rather than the precedent-driven common law tradition of the English system, and its own court structure and legal profession. There are, of course, substantial areas of the law which are the same on both sides of the border, and the way in which legal services are provided is broadly similar. In Scotland legal services are provided predominantly by solicitors and advocates in private practice, with a very limited degree of provision by community law centres, and with advice and a varying degree of representation being provided by Citizens Advice Bureaux and other advice agencies.

The public provision of legal services to those who could not otherwise afford the cost has been achieved largely by means of the legal aid scheme which was introduced throughout the UK in 1950. Although the Scottish scheme has distinctive features, it is essentially the same as that used in England and Wales. The UK scheme has generally been regarded as considerably in advance of similar schemes in other countries, in terms of the extent of state funding and the scope of its coverage[3]. However, the legal aid scheme has come under increasing criticism in recent years as, first, cutbacks in public expenditure have led to the erosion of eligibility and, second, the Government and the legal profession have failed to address other factors limiting its accessibility to consumers. These factors fall into two main categories: those which are faults of the legal aid system itself and those which arise from the fact that legal services are provided through the medium of a self-regulating private profession rather than, for instance, by a publicly funded salaried service.

11.2 Legal Aid

The way in which publicly funded legal services are provided differs significantly from the way in which other public services were provided as a result of the Beveridge reforms after the Second World War, which were characterised by Townsend as "minimum rights for the many"[4]. The legal aid scheme as originally conceived adhered to the Beveridge philosophy in its goal of covering not just those "normally classed as poor", but also those of moderate means, so that "no-one will be financially unable to prosecute a just and reasonable claim or defend a legal right". It nonetheless retained elements more akin to 19th century poor law philosophy, which Townsend has described as "the conditional welfare of the few"[5], with public expenditure being kept down by the use of a means test. The legal aid scheme did not interfere with the existing professional structure and placed no obligations on solicitors either to accept cases or to meet any other conditions which, for instance, might have ensured a widespread geographical availability.

This method of providing legal services is known as the 'Judicare' model and it exists in most western industrialised countries. The main characteristics of this model of provision are that:

- funding comes from the state while the administration of the scheme is the responsibility of an independent body (in Scotland, the Scottish Legal Aid Board);
- it is demand-led with open-ended expenditure;
- it is provided by private practitioners;
- there are complex eligibility criteria;
- it offers a choice to the client of which solicitor to use;
- and, while the poorest get free legal aid, assisted persons may be required to contribute to the cost, depending on their means.

An assessment of eligibility for legal aid takes account of both disposable income and capital after various allowances are taken into account. A lower income limit determines the income level below which no contribution is required. Between this lower limit and an upper limit, contributions are payable on a sliding scale. Above the upper limit clients must meet their full legal costs.

In Scotland legal aid is available for three categories of legal work:

- Advice and Assistance, for advice and preparation in both civil and criminal work;
- Civil Legal Aid, for raising or defending a civil action in court;
- Criminal Legal Aid, for court representation in a criminal case.

Criminal Legal Aid takes 57% of the Scottish Legal Aid Board's (SLAB) expenditure; Civil Legal Aid accounts for 22%; and the remaining 21% going on Advice and Assistance.

While legal aid undoubtedly provides a service to some consumers on low incomes, it is limited by the fact that certain types of legal work cannot be paid for from the legal aid fund, the most significant being representation before tribunals (with the exception of Employment Appeal Tribunals and the Lands Tribunal) and at Small Claims hearings.

(a) **Recent developments**

In the 1980s expenditure on legal aid rose at well above the rate of inflation and faster than other public expenditure. From 1981 to 1991 in the UK as a whole there was an average growth of 17% per annum, or 10% taking inflation into account[6]. In Scotland expenditure almost doubled between 1988/89 and 1992/3, and in 1992/3 £109.5 million was paid out to solicitors and advocates[7]. In England and Wales it has been estimated that 10% of solicitors' total turnover is derived from legal aid[8].

The reaction of a government intent on containing the growth of public expenditure has been to reduce eligibility levels and to consider ways in which efficiency and quality of service could be ensured. The consultation paper *Eligibility for Civil Legal Aid in Scotland* issued by the Scottish Office in July 1991[9] made various suggestions for alternatives to legal aid, such as legal expenses insurance or a contingency legal aid fund. It also included proposals for modifications to the existing system including a legal aid safety net, under which a litigant would start his or her case as a private client and would receive legal aid only when the actual costs of the case reached a certain level.

The Scottish Legal Aid Board which carries out the day to day administration of the scheme was critical of the proposals for alternative methods of provision. Although the Government had attempted to widen the debate about methods of provision, the action which followed was the announcement in November 1992 of changes severely restricting eligibility for Civil Legal Aid. It was proposed to reduce the lower income limit to the income support level, and to increase the levels of contribution payable by those falling within the contributory band. Advice and Assistance would only be available to those who qualified for free legal aid. The proposals were amended on 17 February 1993 when the Government conceded that a contributory band for Advice and Assistance should be retained in Scotland because of procedural differences there[10].

(b) Erosion of eligibility

When legal aid was first introduced it was envisaged that it would cover 'persons of small or moderate means'. In practice, while the poorest members of society have always been covered, and in Scotland there is no contributory element in Criminal Legal Aid, the percentage of the population eligible for Civil Legal Aid has varied according to the prevailing income limits and income levels. In 1950 when the scheme was introduced Civil Legal Aid covered 80% of the population but this fell sharply until 1973 when only 40% were eligible. During this period the eligibility limits had kept pace with inflation but earnings had risen faster, with more wives entering the employment market. In 1979 all the legal aid limits were increased substantially. The effect of these changes was to make 79% of the population eligible.

However, it has been calculated that between 1979 and 1990 11 million adults in the UK lost eligibility for Civil Legal Aid, and that by 1990 only 47% of the population were eligible for Civil Legal Aid[11]. Since 1979 the lower limit has fallen and in the five years before the replacement of supplementary benefit by income support in 1988 was held at around 16% above the long term supplementary benefit rate. In relation to earnings the income limits show a greater fall. Between January 1980 and January 1988 average earnings rose by 107% while the legal aid limits increased by only 37%[12].

To gain a realistic picture of current levels of eligibility it would be necessary to take account of changes in earnings, tax, housing costs, income distribution and household composition. No figures have been produced since the mid-70s and it is undoubtedly time for the Government to conduct a survey of eligibility. Even without these figures there can be no doubt that eligibility has decreased and Glasser has estimated that between 1979 and 1986 the proportion of two-parent families with children eligible for free legal aid halved to 15%[13].

The Scottish Legal Aid Board's annual report for 1992/93 shows that a married couple with two children were ineligible for contributory legal aid when their gross income was £307.77 per week—at a time when the gross normal household income in Scotland was £313.68 per week[14]. Average weekly expenditure in Scotland in 1992 was £237.67 leaving very little to meet the costs of legal action, given that the average cost of a civil case in the sheriff court in 1992/93 was £739.81[15].

As eligibility for free and contributory legal aid is eroded, there is a corresponding rise in the numbers of those who fall outside the system but cannot be described as able to afford the cost of taking a case to court, and of those who, although falling within the contributory band, are unable to afford the level of contribution necessary. This is borne out by statistics in SLAB's annual report for 1992/93 which indicate that £762,943 of contributory payments were written off because the debtor was unable to pay. Statistics do not reveal the numbers who decide against pursuing their case after the cost of contributions is explained to them. Research in England has shown that one in five applicants receiving an offer of contributory legal aid decide not to go ahead with the case[16].

The effect of the reductions in eligibility which came into effect in April 1993 will make the situation considerably worse: in Civil Legal Aid the lower income limit has been reduced from £3,060 to £2,293 a year while the upper limit remains unchanged; for Advice and Assistance the lower income limit has gone down from £75 to £61 per week. The scheme will increasingly help only the very poorest members of society and effectively become a welfare benefit. This represents a fundamental departure from the philosophy behind the introduction of the legal aid scheme, and it has been estimated that as many as a million people in Scotland will be affected by the new rules, either losing eligibility for free legal aid or being required to make a contribution which they cannot afford.

The Law Society of Scotland has given examples of the effects of the changes:

- a single person earning £58.85 a week, who qualified for free civil legal aid before 1 April 1993, must now pay a contribution of £282;
- a 32 year old woman, forced to leave her husband to protect her 7 year old child, with a net income of £86 and £9.95 child benefit, will pay at least £300 for civil legal aid[17].

Payments of contributions are spread over ten months and start when legal aid is granted which may be many months before the action is concluded. If the applicant misses two payments the grant of legal aid is cancelled and the client must reapply.

There is thus a growing problem among that sector of the population which falls just outside the scope of the legal aid system but which increasingly includes members of society whose income is below the level at which they can realistically be expected to make a contribution. Tony Holland, a former president of the Law Society in England and Wales has argued that:

> " the wider you make the band of society without access to the courts, the more you will be building up resentment and, in the end, total disillusionment with the law"[18].

(c) The statutory charge and expenses

The legal aid fund attempts to recoup its costs from three sources: first, if the opposing party is ordered to pay any costs, the fund can reclaim its own expenses; second, from contributions payable by the legally aided party; and third, from any property 'recovered' or 'preserved' in the proceedings although some payments are exempt, notably maintenance payments to spouses or children, and the first £2,500 of lump sum payment in matrimonial disputes. Thus even when clients receive legal aid and no contribution is required, they may find themselves paying back a proportion of any money or property recovered or preserved, under what is called the 'statutory charge'. The effect of this is that for these clients legal aid is in reality a loan rather than a grant. This is most likely to place a burden on a party in a matrimonial case, where costs are not automatically awarded against the losing party. The consequences can be particularly severe where the property preserved or recovered is intended to provide a family home following a marriage breakdown, and in these cases the legal aid fund normally takes a standard security or mortgage over the property. Statistics given in the most recent SLAB report[19] suggest that the average amount recovered from clients in matrimonial and family cases was £727.30 while the average overall cost of those cases was £847.10. A significant proportion of that cost is, therefore, recouped from the client.

Problems with the statutory charge also arise if it is not fully explained to clients and, despite the efforts of the professional bodies to encourage solicitors to do this, it may not always happen. If consumers are to make realistic choices about the desirability of pursuing a legal solution to their problem it is vital that they should be fully informed of the costs and consequences of such an action.

11.3 Alternatives to Court Procedures

One of the ways in which the Government has sought to improve the accessibility of justice has been through the development of alternatives to traditional court procedures such as tribunals or Small Claims. Consumers on low incomes are more likely to be involved with legal issues which will be resolved at a tribunal or by a Small Claim rather than through ordinary court procedures. Any appeal about a welfare payment will be heard by a tribunal, such as the Social Security Appeal Tribunal or Disability Appeal Tribunal. Any consumer dispute with a value of up to £750 may be resolved at a Small Claims hearing. While the amount of money may be small compared to the sums at issue in other courts, the amount will be considerable for consumers on low incomes, and items which are important in maintaining daily life (for example a cooker or a washing machine) may be involved. Most issues arising from employment, such as whether a worker has been unfairly dismissed or is entitled to equal pay, will be decided by a tribunal.

(a) Tribunals

Tribunals have existed as part of the legal system since the last century, but the real impetus for their development came from the Franks Committee which reported in 1957. The Franks Committee identified a number of characteristics of tribunals which gave them advantages over courts, namely cheapness, accessibility, freedom from technicality, speed and expert knowledge in their particular field. The model tribunal was seen as being one in which a citizen was able to present a case adequately without legal or other specialist representation. A tribunal would be a less intimidating forum than a court, with its formal modes of dress and language.

Tribunals in Scotland handle a significant and growing caseload: for example in 1991, 3,561 cases were received by Industrial Tribunals for Scotland; 27,590 cases were received by Children's Hearings; and 20,000 cases were received by Social Security Appeal Tribunals (SSATs). The use of tribunals in social welfare is increasing and it is anticipated that more than 6,000 appeals will be heard by the newly created Child Support Appeal Tribunals. The Independent Tribunal Service in Scotland, which is the umbrella organisation for SSATs, Child Support, Medical, and Disability Appeal Tribunals, and Vaccine Damage Tribunals, estimates that it will handle more than 40,000 appeals in the year 1993-94[20]. By way of comparison the total number of ordinary and summary causes (including Small Claims) disposed of in all the sheriff courts in Scotland in 1991 was 187,063, with Small Claims accounting for 87,769 of this total[21]. (See also section 9.8 in the chapter on social security for further discussion of tribunals.)

It has proved difficult for tribunals to live up to the standards proposed by the Franks Committee. Employers involved in employment disputes have not hesitated to be legally represented and there has been an increasing 'judicialisation' of tribunal procedure and style. To what extent this is a consequence of the complexity of the law involved and to what extent it is due to the involvement of lawyers is a matter for debate. The more legalistic the procedure becomes, the less realistic it is to expect individuals to present their own cases.

(b) Small Claims

Similar problems are evident in the Small Claims procedure in Scotland. The procedure was introduced in the sheriff courts in November 1988 following a recommendation by the Hughes Commission in 1980 that there should be a procedure available for a wide range of claims up to a certain value (currently £750) which was sufficiently simple, cheap, quick and informal to encourage individual litigants to use it themselves without legal representation. The definition of a Small Claim is not restricted to consumer claims, but also covers personal injury and debt collecting actions, such as claims for payment of arrears of rent, and such debt collection actions make up 90% of the cases raised[22]. Although the number of actions raised by individuals in consumer disputes is relatively low, the procedure provides the ultimate remedy to a consumer who has bought a faulty cooker, or when a plumber has not returned to fix the leaking toilet he installed. Research into how well the scheme has operated was published in 1991 and suggests that in some respects the procedure has worked well, particularly in terms of its cheapness. However, there is also evidence of inappropriate formality, a lack of intervention by sheriffs to counterbalance any advantage which a represented party may have, and a tendency for cases not to be settled at one hearing[23]. A recent consultation by Scottish Courts Administration suggested that changes to bring the procedure into line with its original aims were being actively considered[24]. So far nothing has resulted from the consultation.

(c) Representation

There is clear evidence that representation before a tribunal significantly improves the chances of success. At Social Security Appeal Tribunals representation by anyone other than family or friends increased the success rate from 30% to 48%. In Industrial Tribunals it has been shown that where the employer is legally represented and the applicant is not (quite a common scenario) the applicant succeeds in only 10% of cases. Where both are legally represented the applicant succeeds in 30% of cases, while if the applicant is represented in any way and the employer is not, the success rate jumps to 48%[25].

But because legal aid is not available for representation at tribunals or at Small Claims hearings the demonstrated desirability of clients being represented has been ignored and the powerful and wealthy have an advantage. No serious effort has been made to address the question of how the unmet legal need in this area could best be met.

The experience of tribunals in general has been that representatives who are not legally qualified are capable of representing a party to a very high standard. In this area legal services are being provided by agencies which enjoy none of the benefits of legal aid funding but are compensating for the failures of the existing system of provision to meet the needs of consumers, particularly those on low incomes, for advice and representation.

The other consequence of the lack of availability of legal aid is that lawyers have not been encouraged to develop an expertise in areas of law which may bear most closely on the needs of consumers on low incomes. Solicitors are understandably reluctant to spend time preparing a case for which they will be paid only under the Advice and Assistance scheme and not for representing the client. As a result the vast bulk of the legal aid fund is spent on matrimonial and criminal work (84% of the total budget in 1992/93) and solicitors have largely failed to develop an expertise in social welfare law, immigration law, or consumer law, for all of which the likely forum will be a tribunal or Small Claims hearing.

11.4 The Legal Profession—Effect on the Delivery of Legal Services

The fact that publicly funded legal services are provided by solicitors in private practice may also have the effect of limiting their accessibility to those on low incomes.

(a) Geographical distribution

Solicitors will choose to locate their offices according to the dictates of the market in such a way as to optimise access by those clients they seek to attract. Thus it makes sense for a firm which specialises in commercial law to be located in a business centre and firms of criminal lawyers have tended to locate themselves near the courts. There is no obvious financial incentive to open an office in a deprived area although there may be no shortage of legal problems there.

In 1977 in *Why The Poor Pay More* and drew attention to the fact that the distribution of solicitors' offices was uneven with a disproportionate concentration in city centres. The absence of solicitors in areas of social deprivation meant that it was harder for those on low incomes to hear of a lawyer who might be able to help them, and their lower mobility prevented them from being able to make use of a lawyer's services further afield[26]. This is still the case in the deprived areas around Glasgow and Edinburgh and in sparsely populated areas in Scotland the problem may be worse.

In June 1990 the Scottish Office produced a report entitled *Location of and Access to Solicitors in Scotland* which showed that 72% of solicitors' offices were in urban areas with the remaining 28% in rural areas[27]. In relation to access the report showed that less than 1% of the population in urban areas and less than 6% in rural areas lay outwith designated catchment areas, defined as a five mile radius around a solicitor's office for urban dwellers and a ten mile radius for rural dwellers. The report also tried to assess the percentage of the population with access to at least two different firms of solicitors, a consideration of practical importance because of the professional rules as to conflict of interest which prevent one firm acting for opposing parties to a dispute. This is of particular significance in proceedings in relation to separation or divorce. Here the report concluded that while access in urban areas remained at similar levels to access to individual offices, in rural districts just over 10% of the population lay outwith the catchment areas of two firms.

The Scottish Office report was, however, limited in that it did not identify offices which undertook legal aid work, or indicate their opening hours or the specialist areas handled. The Scottish Legal Aid Board has commissioned research into the distribution of offices providing legal aid which answers some of these questions. The report, unpublished at the time of writing, suggests that 78% of the 1,675 legal offices in Scotland are registered to provide legal aid and that access is reasonably adequate throughout Scotland with the possible exception of certain highly rural or low 'access factor' areas. The report defines low 'access factor' areas with reference to the number of offices, size of population and district area, and identifies 14 of these areas, some of which are geographically remote and sparsely populated, such as the Western Isles and Caithness, while others are predominantly rural, such as Clydesdale and Gordon. The report suggests that further research is needed to determine the extent of any unmet legal need in the low 'access factor' areas, both in general, and in relation to an apparently significant degree of unmet need in legal aid work in social welfare areas[28].

(b) Lack of appropriate expertise

In the same way that the market has determined where solicitors have set up in practice, so it has dictated the areas of the law in which they have tended to specialise. In particular areas of the law, solicitors have shown a reluctance to develop the expertise which could be of real help to clients on low incomes. In part this has been caused by the fact that legal aid is not available for tribunal work, as discussed above. A further factor may be the complexity of the law involved. Social security legislation is notoriously complex and in housing law it is widely recognised that solicitors in private practice are failing to provide a good service. The Scottish Homes consultation on the future of housing advice in Scotland issued in 1992 commented that "solicitors do not appear to have adequate information systems to keep them up to date with changes in the housing environment"[29].

The bulk of legal aid expenditure on Advice and Assistance in Scotland has for over 15 years been on matrimonial, criminal and reparation matters (77% in 1991/92) with less than 15% going on social welfare areas (housing, debt, employment and welfare benefits). The SLAB research report suggests that the number of applications for Advice and Assistance payments in relation to these issues is considerably lower than might be anticipated during a period of severe recession. At the same time Citizens Advice Scotland statistics indicate considerable increases in enquiries on these issues, and in England and Wales during the same period 27% of advice expenditure under the legal aid scheme related to social welfare matters. While this appears to be a significant area of unmet legal need, there are substantial regional variations, and in certain districts, notably Lochaber, Perth and Kinross, and Wigtown, solicitors appear to have recognised the need for advice in these areas and have responded positively to this need[30].

Even in areas in which lawyers can claim expertise, such as matrimonial work, the advice offered to clients may be deficient if they have only a limited knowledge and understanding of the benefits system. A recent study of ten firms of solicitors in Liverpool showed that a lack of such knowledge led to deficient advice being given on the financial implications of divorce[31].

11.5 Other Factors Limiting Access to Legal Services

(a) Lack of knowledge about legal rights and services

Consumers on low incomes may suffer additional detriment in relation to legal services because of a lack of awareness of their legal rights, the fact that there may be a legal solution, or the fact that they qualify for legal aid. There may equally be a low level of knowledge about how to find a solicitor, how to choose between different solicitors, or what the likely costs will be. Studies in England have shown low levels of awareness of legal aid among accident victims[32], those with housing problems[33], and in the population as a whole[34]. This lack of awareness can have devastating consequences for the individual. In cases involving arrears of rent the result may be that the landlord obtains a housing repossession order. So a tenant who fails to understand the consequences of the debt recovery process or who fails to attend court to ask for a time-to-pay order may lose his or her home. In Scotland research conducted for the Scottish Consumer Council found that one year after the introduction of the Small Claims procedure, more than 60% of the population were unaware of its existence and that 60% of those who had brought cases thought that greater publicity should be given to it[35].

While the ability of lawyers to advertise their services since 1985 may have helped the public to choose a lawyer, research has shown that traditional areas of legal activity predominate in advertisements, with areas such as consumer law, landlord and tenant, and social security featuring in only 5%, 8% and 2% of advertisements respectively[36]. Finding a solicitor with the necessary expertise may mean the difference between success and failure, as research in the field of personal injury has indicated[37]. Advice agencies often provide a useful service in this field, referring clients to solicitors with a particular expertise, but for the majority of clients recommendations come from family and friends[38].

While solicitors are allowed to state areas of expertise in their advertising, this is not subject to any controls. In contrast to this self-accreditation, the Law Society of Scotland now maintains panels of accredited specialists in 11 fields, including employment law and child law, with family law due to be added soon. The existence of these panels is primarily for the benefit of other lawyers who may need specialist advice, but inevitably the specialist lawyer will wish to advertise this fact to the general public. While greater information about specialisations is useful to the consumer, the needs of consumers in remote and sparsely populated areas will continue to be for general legal practitioners.

(b) Perception of the legal system and fear of cost

To any consumer the courts may be intimidating places, associated with the enforcement of the criminal law rather than a forum for enforcing the rights of the individual. A study conducted by the Welsh Consumer Council showed that, even among consumers who knew there was a legal remedy in cases involving faulty goods and services, there was a reluctance to go to court. Forty-five per cent mentioned the cost; a third said they would be worried about the whole atmosphere; a quarter mentioned the formalities; and a quarter mentioned the disappointment of losing.

Also, 27% were worried about getting their name in a newspaper. 'Going to court' for these people represented personal disgrace[39].

In a study of accident victims in 1984, fear of legal expenses was one of the main reasons given for not going ahead with an action. The study found that 85% of injured people did not make a claim for compensation, and around three-quarters did not even consider it[40]. Comparing the caseload statistics of Citizens Advice Bureaux in Scotland with the number of applications for Advice and Assistance under the legal aid scheme also suggests that many consumers are reluctant to approach solicitors, and find CABx more accessible[41].

11.6 Alternative Forms of Provision of Legal Services

(a) Law centres

In the 1970s law centres emerged as a possible solution to the problem of unmet legal need for those on low incomes. Located in areas of social deprivation, they were able to develop expertise in aspects of work which lawyers in private practice chose not to; and, because their funding was not dependent on legal aid, they were able to represent their clients before tribunals. In addition they undertook educational and training work which was of benefit to other agencies working in related fields. The service provided was free; the approach was less formal; and they could work for communities or groups as well as for individuals. The growth of law centres in England from 1970 was not matched in Scotland where the first law centre, in Castlemilk, did not open until April 1979.

Unlike the 54 law centres in England and Wales which are now primarily dependent on local authority funding, the three community-based law centres in Scotland (Castlemilk, Drumchapel and Dumbarton) have recently been or are being funded by central government through the Urban Programme. Urban Programme funding is available for community law centres for an initial period of four years which may be extended to a maximum of seven years. Thereafter the law centre is dependent on local authority funding on a year to year basis. Castlemilk Law Centre now receives funding from the Regional and District Councils and generates some of its income from legal aid work. Drumchapel Law and Money Advice Centre has been funded for two years under the Urban Programme, while the law centre in Dumbarton is not yet fully operational.

Scotland has also begun to see the development of specialised law centres which provide a service to clients throughout Scotland in particular areas of legal need. The Scottish Child Law Centre, established in 1988, provides advice and information to the public, social workers and other professionals in the field of child law, and in addition is involved in educational work, representation and in active lobbying for improvements in legislation. The Legal Services Agency (LSA) based in Glasgow operates on a national basis setting up local advisory committees where local funding exists. It is currently funded by Strathclyde and Lothian Regional Councils and has offices in Glasgow and Edinburgh. The LSA combines the role of a community law centre with specialised work of an educational and training nature in the fields of housing law, mental health and other areas of unmet legal need. Also, in October 1991 an Ethnic Minorities Law Centre—involving both a casework and training function—was established in Glasgow to address the unmet legal need of people from ethnic minorities. In the year 1992/93, 51.5% of its cases involved immigration and discrimination, both areas in which it has been suggested that the majority of solicitors in private practice lack expertise[42], while a further 19.5% concerned housing, debt and welfare issues[43]. In April 1993 it was announced that the Scottish Office had granted Shelter (Scotland) £65,000 to establish a Scottish Housing Law Centre to provide independent legal advice to agencies throughout Scotland.

Law centres provide an alternative model of provision using public funds to support a salaried staff not motivated by the need to make a profit. They make use of, and work effectively with, non-legally qualified advisers, and are able to look beyond the boundaries of a single case to the legal and social needs of a particular community, or part of it. The development of specialised law centres will provide an expertise which can be tapped by other law centres as well as other advice agencies. An increase in the number of law centres would lead to improvements in the accessibility of legal advice, a greater choice of advisers, a raising of the quality of advice available, and the possibility of securing representation before tribunals.

There is evidence that the Legal Aid Board in England and Wales is beginning to recognise the advantages of channelling a greater part of the legal aid budget through law centres[44] and it is to be hoped that this will also be the case in Scotland. However, the need for law centres is not necessarily restricted to Urban Programme areas, and the question of how law centres could be funded in rural areas should be addressed.

(b) Advice agencies

In addition to the 64 Citizens Advice Bureaux (CABx) throughout Scotland, and the 24 independent advice agencies affiliated to Citizens Advice Scotland (CAS), there are other centres providing consumer advice, money advice, housing advice, legal advice and advice about welfare rights to the general public. In addition agencies such as the Immigration Appeals Advisory Service and organisations such as Enable offer specialised advice in their field. Some agencies will pass a client on to a solicitor if the problem is identified as requiring a legal solution. Others will themselves have developed a far greater expertise in their area than would be available from a solicitor. CABx are staffed by volunteers but, while volunteers may develop an expertise in particular areas, many cases will be referred to solicitors when the lay adviser can proceed no further. Some CABx also make use of solicitors who provide legal advice on a voluntary basis.

CABx in Scotland dealt with 629,570 enquiries in 1992/93. The largest single category of enquiry was about money (including enquiries about welfare benefits as well as debt cases), representing 47% of all enquiries; while 39% were about employment, goods and services, housing and family or personal matters, in all of which there is a significant legal content. (See also section 10.5 in the chapter on credit and debt.)

CAB volunteers also take a more active role in legal work, for example by representing clients at tribunals or Small Claims hearings. In Scotland in 1992/93, CAS statistics show that 777 clients were represented at tribunals and 227 in cases in the sheriff court. As the erosion of eligibility for legal aid continues, so the need for clients to obtain advice and representation from another source will increase.

If advice agencies are to be seen as a part of the overall provision of legal services it will be important to consider how they can most effectively be incorporated into a coherent nation-wide service with secure funding, whether operating as initial points of access to legal services or, as a result of improved funding, being able to employ solicitors.

11.7 Quality Of Service

While access to legal services is limited in the various ways discussed, a second and no less important question concerns the quality of service that the client can expect from a solicitor. While the professional bodies have always had the power to remove a solicitor's practising certificate if he or she is incompetent or negligent, they have only recently begun to consider how to lay down standards of competent service. In England and Wales the Client Care rule requires every firm to have a complaints handling procedure, to keep clients informed as to the progress of their case, and to inform them of who to approach with a problem; and there are written standards covering other matters, such as requiring clients to be given advance information about costs. In Scotland there are as yet no such explicit standards, although the Scottish Legal Services Ombudsman, created in 1991, has specifically called on solicitors to provide clients with better information about the service provided and how a client can tell when that service is inadequate[45]. The Law Society of Scotland has established a client care committee to consider issues relating to quality of service.

It would seem reasonable to require that any legal work done under the legal aid scheme should meet specified standards, and this is recognised by both the legal aid boards. Although the professional bodies argue that the legally-aided client is entitled to the same standard of service as the non-legally-aided, there is concern that the low level of fees paid for legal aid work inevitably means that junior or inexperienced staff are given this work. For every expert witness secured for the legally-aided client a wealthy opponent may be able to secure several.

Legally-aided clients may not be in a strong position to assess the standard of service they have received, and the boards act on their behalf, although it has been argued that there is scope for taking clients' views into account[46]. The Legal Aid Board (LAB) for England and Wales has taken a more interventionist position than the SLAB in this area. The system of franchising which is now being introduced in England and Wales following a three year experiment in Birmingham allows solicitors and advice agencies which satisfy required quality standards to be freed from administrative restrictions and to get speedier settlement of their accounts. There does, however, appear to be a danger that there may be a conflict of interest between the LAB's role as the funding body and as the body concerned with setting standards, and the Legal Action Group (a legal pressure group based in England whose remit is to improve legal services) has argued that the Law Society should take a more active role in the setting of quality criteria, with an independent inspectorate enforcing them[47]. There is also a fear that franchising will lead to competitive tendering for franchises resulting in pressures to cut costs to the bare minimum.

The franchising experiment in Birmingham drew attention to the role which advice agencies can play in legally-aided work and also showed that requirements laid down by LAB can have positive benefits in other areas of practice, such as the requirement that all franchisees have a minimal level of welfare law knowledge[48]. The effect of franchising may be to improve the financial security of alternative forms of provision, creating a counterbalance to the prevailing dominance of the private practitioner and improving the viability of legal work in areas of unmet legal need.

The SLAB's 1992/1993 annual report states that "questions of quality and value for money are given a high priority", but it has expressed doubt as to the value of franchising in Scotland. Its research report on the supply of legal aid argues that because of the concentration of legal aid work (20% of offices handling 65% of all

Advice and Assistance, and 60% of Civil Legal Aid) there would be a danger that firms handling fewer applications would fail to win franchises, thus jeopardising the position of firms in low 'access factor' areas[49].

The Scottish Legal Action Group has argued in favour of franchising provided safeguards are built into the system to ensure a choice of providers in urban and rural areas, adequate remuneration, no competitive tendering, and monitoring of franchisees[50].

11.8 Conclusion

The low income consumer is to a large extent dependent on the adequacy of the provision of publicly funded legal services. The legal aid system meets the legal needs of the poorest members of society who seek help in traditional areas of legal expertise, notably family and criminal law. Those who qualify only for contributory legal aid or who fall outside the contributory band are increasingly excluded from the justice system.

The poor and the not quite so poor fail to assert their rights as a result of lack of knowledge and information about legal services and their cost. The limitations on the scope of legal aid and the control which the legal profession has enjoyed have prevented the development of areas of expertise which would be of particular relevance to consumers on low incomes.

The debate which recent cutbacks in eligibility has provoked has called into question whether the existing system is the best way of providing legal services to those unable to afford the services of a private practitioner. The need to find a cost-effective system which is accessible to the greatest number and which provides an appropriate standard of service has led to alternative models of provision being considered. A greater use of salaried lawyers, a more effective use of advice agencies, the use of standard fees in legal aid work and contingency fees have all been suggested. The way legal services are provided in other countries may suggest alternatives. In the Netherlands salaried lawyers working in legal aid bureaux provide initial advice and refer clients to accredited lawyers on a rota basis. In Germany and Sweden, a larger proportion of the population has legal expenses insurance and in Sweden this is combined with a legal aid system which allows any citizen one hour of legal advice free of charge. Both public and private lawyers can provide legal aid and are in competition[51].

Whatever modifications emerge from the present debate, the fundamental requirements which must be borne in mind are that the method of provision should be comprehensive, encompassing advice, assistance and representation; it should promote education and information about legal rights and legal services; and it should monitor the need for changes to substantive law and procedure.

The need to improve the service provided to those on low incomes must be a priority. The current initiatives being pursued in England and Wales suggest grounds for optimism that some account will be taken of the need to expand the system to make greater use of law centres and advice agencies, and it is clearly desirable that these bodies which play such a significant role in addressing areas of unmet legal need should have more secure funding arrangements.

While legal services in general are subject to increasing scrutiny from the consumer perspective, it does appear that for consumers on low incomes there are particular problems which should be explicitly addressed if an increasingly large section of the population is not to be excluded from our system of justice. A wide-ranging review of the civil justice system, which has been called for by the Scottish Consumer Council, Citizens Advice Scotland and the Law Society of Scotland, would help to delineate the extent of the problem and would be able to propose solutions in the context of the legal system as a whole.

References and footnotes to Chapter 11

1. National Consumer Council, *Ordinary Justice,* HMSO, 1989.
2. Royal Commission on Legal Services in Scotland (Chairman: Lord Hughes), Report, Cmnd 7846, HMSO, 1980.
3. M. Cousins, 'Civil legal aid in France, Ireland, the Netherlands and the UK', *Civil Justice Quarterly,* Vol.12, p. 154, April 1993. This article shows that in 1989 the total cost of the legal aid scheme in the UK represented 0.05% of GDP, compared with 0.04% in the Netherlands, and less than 0.01% in France and Ireland.
4. P. Townsend, *Poverty in the UK,* Penguin, 1979.
5. P. Townsend, see reference 4.
6. O. Hansen, 'A future for legal aid?', *Journal of Law and Society,* 1992(1), p.85.
7. Scottish Legal Aid Board, *Annual Report, 1992/93.*
8. Editorial, *Legal Action,* October 1992.
9. The Scottish Home and Health Department, *Review of Financial Conditions for Legal Aid: Eligibility for Civil Legal Aid in Scotland,* Scottish Office, July 1991.
10. *Hansard,* 17 February 1993, column 226.
11. M. Murphy, *Civil Legal Aid Eligibility Estimates 1979-1990,* 1990.
12. National Consumer Council, see reference 1, p.85.
13. C. Glasser, 'Legal aid eligibility', *Law Society Gazette,* 9 March 1988, pp.11-13.
14. Central Statistical Office, *Family Spending: A Report of the 1992 Family Expenditure Survey,* HMSO, 1993, Chart E.
15. Scottish Legal Aid Board, see reference 7, p.27.
16. Lord Chancellor's Department, *Legal Aid Efficiency Scrutiny,* 2 vols, June 1986.
17. The Law Society of Scotland, *Briefing Papers on Access to Justice* issued in February 1993.
18. T. Holland, 'Priorities for funding', *New Law Journal,* Vol.143, 1993, p.102.
19. Scottish Legal Aid Board, see reference 7, pp.22, 30.
20. J. Burns, 'The future of tribunals', *SCOLAG,* May 1993, p.71.
21. Scottish Courts Administration, *Civil Judicial Statistics, Scotland, 1991,* HMSO, 1993.
22. Scottish Office Central Research Unit, *Small Claims in the Sheriff Court in Scotland,* The Scottish Office, 1991.
23. Scottish Office Central Research Unit, see reference 22.
24. Scottish Courts Administration, *Small Claims Procedure in the Sheriff Court,* Scottish Courts Administration, 1991.
25. H. Genn and Y. Genn, *The Effectiveness of Representation at Tribunals,* Lord Chancellor's Department, 1989.
26. M. Zander, 'Legal Services', in National Consumer Council, *Why the Poor Pay More,* MacMillan, 1977.

27. Scottish Office, *Location of and Access to Solicitors in Scotland*, Central Research Unit Papers, June 1990.
28. Scottish Legal Aid Board, *Research Report on the Distribution of the Supply of Legal Aid in Scotland*, 1993.
29. Scottish Homes, *Housing and Information Advice: you can't ask a leaflet questions*, July 1992.
30. Scottish Legal Aid Board, see reference 28.
31. N. Harris, 'Judging the quality of welfare benefits work by firms of solicitors', *Civil Justice Quarterly*, Vol.10, 1991, pp.311, 325-6.
32. D. Harris et al., *Compensation and Support for Illness and Injury*, Oxford Socio-Legal Studies, Clarendon Press, 1984.
33. School of Advanced Urban Studies, University of Bristol, *Study of Housing Cases: final report to the Chancellor's Department*, produced for the Civil Justice Review, Lord Chancellor's Department, January 1987.
34. J. Baldwin and S. Hill, *The Operation of the Green Form Scheme in England and Wales*, Lord Chancellor's Department, January 1987.
35. Scottish Consumer Council, *Small Claims in Scotland, a discussion paper*, August 1990.
36. Taylor Nelson Media, *An Analysis of Solicitors' Advertising*, prepared for the National Consumer Council, October 1987.
37. H. Genn, *Hard Bargaining: out of court settlement in personal injury actions*, Oxford Socio-Legal Studies, Clarendon Press, 1987.
38. D. Harris et al, see reference 32.
39. National Consumer Council/Welsh Consumer Council, *Simple Justice: a consumer view of small claims procedures in England and Wales*, NCC/WCC, 1979.
40. D. Harris et al., see reference 32.
41. Scottish Legal Aid Board, see reference 28.
42. Scottish Consumer Council, *Access to Justice for Ethnic Minorities*, SCC, May 1993.
43. Ethnic Minorities Law Centre Ltd., *Annual Report, 1992-93*, p.6.
44. Legal Aid Board, *Annual Report 1990-91*, HMSO, para 8.1.
45. Scottish Legal Services Ombudsman, *Second Annual Report*, HMSO, 1993.
46. T. Goriely, 'Quality of legal services: the need for consumer research', *Consumer Policy Review*, Vol.3(2), 1993, p.112.
47. Legal Action Group, *A Strategy for Justice*, 1992, pp.146-7.
48. F. Bawdon, 'The Birmingham Pilot', *Legal Action*, May, 1993.
49. Scottish Legal Aid Board, see reference 28.
50. Scottish Legal Action Group, *Response to consultation paper on eligibility for civil legal aid in Scotland*, 1991, p.6.
51. A. Paterson, 'Legal aid at the crossroads', *Civil Justice Quarterly*, Vol. 11, 1992, p. 124.

Index

Note:: Titles are in italics

Access cards 155
advertising 123, 132
    lawyers' services 182
advice
    agencies 182, 184, 186
    affording on low incomes 13–14
    Scottish services 14
advocacy
    learning difficulties support 81
agriculture
    Common Agricultural Policy 58, 63
air services 108, 111, 117, 118
Air Transport Users Council 108
Audits of Great Britain 42, 43

banking
    Code of Practice 168–9
    credit in Scotland 155–6
    debt settlement 162
    direct debit 162, 163. 169
    low income and 162, 163, 169
    maintenance charges 169
    overdraft facilities 163, 169
    standing orders 162, 163, 169
bankruptcy 163
Bankruptcy (Scotland) Acts 163
Benefits Agency
    Customer Charter 149
    debt advice 160
    fraud targets 147
    performance targets 148
Berthoud, R. and Kempson, E. 160
Beveridge Report 137, 140, 142, 174–5
Beyond Draughtproofing 48
Breadline Britain Survey (1991) 141
British Airways 118
British Dental Association 77
British Paediatric Association 76
British Rail
    fares 109, 111, 113, 116–19
    financial controls 109
    lower income groups' use 114
    Passenger's Charter 108
    privatisation 111, 119
    Scottish network 109
British Standard kitemark 47
Building Regulation Standard 39
Building Research Establishment 44

Building Society, Class 3 loans 154
bureaucracy, access problems 13
buses *see* transport

Caledonian MacBrayne 108, 111, 118
cancer deaths in Scotland 70, 72
carbon tax 112
car boot sales 131
care *see* community care services
carers' dependence on benefits 137
car ownership
    carbon tax 112
    catalytic converters 112
    costs 108
    exhaust emission standards 112
    fuel prices 112, 118
    low income 112, 113, 118, 123
    mobility 113–14, 127
    shopping behaviour patterns 124–5,
        127, 128, 131, 132–3
    statistics 106, 113, 123
Central Statistical Office
    Credit Business Bulletin 154, 156
    Family Expenditure Survey 2, 4, 9, 10, 19,
        22, 28, 29, 36, 37, 38, 106, 122
    Financial Statistics 154
    General Household Survey 19, 21, 24, 81,
        106
    Regional Trends 8
charities
    Oxfam 127
    shops 131
    surplus food distribution 65–66
check traders 159, 164
child benefit
    raising recommended 145
    statistics (table) 8, 136
child health
    dentistry 77
    schoolchildren study 72
    services 76
child law
    accredited specialists 182
    Law Centre 183
Children Act 1989 76
Children's Hearings 179
Child Support Agency 149, 150
Child Support Appeals Tribunal 179
Citizens Advice Bureaux 14, 148, 160, 173, 174,
    181, 183, 184

Citizens Advice Scotland (CAS) 184, 187
Citizen's Charter 13, 87
class *see* social class
Committee of Scottish Clearing Banks
    credit personal loans (table) 155–6
community care services
    assessment and care management 79–80
    co-ordination between agencies 79
    housing policy changes 25
    mental health 80–81
    nursing care in 79
    representation needed 14
    residential care 79
    transfer of responsibilities 75, 78–79
Community Charge 141
community health services
    reform process 80
community ventures
    development 12
    food poverty responses 64–65, 68
    health development projects 76
complaints
    consumer credit market 167
    goods and services 132
    legal services 185
    Ombudsman, Banking and Building Society 168
    transport 108
comprehensive schools 93, 98, 99–100, 101
Co-operative Wholesale Society 65
Conservative Party
    conference 147
    Government *see* Government
Consumer Advice Centres 14
Consumers' Association 132, 168
Consumer Credit Act 1974 168
consumer detriment
    access to goods and services 11–13, 121, 133
    advice and information 13–14
    consultation needed 14
    definition 1
    discriminatory rules 14–15
    education 1, 96, 98
    food 11, 64, 67
    housing 17, 25
    information costs 132
    lack of capital 11–12
    lack of choice 13
    lack of income 125
    legal services 12–13, 149–50, 173–4, 180, 182
    representation lacking 14
    Scotland 133
    transport 1, 12–13, 14, 71, 125–6
    Why the Poor Pay More (NCC report) 1, 5, 17, 96, 121
    women 150
consumerism
    advice 184
    changes in shopping habits 127
    choice 3, 13, 87
    Citizen's Charter 13, 87
    disadvantaged 1, 2–3, 11, 13, 15, 25–26, 122, 124–5, 128
    durables *see* durable goods
    expenditure, Lothian (table) 123
    goods *see* goods
    information for 131–2
    low income *see* low income
    market forces *see* market forces
    pressures to buy 123
    price-quality relationship 129–31, 133
    price-volume relationship 131
    representation of interest 3, 108
    services *see* services
    transport grievance redress 108
Contributions Agency 149
Costco warehouse club 62
Council of Europe
    low income definition 3
Council tax 142
credit
    ability to pay 158–9
    agreements 168
    Annual Percentage Rate (APR) 168
    arrears on agreements 153
    bank loans 159
    banks, Scotland (table) 155–6
    borrowing from family and friends 164
    building society loans 154, 156, 159, 168, 169
    cards advances (table) 154–5, 156
    costs of different forms 158–9
    expansion 169
    'extortionate' 168
    finance houses (table) 155–6, 159, 164
    fraud 168
    hire purchase agreements 164
    levels outstanding (table) 153–4
    low income 157–8, 159, 162, 165–6, 169, 170
    mail order 127, 129, 159, 164
    money lenders 158–9, 164, 168
    payments, weekly 159
    pensioners' attitude 159
    'red-lining' 158, 159
    referencing 155, 156–8
    regulation 166–8
    scoring system 157, 158
    Social Fund *see* Social Fund 165

INDEX

systematic rationalisation 162
unions development 12, 165,
    (table) 166, 169
see also banking *and* debt
Credit and Debt: the PSI Survey 160
Credit Union Working Party 12
Cruikshank, Don 78

Dalmuir Credit Union 166
Data Protection Agency 157
death causes, Scotland 51, 70–71
debt
    advice 160, (table) 161, 169, 184
    bank facilities 162, 163
    bankruptcy 163
    causal factors 159–60
    counselling services 162, 169
    court procedures 161–2, 169
    early warning system 158
    enforcement 169
    household income (table) 160
    increase 169
    licences for collection agencies
        (table) 167
    patterns 153
    sequestration awards (table) 163
    settlement developments 162
    Small Claims procedure 162–3, 175,
        178, 179, 180, 182, 184
    Social Fund *see* Social Fund
Debtors (Scotland) Act 1987 162
dental care changes 77–78
Department of Health
    Dietary Reference Values 59
Department of Health/Social Services
    nutritional standards review 59
Department of Social Security (DSS)
    administrative costs 145
    claims determination targets 145
    division into five agencies 149
    Expenditure Plans 149
    fraud targets 147, 149
    *Households Below Average
        Income* 6
    information on benefits 148, 149
    residential care allowance 80
    Social Fund evaluation 144
    Statistics 139, 149
deprivation *see* poverty
*Diet, Nutrition, and Healthy Eating in Low
    Income Groups* 56
diet *see* food *and* nutrition
disability
    cash benefits (table) 8, 136, 137,
        139, 140
    claims investigation 145
    housing 25, 28
    transport concessions 107, 111,
        116, 117–18, 119
    tribunal 178, 179
Disability Appeal Tribunal 178, 179
discrimination
    diet 61, 62, 64
    ethnic minorities 94
    housing problems 28
    retail pricing policies 15
    rules creating disadvantage 14–15
    see also quality of life
Dumfries and Galloway
    assessment and care management
        79–80
    health survey 71, 73
durable goods
    assistance to buy 11–12
    households purchase (figure) 2, 11
    ownership, housing tenure
        indicator 123, (table) 124

Economic and Social Research Council
    Data Archive 106
    food choice research 58
economic recession effect 131, 153, 181
Edinburgh University
    Students' Association survey 160
education
    academic and manual 91–92, 96
    accountability 102
    Afro-Caribbean pupils 94, 95
    Asian pupils 94, 95
    Chinese pupils 94
    choice 13, 87, 88, 100, 101–2
    class size and pupil progress 98
    comprehensive schools 93, 98,
        99–100, 101
    consumer detriment 1, 96, 98
    disadvantage 87–88, 99–102
    disadvantage, ethnicity 94–95
    disadvantage, single parent 95
    disadvantage, social class 88–94,
        97, 98
    domestic science introduction 55
    equalisation of opportunity 99–102
    exclusions 101
    exam results 89–93
    exam results publication 100
    financial delegation to schools 100–1
    Government policy 87, 88, 100–2
    higher participation 89–94, 98,
        99, 101
    inequality 96
    learning difficulties 98, 101
    market forces 100, 101
    parental education level 89
    parental involvement 102
    parentocracy 101
    pre-school 96

primary pupils' attainments
  88–89, 91
pupils' achievements 98–99, 101
school effectiveness 95–99, 100, 102
teachers' expectations 96, 97, 98, 99
truancy rates 100
unemployment effect on 92
value-added data 100
Educational Priority Area (EPA) 96
Education Reform Act 1988 101
Education (Scotland) Act 1981 98, 100
elderly *see* pensioners
electricity *see* energy
employment
  Appeal Tribunal 175, 178, 179, 180
  benefits administration by
    employers 146–7
  deregulation of labour markets 6
  health and lifestyle data 71, 72, 73
  health protection 73
  law, accredited specialists 182
  low pay *see* low pay
  part-time statistics 6, 8
  transport facilities and 113, 114
  Wages Councils abolition 6, 145,
    173
Enable 184
energy
  audits 44, 45
  choice of fuels 36, 51–52
  consumer detriment 11, 14
  customised advice packages 52
  efficiency 35–36
  expenditure by income (tables)
    36–38, 39, 43–44, 49
  market forces 35
  see also fuel
Energy Efficiency Office 44, 45, 47
environment
  carbon tax 112
  exhaust emission standards 112
  hazards 73
  health influence 71–72
  pollution 71, 73
  transport policy 109, 111–13, 119
ethnic communities
  educational disadvantage 94–95
  food choice 58
  housing 25
  intimidation of 94
  law centre 183
  legal access 13
  Scottish survey 94
European Commission (EC)
  poverty threshold 3, 4

family allowance 140
family credit 137, 142, 145, 147, 149

Family Expenditure Surveys 2, 4, 9, 10, 19, 22,
  28, 29, 36, 37, 38, 106, 122
family income supplement 145, 149
ferry operations 108, 111, 116, 117
finance houses credit (table) 155–6
financial services deregulation 155
food
  advertising and marketing 54, 58, 66
  Common Agricultural Policy
    regulation 58, 63
  community initiatives 64–65
  consumer choice 55, 58
  consumer detriment 11, 64, 67
  consumption behaviour 55–58, 72
  co-operatives 12, 64–65
  cultures 54
  dietary expectations 54
  frozen and chilled 54, 62
  Government policy 64, 67–68
  health effects *see* health problems
  healthy diet cost 59–62
  low income diets 56–58, 68
  low income expenditure on 59,
    63, 64, 65, 68, 141
  market forces 63, 64, 66
  National Food Commission
    proposal 68
  national food policy (1940s) 54
  nutrition *see* nutrition
  prices 63, 64
  rationing in war 54
  retail price maintenance 54, 68
  shopping requirements 54, 61,
    62–63, 64–65, 66, 67, 127, 129
  snacks, sweets and drinks 57, 59
  storage 54, 61, 62
  street market trading 63
  supermarkets 13, 62, 66
  surplus items to charities 65–66
  warehouse clubs, Costco 62
*Food Patterns Amongst Lower Income Groups in
  the UK* 56
Franks Committee on tribunals 178–9
Fuel
  actual and estimated expenditure
    (figure) 46, 47
  annual costs estimate for different
    house sizes (table) 44
  annual heating cost and consumption
    (tables) 40–41
  audits 44, 45
  central heating ownership (table)
    42–43
  cold/damp/mouldy houses health
    problems 50–51
  condensation/mould growth
    problems 50
  consumer detriment 11, 14

INDEX

customised advice packages 52
debts and disconnections 46, 49–50
discriminatory pricing policies 14
domestic consumption end use 39
domestic consumption VAT 34–35, 38
efficiency 35–36
expenditure by income (tables) 36–38, 39, 43–44, 49
flat temperature and costs (figures) 48
franchise customers 36
'fuel direct' prepayment meters 46, 49–50, 170
gas contracts 36
heating appliances and systems 36, 39, 41, (table) 43, 44
heating fuel costs weekly (table) 45–46
heating Tolerable Standard 47, 49
income support less 'fuel direct' 46, 164
insulation improvements 12, 35, 39, 51
insulation lacking 44, 45, 47, 49
insulation levels (table) 41–42, 43
low income households 35–37, 43, 46–47, 49, 51–52
market forces 35
monthly payment schemes 164
one room only heated 51
prepayment meters 46, 49–50
price increase effect 37
privatisation effect 36
quality of life and use 36, 51
room temperatures in Easterhouse, Glasgow 43–44, 45, 46, 47, 49
room temperatures of elderly survey 35
rural areas 36
Severe Weather Payment Scheme 41
switching fuel or suppliers 36
temperature standards 39, 43, 47, 51
see also energy

gas *see* fuel
General Household Survey 19, 21, 24, 81, 106
Germany, legal expenses insurance 186
Glasgow
  death rate 70–71
  Drumchapel health profile 78
  Easterhouse energy audit and fuel cost survey 43–44, 45, 46, 47, 49
  fuel utilities, debts to 49
  health and poverty report 55
  health centres location 77
  health inequality 70, 71
  Healthy Cities Project 76

shopping facilities 129
women, deaths from lung cancer 72
women's health policy 76
goods
  access, consumer detriment 12, 121, 133
  changes in provision 125–8
  complaints about 132
  credit card purchases 155
  definition 121
  durable *see* durable goods
  expenditure on 122
  low income cost higher 121
  price-quality relationship 129–31
  price-volume relationship 131
Government
  Budget (1993) 34
  costs of welfare state 135, 138
  education policy 87, 88, 100–2
  food poverty problem 64, 67–68
  housing policy 17–18, 25, 27, 31
  low income groups 133, 145–6
  social security policy 141, 146–7
  transport policy 109
Government's Expenditure Plans 1993–94 136
Grampian Healthcare
  community liaison manager 81

Headstart programme 96
health
  centres' location in Glasgow 77
  children's 72
  data on health and lifestyle 71–73
  differences and death rates 70–71
  Eating for Health guidelines 56
  environmental influences 71–72
  equity policies 82
  GP surgeries' location 77
  inequality 70–73
  local consultation on needs 78
  Patient's Charter 81
  problems *see* health problems
  public health departments 76
  public policies in Scotland 73–75
  rural areas 72
  Scotland's Health White Paper 66–67
  social support importance 71
  socio-economic influences 71–73, 74–75
  see also National Health Service
Health and Lifestyle data 71–73
Health Boards, Scotland 70, 71, 73, 74, 75–79, 81
Health Education Authority
  healthy eating report 56
Health Education Board for Scotland 74
health problems

alcoholism 76, 79
cancer 70, 72, 74
cold/damp/mouldy houses 50–51
death rates, Scotland 70
dental and oral health 74
diet related disorders 54, 55,
   57–58, 64, 66–67, 75
diet requirements 61
heart disease 55, 67, 70, 74
HIV/AIDS 74, 79
housing people with 25, 28
lifestyle changes 74
mental illness 71, 76, 78, 79, 80
poverty and 55–56, 70–73, 82
psycho-social 71
health service *see* National Health Service
heart disease in Scotland 55, 67, 70
Heating Costs in Easterhouse 44, 45, 46
Home Energy Efficiency Scheme 12, 35–36, 39
homelessness 24, 26, 29, 31, 56, 62, 140
   bed and breakfast accommodation
      57, 62
   health needs 76
   statistics 23
hospitals
   discharge of patients care 80
   Patient's Charter 81
   transport for visits 110
   trust status 80, 81
households
   casualties of consumer credit
     boom 169
   credit *see* credit
   durable goods purchases (figure) 2,
     11, 123, (table) 124
   expenditure (figures) 9, (table) 10
   food *see* food
   fuel expenditure (tables) 36–38, 39
   incomes statistics 2, (table) 4,
     6–7, 122
   low income 157–8, 159, 162,
     165–6, 169, 170
   mobility 114–15, 118
   poverty threshold 3, 141
   Scotland, incomes (table) 7, 122
   Scotland, weekly expenditure 10
   size decrease 5
   social security benefits 2, 6, 8,
     137, 145–6
   surveys in Grampian 114
   'traditional family' 5
   weekly expenditure (table) 10
Households Below Average Income 6
housing
   advice, counselling, advocacy 28–31,
     184
   Below the Tolerable Standard
     (BTS) 24, 50

Care and Repair schemes 29
choice 13
cold/damp/mouldy health problems
   50–51, 71
Conservative Government
   policy 17–19, 25, 31
consumer detriment 17, 25
council housing policy 18
definition of 'house' 49
finance changes 26–28, 31–32
home ownership extension 18, 19,
   20
information requirements 28–31
insecure 56
low income consumers 17, 18–19, 49
management, compulsory
   competitive tendering 32
mortgage arrears advice 29
mortgage finance 26
owner occupier subsidy 26, 31, 32
private sector definition 17
public expenditure constraints 32
public renting definition 17
public sector estates renewal 18
public sector policy 17–18
repair or improvement grants 26
tenancy changes advice 29, 173
tenant liaison 14
Housing and Planning Act 1986 18
housing associations
   definition 17
   expansion 18, 20, 22, 23, 28, 31
   finance changes 27
   Government grant changes 28
   older people dwellings 20
   rent levels 27–28
   rural areas 26
   special needs developments 32
housing benefits
   application procedures 147
   costs not effectively met 142
   means testing 142, 143
   payable to households 18, 23,
     32, 137, 138
   reforms 27, 28, 31, 138
   rent rises cushioning 23
   Scotland 138
housing, Scotland
   advice services 29–30
   amenities and dwelling type by
     income and tenure (table) 21
   costs by income group (table) 29
   council estates 24, 25, 32, 128
   council housing improvement
     20, 22–23, 26, 27, 32
   disadvantaged groups 25–26
   Government policy 18–19, 25, 27
   homelessness 23, 24, 26, 29, 31

INDEX

household income by tenure
(table) 22
Housing Plans 25
law centre 184
low income choice 20, 23, 24–25,
31–32
legal expertise 181
match, stock and applicants 24
mortgage arrears 23
owner occupied increase 20, 22,
23, 31
physical conditions 24–25, 26, 27, 71
popularity 24
private rented stock 20, 22, 23,
24, 25, 31, 32
public rented stock 20, 24–25, 26,
31, 32
public sector capital expenditure 27
rent changes in public sector 27–28
rent deregulation, private sector 27
Rent-to-Mortgage scheme 18, 19, 20
repair or improvement grants 26–27
Right-to-Buy 19, 20, 22, 23, 24,
27, 31
social isolation/stigmatisation 25
stock by tenure (table) 19
tenure changes 19–20, 25
Tolerable Standard 24, 47, 49, 50
transfer of ownership 26
waiting lists 24
Housing (Scotland) Act 1987 23
Housing (Scotland) Act 1988 18, 28, 31, 32, 173
Hughes Commission 173, 174

Immigration Appeals Advisory Service 184
income
benefit interaction poverty trap 15
distribution 6–7, 145
household incomes and benefits 2,
6, 8, 137
low *see* low income
wages levels 143, 144
income support
administrative costs 145
cash benefits statistics (table) 8, 122,
138, (table) 139, 140
claims administration 145, 147,
Community Charge compensation
141
cost of children 141
dietary consideration 59, 68
non-claimants 138
Scotland 138
subtraction for 'fuel direct' 47,
164, 170
take-up rate 149, 150
Independent Money Advice Centres 160
Independent Tribunal Service, Scotland 179

Industrial Tribunals 179
information
affording on low incomes 13–14
informed choice 131–2
Information Technology Services Agency 149
Institute of Grocery Distributors 65
insulation *see* energy
invalidity benefits
cuts forecast 6
statistics (table) 8

Labour Party
Commission on Social Justice 135
Lands Tribunal 175
land-use planning, Scotland 128, 133
language
access, consumer detriment 13
Law Society 185
Law Society of Scotland 177, 182,
185, 187
learning difficulties
advocacy for 81
schools 98
Legal Action Group 185
legal advice
availability 173–4, 182, 184,
185, 186
community law centres 174, 183–4,
186
consumer detriment 12–13,
149–50, 180, 182
Ethnic Minorities Law Centre 183–4
law centres, England and Wales 183,
84, 186
Scottish Child Law Centre 183
Scottish Housing Law Centre 184
legal aid
Advice and Assistance scheme 176,
180, 181, 183, 186
advice for benefit claimants 148
alternatives to 176
Board 174, 184
Civil Legal Aid 176, 186
contributory 177
Criminal Legal Aid 176, 181, 186
debtors' petitions 163
eligibility 176–7, 182, 186
European countries 186
expenditure on 175–6, 180, 181
franchising 185–6
matrimonial disputes 178, 180,
181–2
provision 174–5, 186
social welfare matters 181–2
solicitors 163, 176, 180
standard of service 185, 186
statutory charge and expenses 178
Legal Aid Board (LAB) 185

legal services
  access 173, 180–1, 182, 186
  accident victims fears of 183
  accredited specialists panels 182
  alternatives 178
  civil justice system review call 187
  Client Care rule 185
  complaints handling procedure 185
  court procedures 161–2, 169
  fear of, by consumers 182–3
  'Judicare' model 175
  low income and 174, 180, 181, 182, 186
  provision 174–5
  quality of service 185–6
  Scottish 174
  Small Claims see Small Claims
  solicitors 180–1, 182, 184
Legal Services Agency (LSA) 183
local authorities
  community care changes 78–79
  debt advice 160
  equity objectives prioritising 82
  health strategies 76, 77
  housing advice/information 30–31
  housing construction 20
  housing costs 18, 27
  housing revenue accounts 27
  housing sales 19
  Joint Liaison Committees with Health Boards 79
  law centres funding 183
  Scottish reorganisation 76
  transport 108, 109, 110
  welfare rights services 148, 149
Local Health Councils
  representation 3
Loganair 118
Lothian Regional Council
  consumer expenditure estimates 122–3
  credit unions (table) 165–6
low income
  claims delays 145
  credit scoring 157–8, 159
  debt 159
  definition 2–4
  disadvantages of 1, 2–3, 11, 13, 15, 122, 128, 142–3, 145
  disincentives to work 15
  education see education
  energy consumption see energy
  ethnic minorities 94
  food see food and also nutrition
  Government policy 133
  health and lifestyle data 71–73
  health service reforms 76–77
  households see households
  housing see housing, Scotland
  identifiable sub-groups 107
  large families and 143
  legal services see legal services
  low cost budget 141
  making best use of money 12
  mobility 114–15, 118, 119, 122, 124–5, 127–8, 129, 131
  pensioners see pensioners
  percentage of people on 1, 7
  protection decreasing 6, 145
  Scotland 7–8, 20, 122, 145
  shopping see shopping
  social deprivation indices 98
  transport see transport
  walking importance 114, 116
  women 8, 144–5
  women smoking 72
  see also poverty
low pay
  Scotland 7–8
Low Pay Unit
  low income definition 3
  Scottish 7, 8

Mackay Consultants
  Rural Scotland Price Survey 112
Maguiness, H. ed. Educational Opportunity (figures) 90–93
mail-order
  catalogues 127, 129
  credit 159, 164
market forces
  education 100, 101
  food purchases 63, 64, 66
  transport 109
maternity pay, statutory 146
matrimonial disputes legal aid 178, 181–2
Maxwell pension fraud 146
means testing 137, 138, 139, 141, 142, 144–6, 148, 149
Medical Appeals Tribunal 179
mental illness 71, 76, 78, 79, 80
Ministry of Agriculture
  Consumer Panel 57, 59
  Cost of Alternative Diets 60, 67
mobility 114–15, 118, 119, 122, 124–5, 127, 129
money
  advice 160–1, 169, 184
  lenders 158–9, 164, 168
  value for 1, 127, 131
  see also credit
Money Advice Scotland 160
Monopolies and Mergers Commission 154
motor cars see car ownership

National Assistance Board
  assistance scales 59

INDEX

National Children's Home
  Poverty and Nutrition Survey
  56, 57, 67
National Consumer Council
  housing, consumer detriment 25
  shopping research 129
  Why the Poor Pay More 1, 5,
    17, 96, 121
  Your Food: Whose Choice 58
National Food Survey 56, 59
National Health Service
  consumer detriment 1, 11
  consumer voice 81–82
  dental care 77–78
  equity objectives prioritising 82
  Framework for Action, Scotland 74
  Health Boards, Scotland 70, 71, 73,
    74, 75–79, 81
  high technology medicine 76
  local consultation in needs
    assessment 78, 81
  Management Executive 81
  Patient's Associations 81
  Patient's Charter 81
  Patient Supporter scheme 13, 81
  prescription charges 77
  provision assessment 77
  purchasing health contracts 76
  quality of services 78
  resource allocation 75, 77
  targeting resources 75
  user views 81
  Working for Patients 75
  see also health
National Insurance 137, 138, 139, 144, 145, 146,
  148
National Insurance Act 1911 136–7
National Insurance Fund 136, 139, 146
National Travel Survey (table) 115
Netherlands
  benefits 140
  legal aid bureaux 186
New Town Development Corporations 19
nutrition
  Eating for Health guidelines 56
  efficient purchases 56, 57–58
  healthier diet promotion 67, 68
  lower income groups 54–58
  malnutrition 55, 59
  over-nutrition 55
  standards 55
  value 54
  see also food

occupational pension 143, 146–7
Office of Fair Trading 157, 158, 166–8, 170
old age *see* pensioners
Ombudsman

Banking and Building Society 168
Scottish Legal Services 185
one parent *see* single parent families
Orkney assessment and care management 79–30
Oxfam 127

P & O Ferries 111, 116
Paisley College, Local Government Centre
  (figures) 90–93
Parents for Safe Food 66
Patient's Charter 81
part time employment 6, 8
Paterson, L. *Social origins of under-achievement
  in school leavers* 90–93
pensioners
  benefits 135, 136, 137, 138,
    140–1, 144
  car ownership 123
  credit, attitude to 159
  debt problems 159
  fuel, domestic, VAT effect 34–35
  fuel expenditure 38
  home care 81
  housing 25, 29
  low cost budget 141
  low income 4, 5, 35, 138
  mobility 114, 123
  nursing care in community 79
  occupational pension 143, 146–7
  private pension schemes 147
  residential care 79
  Retirement Pension 142
  shopping 132
  standard of living 140
  State Earning Related Scheme 147
  statistics 5, (table) 8, 122
  transport concessions 107, 109,
    117–18, 119
  trap 143
planning land use 128
population
  ageing 5
  death rate, Scotland 51, 70–71
  life expectancy factors 71
  lung cancer deaths, women 70, 72
poverty
  credit *see* credit
  debt *see* debt
  definition 3–4, 82
  education *see* education
  ethnic minorities 94
  feminisation of 95
  food *see* food *and also* nutrition
  health problems 55–56, 57, 70–73,
    82
  housing association tenants 28
  isolation factor 71, 82
  lack of capital 11–12

197

paying for 11
review of measures supporting 15
Scotland 137
single parent families 95
social security system and 135–7, 145
surplus food distribution effect 66
taxation shift effect 141, 147
trap 15, 135, 142, 150
women smoking 72
see also low income
Poverty and Nutrition Survey 56, 61
pre-school education 96
prices *see* retailing
PSI survey 159, 164
public expenditure
  costs of welfare state 135, 138, 141
  legal aid reduction 176
  social security 6, (table) 8, 135, (table) 136
public services
  consumer detriment 1
  Public Service Obligation grant 109
  see also services

quality of life
  definition 3–4
  energy determinant 36, 51
  food poverty 54–56, 61
  structural changes for 11
  transport facilities 106
  see also discrimination *and* standard of living

recession 131, 153, 181
'red-lining' credit rating 157, 159
Regional Trends 8
Registrar General's Classification of Occupations 88, 89
Registrar of Friendly Societies 17
Resettlement Agency 149
retailing
  changes, Scotland 125–9
  discount outlets 131
  discriminatory pricing policies 15
  economic recession effect 131
  mail order catalogues 127, 129
  operational changes 126–7
  price changes 126, 141
  price maintenance 54
  price-quality relationship 129–31, 133
  price-volume relationship 131
  Retail Price Index 68, 110, 111, 126, 141
  retail revolution 124–5, 128, 132
  rural areas 129
  see also shopping
Retailing in Scotland 2005 126

retired *see* pensioners
Road Traffic Act 1930 109
Royal Commission for Legal Services in Scotland 173, 174
Rural Scotland Price Survey 112

schools *see* education
Scotland
  Health Boards *see* Health Boards
  Regional and Islands Councils 107, 109, 111, 116
Scotland Patients Association 81
Scotland the Tenants Rights, etc, (Scotland) Act 1980 18
Scottish Abstract of Statistics 7, 124
Scottish Bus Group 109
Scottish Building Regulations 39, 41, 44
Scottish Consumer Council
  civil justice system review call 187
  commissioning for this book 1, 15
  education consultation paper 100
  Small Claims research 182
Scottish Council for Voluntary Organisations 82
Scottish Courts Administration 179
Scottish Health Authorities Revenue Equalisation formula (SHARE) 75
Scottish Heart Health Study 57
Scottish Homes
  council housing improvement 22–23
  establishment 18
  finance for upgrading 26
  housing conditions survey 19, 24
  housing for rent 17
  information/advice evaluation 30
Scottish House Condition Survey 19, 24, 50
Scottish Hydro-Electric 36
  card meter 49
Scottish Legal Action Group 186
Scottish Legal Aid Board 175, 176, 177, 178, 181, 185
Scottish Legal Services Ombudsman 185
Scottish Low Pay Unit 7, 8
Scottish Office
  Accountant in Bankruptcy Annual Report 163
  Central Research Unit 94
  Education Department 100
  Eligibility for Legal Aid 176
  Framework for Action 74
  heating guidance 49
  Location and Access of Solicitors 180–1
  Scotland's Health White Paper 66–67, 74
  Scottish Abstract of Statistics 7, 124
Shelter (Scotland) grant 184
Social Work Services Group 82

INDEX

Statistical Bulletin 19
Scottish Power
    franchise consumers 36
    monthly payments scheme 164
    Powercard Register 49, 50
Scottish School Leavers' Survey 99
Scottish Special Housing Association 19
Scottish Transport Statistics 110
Scottish Young People's Surveys 89
Second Harvest 66
Secretary of State for Trade and Industry 167
services
    access, consumer detriment 12, 14, 133
    changes in provision 125–8
    complaints about 132
    consultation 14
    credit card purchases 155
    definition 121
    discriminatory rules 14–15
    expenditure on 122
    information on 131
    low income cost higher 121
    quality 1
    statutory representation 14
    see also public services
Severe Weather Payment Scheme 41
Shelter (Scotland) 184
Sheriff Court 163, 179, 184
shopping
    bulk buying 132
    car boot sales 131
    car ownership effect 124–5, 127, 128, 131, 132–3
    centralising of facilities 54
    charity shops 127, 131
    consumer changes 127
    council estates neglect 128
    food 54, 61, 62–3, 64–65, 66, 67,127, 129
    income influence 129–31, 133
    land-use planning 128, 133
    locational trends 127, 128
    mail order *see* mail order
    one-stop 127
    pensioners 132
    public markets 131, 132
    retail revolution 124–5, 128
    retail warehouses 62,128, 131
    second-hand shops 131, 132
    shop numbers estimates (table) 126
    supermarkets 13, 62, 66, 114
    transport to 61, 113, 114, 124–5
    see also retailing
Shopping Needs in Lothian Region 123
sickness benefits
    dependence on 137, 144
    statistics (table) 8, 136, 140

statutory 146
single parent families
    benefits disadvantage 150
    child care costs 143
    criticism of 135
    educational disadvantage 95
    food and diet 54
    fuel expenditure 38
    housing 25, 29
    income support 6, 122, 139, 140, 141
    increase 5
    marginal tax rates effect 143
    poverty 95, 143
single people
    fuel expenditure 38
    housing 25
    low income 5, 122
Small Claims procedure 162–3, 175, 178, 179, 180, 182, 184
smoking
    children 72
    health and 75
    tobacco advertising ban 73
    women 70, 72
social class
    educational outcomes 88–94, 96, 97, 98
    ethnic groups 95
    hierarchy of British society 13
    Registrar General's Classification of Occupations 88, 89
    structural changes 2, 11, 15
Social Fund
    administrative costs 145
    Annual Report 166
    debt advice 160
    loan repayments 12, 143, 165
    loans (table) 166
    objectives 143–4, 147, 150
    survey 141
Social origins of under-achievement in school leavers (figures) 90–93
social security
    advice for claimants 148
    appeal and adjudication 147–8
    Benefits Agency 147, 148, 149
    claims administration 145, 147–8
    consumer interests 135
    cross-party interest 135–6
    deductions 47, 164, 169, 170
    dependence on system 137
    disadvantaged claimants 143
    eligibility curtailed 137–8
    employer delivered benefits 146–7
    entitlement not taken up 138
    food and benefit level 59, 67, 68
    fraud investigation 147, 149

Government expenditure on 6,
  (table) 8, 135, (table) 136, 138
Government objectives 141, 146–7
household incomes and benefits 1,
  6, 8, 137
inadequacies 137, 140–2, 149–50
income interaction poverty 15
income related system 142–3, 146
inflation uprate 141
legal aid advice 181–2
legislation complexities 181
marginal tax rates effect 142
means testing 137, 138, 139, 141,
  142, 144–6, 148, 149
'perverse incentives' 135
poverty trap 15,135, 142–3
quality service targets 149
take-up of benefits 149
tribunal 147, 178, 179
universal categorical system 146
see also child benefit, Family
  Credit, housing benefit, income
  support, invalidity benefit,
  National Insurance, sickness
  benefit, Social Fund *and*
  unemployment benefit
Social Security Appeals Tribunals 147, 178, 179
social services
  assessment and care management
    79–80
  inequalities in access 82–83
society *see* social class
solicitors 163, 176, 180–1, 182
standard of living
  benefits level and 141–2
  pensioners 140
  unemployed 135, 140
standards
  British Standard kitemark 47
  transport (BS 5750) 108
Stirling University
  Social Work Research Centre 79
Strathclyde
  car ownership 123
  Community Charge cost 141
  Community Enterprise 65
  Dial-a-Bus service 107
  food co-operatives research 64–65
  Healthy Cities Project 76
  Passenger Transport Executive
    107, 109. 110, 111
  Poverty Alliance 61
  Trading Standards Dept 167–8
students
  grants and loans 160
  low income group 2, 107
supermarkets *see* shopping
supplementary benefit 6, 139, 140, 176

see also income support
Swansea study of disadvantage 124–5
Sweden, legal expenses insurance 186

tallymen 159, 164
taxation
  direct and indirect 141
  fraud 147
  income tax rates 142
  marginal tax rate 142, 143
  occupational pension schemes
    146, 147
  relief 147
Tolerable Standard (BTS)
  housing 24, 47, 49, 50
trade union officers 174
trading checks 159, 164
Trading Standards Authorities 166–8, 170
trading standards officers 173
transport
  accessibility 107
  air services 108, 111, 117, 118
  bus fares 107, 109–11, 113, 115–19
  bus services 107–11, 113, 114,
    118,119
  carbon tax 112
  cars *see* cars
  concessionary schemes 107,
    116–18, 119
  consumer detriment 1, 12–13, 14, 71
  dial-a-ride service 107
  deregulation and privatisation 109,
    110, 111, 118
  disabled concessions 107, 111,
    116, 117–18, 119
  discount schemes 107, 116–18
  environmental consideration 109,
    111–13, 119
  exhaust emission standards 112–13
  ferry operations 108, 111, 116, 117
  Government policy 109
  GP surgeries' location 77
  grievance redress 3, 108
  hospital visits 110
  housing estates 62, 108
  information on services 107,
    110, 113, 118
  local authorities' provision 108,
    109,110
  low income consumer needs 108,
    110, 111, 114
  market forces 109
  mobility 114–15, 118, 119,
    122, 124–5, 127, 129
  pensioners' concessions 107,
    109, 111, 116, 117–18, 119
  petrol prices 112
  public affordability 107, 109–11

INDEX

public services 107–8, 109, 114–15
quality of life 106, 108
rail *see* British Rail
recreation activities and 113
rural areas 108, 110, 112, 114
shopping requirements 54, 61, 62–63, 64–65, 107, 113
standards (BS 5750) 108
student concessions 109, 111, 118
traffic regulation 73
unemployment effect 110
urban congestion 119
Transport Act 1985 110
Transport Users Consultative Committee for Scotland 3, 108
tribunals
alternative to court procedures 178
claimants' representation at 148, 175
development of 178–9
'judicialisation' 179
representation 179–80, 181

unemployment
benefits 6, 137, 138, (tables) 139, 140, 141–2, 144
education attitudes affected by 92
ethnic minorities 94
food costs 57
housing association tenants 28
long-term disadvantaged 150
mobility 114
Scotland 8, 20, 138
standard of living 135, 140
statistics 5–6, (table) 8
transport use lessened 110
trap 142–3, 150
University of Edinburgh
Centre for Educational Sociology 89, 97
University of York
Family Budget Unit 141
Urban Programme Funding 183, 184

Vaccine Damage Tribunals 179
VAT on domestic fuel consumption 34, 38
Visa card 155
Vital Travel Statistics (table) 115
voluntary organisations
benefit claimants advice 148, 149
community care planning 82
housing advice 30, 31

wages *see* income
Wages Councils abolition 6, 145, 173
welfare benefits *see* social security
welfare rights
advice 184
services 148

welfare state, cost of 135, 138, 141
Welsh Consumer Council 182
Western Isles
assessment and care management 79–80
Why the Poor Pay More 1, 5, 17, 121
women
benefits system detriment 144–5, 150
low income 8, 144–5
part time work 8
smoking 70, 72
see also single parents
World Health Organisation
room temperatures guidelines 35

Your Food: Whose Choice 58